THE ART OF THOMAS HARDY

THE ART OF
THOMAS HARDY

BY LIONEL JOHNSON

TO WHICH IS ADDED A CHAPTER ON
THE POETRY BY J. E. BARTON AND
A BIBLIOGRAPHY BY JOHN LANE
TOGETHER WITH A NEW PORTRAIT BY
VERNON HILL AND THE ETCHED
PORTRAIT BY WILLIAM STRANG

HASKELL HOUSE
Publishers of Scholarly Books
NEW YORK
1966

published by

HASKELL HOUSE
Publishers of Scholarly Books
30 East 10th Street • New York, N. Y. 10003

New Edition.

First printed in 1923.

PRINTED IN UNITED STATES OF AMERICA

PUBLISHER'S NOTE

THIS book was originally published in 1894, the first of many dealing with Mr. Hardy's works.

At that time, though *Jude the Obscure* was still unfinished, Mr. Hardy had long been hailed as one of our most distinguished living novelists, his fourth novel, *Far from the Madding Crowd*, having brought him not merely a name, but popularity.

In 1894, however, his reputation as a poet was still to make. Much of his earliest work—I have been told on good authority, the entire work of two years—was in verse, but of this everything, with the exception of one poem, was destroyed. It was not until 1898 that Mr. Hardy at the age of fifty-eight (he was born on June 2, 1840) issued his first volume of poetry under the title of *Wessex Poems and Other Verses*, and with the exception of a collection of short stories every volume appearing from his pen in the last quarter of a century has been in verse, until to-day, in his eighty-third year, he is regarded by many not only as our greatest living novelist, but also as our greatest living poet. What a record!

The Art of Thomas Hardy, though long since out of print, is still eagerly sought after by Hardy enthusiasts. Lionel Johnson, who was born on March 15, 1867, and died on October 4, 1902, at the age of thirty-

v

five, was a brilliant critic and his discerning appreciation is as valuable to-day as it was in the nineties. In response to many inquiries I should doubtless have republished the volume long ago, but for my feeling that a book with such a title demanded a section dealing with Mr. Hardy's great and still growing reputation as a poet. At last, however, I have been fortunate enough to enlist the services of Mr. J. E. Barton, the Headmaster of Bristol Grammar School, whom I have known for some years as an enthusiastic admirer and withal a discriminating critic of Mr. Hardy's poems, and I believe that the chapter contributed by him will fully justify my selection.

When this book was first planned I arranged for Mr. Hardy to sit to the late William Strang, then a young artist, for the powerful etching which was used as a frontispiece. Many connoisseurs have considered this to be Strang's finest etched portrait, and it certainly did much to popularize his portraiture.

For this reprint Mr. Hardy has again consented to sit for his portrait, this time to Mr. Vernon Hill. Both portraits will now adorn the work.

A word remains to be added on the subject of the bibliography.

Bibliography has now become an exact science and altogether too exacting for a busy publisher personally to undertake. Besides, there are already in existence two or three excellent Hardy bibliographies which I have no desire to supersede. The one, therefore, compiled by me for the first edition of this work will not be reprinted in its original form, as I have decided to make it a bibliography of first editions only, and the titles of short stories and poems will all be included in the contents list under the title of each volume, so that any given story or poem can be located at a glance.

To this I have added when possible the dates of the various poems, the notes, traditions, and sources when given of the subject dealt with, also what is perhaps of even greater importance, the places where the poems and stories were written, for it will be generally admitted that a knowledge of the *genius loci* is as important for the study of Mr. Hardy's work as it is in the case of Scott, Kingsley, and Blackmore. It is indeed possible to argue that the spirit of place dominates his poems more than those of any other great English poet. Would that some Irish poet and romancer might arise who would achieve for Ireland what Scott has done for Scotland, Kingsley and Blackmore for Devon, and Thomas Hardy for the kingdom of Wessex.

The poem, *The Fire at Tranter Sweatley's*, has been omitted from the present volume because it is now reprinted in *Wessex Poems*, but the very useful note on Dialect and the admirable article on Barnes have been retained as these are not to be found in any of Mr. Hardy's volumes. I have also included the note on Anatole France which appeared in the Press when that distinguished author was entertained in London in 1913.

A tribute of admiration is also due to Mr. Hardy for the exquisite designs drawn by him and reproduced in the *Wessex Poems*—they are worthy of a place among the works of the ' Little Masters ' at least, and it may perhaps cause many lovers of the graphic arts to regret that Mr. Hardy should have forsaken the pencil for the pen.

My grateful thanks are due to Mr. Edmund Gosse, C.B., Miss Margaret Lavington, Mr. Clement Shorter, Mr. Stanton Whitfield, Mr. J. Carroll, Mrs. Paul Taylor, and Mr. Thomas Wise for their very valuable assistance in the revision of the bibliography.

JOHN LANE.

THE BODLEY HEAD,
LONDON, *March* 1923.

AUTHOR'S PREFACE

IT is held, upon all hands, that to write about the works of a living writer is a difficult and a delicate thing : I have felt the inevitable difficulty ; I have tried to preserve the becoming delicacy. Throughout these essays upon the works of Mr. Hardy, there will be found, I trust, no discourtesy in my censure : I trust still more, no impertinence in my praise. Dr. Johnson assigned two meanings to the word *Critick* ; in the first place, it means ' A man skilled in the business of judging of literature ; a man able to distinguish the faults and beauties of writing ' : in the second place, it means ' A snarler ; a carper ; a caviller.' This evil kind of critic is prettily described by Drayton :

> ' This Critick so sterne,
> But whom, none must discerne
> Nor perfectly have seeing,
> Strangely layes about him,
> As nothing without him
> Were worthy of being.'

But there is another critic, equally abhorrent : a creature of adulation, prying and familiar, whose criticism is founded upon personal gossip about his victims : a rude fellow, who holds a writer's private life and history, to be public concerns. To all such *canaille écrivante*, I would apply these verses of Cowper :

> ' The man who hails you Tom, or Jack,
>   And proves by thumping on your back,
>   His sense of your great merit,
>   Is such a friend, that one had need
>   Be very much his friend indeed,
>   To pardon or to bear it.'

All varieties of evil criticism flourish exceedingly in books upon the works of living writers : so many and so great are the vices incident to them, that some judicious persons would have them discouraged altogether. Yet there is much to be said on their behalf : somewhat of this kind. Most of us accept with equanimity the reviews, the journals, the magazines, which contain an abundance of criticism upon living writers ; criticism, of necessity hastier, than the criticism contained in a deliberate book. But reviews, I may be told, and journals, and magazines, are published for the passing day : a book makes the greater pretension to some lasting value. The reply had its force, did all journals die with the day, the week, the month, the quarter, of their production : did all books remain ever in the public way. But the review, be it good or bad, once published, is indestructible ; posterity can excavate it from the stores of newspapers in libraries and in museums ; can light upon it among the volumes of old magazines ; *litera scripta*, it must remain. Ephemeral it may be, in value ; it cannot be ephemeral, in duration : whilst for such books, as this of mine, I claim

that, if they be worthless, they will but exist in equal
obscurity with the reviews, an offence to no one ; and
that, if they have some little value, they may, by the
more careful workmanship and preparation, which
alone can justify them, be of greater interest and worth,
than the criticism produced under conditions, not so
favourable to thought and care.

But the reviews, it may be urged, deal with a writer's
books, singly and in succession, without attempting to
consider his life's work, as though it were ended ; they
remember, that he may yet write a great number of
books : it is premature to write a book about a living
writer's books : he may write books of so new and
fresh a kind, as wholly to overthrow his critic's general
positions. Certainly, that is possible : and, certainly,
it is improbable. But, be it so or not so, when a writer
has published fifteen volumes, the critic is at no loss
for materials of criticism. Mr. Hardy may write as
many works, as Sophocles or Shakespeare, Voltaire or
Goethe, Balzac or Hugo, Dumas or Scott : that does
not deter me from considering, nor from expressing,
the character of his fifteen published works : for I make
no silly claim to pass sentence upon them, to determine
their absolute value, to assign them their rank and
place. It amply contents me to dream, that some
gentle scholar of an hundred years hence, turning over
the worn volumes upon bookstalls yet unmade, may
give his pence for my book, may read it at his leisure,
and may feel kindly towards me. For we look back
with eagerness upon memories of the *Mermaid Tavern*
and of the *Apollo Room*, of *Will's* and of *Button's* and

of *The Club* : we are grateful to Drummond of Haw-
thornden, to Boswell, and to Spence : and this, because
we love to know how the great, or the little, writers of
those days were esteemed by the great, or by the little,
critics.   Criticism of living writers need not be presumptuous, nor impertinent ; let the critic feel but the
reverence of a novice in the tribes of Ben, of Dryden,
of Addison, of Pope, of Johnson ; he may take heart
of grace, and speak his mind upon the seeming masters
of his own day.   I do not know, that he will do well
to think much about the ' Science of Criticism ' :
about the ' Science of Fiction,' Mr. Hardy has written
that an attempt to set it forth ' is to write a whole
library of human philosophy, with instructions how
to feel.'   I have but brought to these essays the best
of my thought and of my knowledge : remembering,
how it is held, upon all hands, a difficult and a delicate
thing, to write about the works of a living writer.

LIONEL JOHNSON.

CADGWITH : 1892.

CONTENTS

		PAGE
PUBLISHER'S NOTE, ...	v
AUTHOR'S PREFACE, ...	ix
I. CRITICAL PRELIMINARIES, ...	I
II. DESIGN AND COMPOSITION, ...	35
III. WESSEX, ...	83
IV. COUNTRY FOLK, ...	122
V. CHARACTERS OF MEN AND WOMEN, . . .	167
VI. SINCERITY IN ART, ...	208
THE POETRY OF THOMAS HARDY, ...	257
BIBLIOGRAPHY, ...	297
WILLIAM BARNES : A BIOGRAPHICAL NOTE . .	347

ILLUSTRATIONS

| PORTRAIT BY VERNON HILL, . . . | *Frontispiece* |
| ETCHING BY STRANG, . . . | *facing page* 257 |

THE ART OF THOMAS HARDY

THE ART OF THOMAS HARDY

I

CRITICAL PRELIMINARIES

LITERATURE has commonly been called humane, by way of precept and of praise : if that fact be well taken to heart, it rebukes our solitary pride in our own works, and it calms our feverish concern for our own times : it fills the mind with a cheering sense of security and of companionship. In the humanities of literature, its various occupation with the whole mind of man, consist its value and its power : and the famous phrase in Terence, which declares the natural sympathy of man with man, serves further to declare the natural sphere of men's most natural art, the art of letters. The most enduring things, in a world of growth and change, are the human passions and the human sentiments : it is the office of good literature, the distinction of classical literature, to give form in every age to the age's human mind. Knowledge increases ; the history of one age is the intellectual inheritance of the next : the sciences appear to conquer the natural world, and the philosophies attempt the mysterious : but literature must always have a supreme care for those original

A

elements of human passion, and of human sentiment, which knowledge trains, and experience edu-
cates, without changing their essential quality. Life,
in contact with the passions and with the emotions
of men, and so provoking their minds to expression,
is the occasion, the origin, of literature. From Homer
or Virgil, to Wordsworth or Goethe, the great books
and utterances tell all one story, under diverse forms :
with accumulating wealth of matter, and with increasing complexity of thought, but with the same
animating spirit of ' fair humanities.' To the apprehensions of some hasty and impatient minds, the
lucid wisdom of the ancients is poor and stale : the
Eastern sages, the Greek tragedians, Homer and
Pindar, Theognis and Herodotus, Virgil and Horace,
Hafiz and Omar : how much of all these seems flat
and frigid, mere proverb, parable, allegory, personifi-
cation ! For our century has in succession enjoyed
the *Welt-Schmerz* of Germany, and the *Névrose* of
France : an immense and desolate melancholy from
Russia, a perverse and astringent misery from Scan-
dinavia. We ' refine upon our pleasures,' as Congreve
has it ; and our refinement takes the form of that
paradoxical humour, which confounds pleasure with
pain, and vice with virtue. It is a sick and haggard
literature, this literature of throbbing nerves and of
subtile sensations ; a literature, in which clearness is
lost in mists, that cloud the brain ; and simplicity
is exchanged for fantastic ingenuities. Emotions
become entangled with the consciousness of them :
and after-thoughts or impressions, laboured analysis

or facile presentation, usurp the place of that older workmanship, which followed nature under the guidance of art. Ages of decay, seasons of the falling leaf, are studied for love of their curious fascination, rather than ages of growth and of maturity : ' the glory that was Greece, and the grandeur that was Rome,' are chiefly welcomed in the persons of those writers, whom it is convenient to style *Cantores Euphorionis*. Literature, under such auspices, must lose half its beauty, by losing all its humanity : it ceases to continue the great tradition of polite, of humane letters : it becomes the private toy of its betrayers. Many and many a book, full of curious devices, and of distorted beauties, full of hints and of suggestions, can charm our modern taste, with its indulgence, not to say its appetite, for all sorts of silly audacity : but we dare not prophesy for such books an immortality, nor contemplate them by the side of the classics. Yet the classics, of all ages and in all tongues, are a catholic company : in their fellowship is room for comers from the four winds, laden with infinitely various gifts and treasures. But, as the Church Catholic, *la seule Église qui a mis l'humanité dans sa voie*, embracing Tauler and Saint Teresa, excludes Swedenborg and Behmen : so too acts the catholic company of the classics. Diversity is admirable : perversity is detestable : the distinction may be delicate, but it is decisive, and separates, according to the judgment of time, the cleverness of to-day, from the genius, that is at home throughout the centuries. I profess my faith in too many writers of this age, to accuse myself of a backward tendency in my appreciations, of an over conservative spirit in my attempts upon criticism : but at the outset of these essays, and before I venture to approach the art of Mr. Hardy, I wish to declare my loyalty to the broad and high traditions of literature ; to those humanities, which inform with the breath of life the labours of the servants, and the achievements of the masters, in that fine art.   There are theorists, who maintain the absolute independence of the artist ; his ' unchartered freedom ' from all traditions, and from all influences ; his isolated station, his spontaneous powers : and there are theorists, who maintain the entire dependence of the artist upon hereditary impulse, upon circumstantial influence, upon local forces, and upon social tendencies ; they rob him of his originality, that they may fit him into their theory. The great name of Carlyle, and the distinguished name of M. Taine, may stand sponsors for the two doctrines.   And yet the truth would seem to lie between these two desperate extremities, of plenary inspiration and of mechanical necessity : between that doctrine, which detaches the artist from his fellow men ; and that doctrine, which forbids them to see, even in the artist, an example of free and of creative will.   At the least, it is of interest to consider the middle position : to contemplate the artist, the man of letters, in his relation to past times and to his own, with something of a Positivist spirit, tempered by a saving disbelief in Positivism.   The result of such a meditation might be of this kind ; with due allowance for ' accidental variations.'

The supreme duties of the artist toward his art, as of all workmen toward their work, are two in number, but of one kind : a duty of reverence, of fidelity, of understanding, toward the old, great masters ; and a duty of reverence, of fidelity, of understanding, toward the living age and the living artist. There are times, when the two duties are hard to reconcile ; when the artistic conscience must put forth all its honest casuistry, and determine the true solution with laborious care. The law of restraint seems to say one thing : and the liberty of power, another. Is this, asks the artist of his conscience, a fine discovery of beauty, a fine exercise of strength ? or is it a temptation, a vicious thing disguised, for the moment, in the semblance of beauty and of strength? Am I dishonouring art, by the rejection of fine chances ? or honouring art, by obedience to fine traditions ? As the artist decides, so does he find his salvation, or pronounce his own sentence of failure : if he decide well, his work is alive, vigorous, and sure. But the difficulty of decision ! for it requires no less than a science, to lay at rest questions of the artistic conscience : a knowledge of the ends of art, an insight into the perplexed issues, the tangled ideas, which beset the artist's mind, and confound his plain morality. It is not in estimates of the past, that the difficulties come : it is in estimates of the present. That the habit and the drift of our own age are good, and to be praised, who shall assure us ? The facts of life, its energies and activities in play about us, we can recognize with some clearness ; and the fashions, ventures, experiments, of contemporary artists are' almost too prominently in sight. But we require a touchstone and a test ; some image, as it were, of that perfect state ' which lieth in the heavens,' seen there by Plato, ' eternal in the heavens,' proclaimed by Paul ; before we can accept with joy, and follow with readiness, the ways of our living age, of our living artists. And in the old, great masters, and even in the excellent, old writers of less excellence, we have our test, a test of the widest application, whereby to assay ourselves and others. For, *securus iudicat orbis terrarum* : sure and sound is the whole world's judgment : in Homer and in Virgil, in Milton and in Dante, virtue and truth shine clearly. The general voice of men, the authoritative voice of artists, go together in praise of the old, great masters. ' But they lived in their times, we live now ; what have we to do with them ? ' asks many a man, whose illiteracy has made him petulant. Neither did the old, great masters flourish together : yet examine, I pray you, the debt of Virgil to Homer, the debt of Dante to Virgil, the debt of Milton to Dante, to Virgil, and to Homer. Do you not find it an inestimable debt of reverence, of fidelity, of understanding ? Or can you discern in those masters, for the most part, any sign of a servile obedience to each other ? Call it rather, not a debt due, but a grace sought and received. Great art is never out of date, nor obsolete : like the moral law of

Sophocles, ' God is great in it, and grows not old ' ;
like the moral law of Kant, it is of equal awe and
splendour with the stars. A line of Virgil, written
by the Bay of Naples, in some most private hour
of meditation, all those long years ago ! comes home
to us, as though it were our very thought : upon
each repetition, experience has made it more true
and touching. Or some verse of Arnold, written
at Oxford or in London, some few years past : it
comes home to us, as though a thousand years had
pondered it, and found it true. In beauty and in
strength, in beauty of music and in strength of thought,
the great artists are all contemporaries : ' Vandyke
is of the company,' now and always : an eternal
beauty and strength are upon the great works of art,
as though they were from everlasting. Be we artists
then, or students merely, let us value our age and
ourselves, according to the *mind* of the great masters,
and in their *spirit*. ' There is but one way for me,'
wrote Keats, in the very accents of Milton : ' The
road lies through application, study, and thought. I
will pursue it.' To his disciples in art, Sir Joshua
Reynolds, sanest and most refined of English painters,
gave the same counsels : ' The daily food and nourish-
ment of the mind of an artist is found in the great
works of his predecessors. There is no other way
for him to become great himself. *Serpens, nisi
serpentem comederit, non fit draco*, is a remark of a
whimsical Natural History, which I have read, though
I do not recollect its title ; however false as to dragons,
it is applicable enough to artists.' In his old age,

Michael Angelo was met among the ruins of the Colosseum, by the Cardinal Farnese : who enquired of him, to what end he meditated there. ' I go yet to school,' said Michael Angelo, ' that I may continue to learn.' But in our day, many men of admirable powers love to think of themselves, as alone in the world, homeless in the universe ; without fathers, without mothers ; heirs to no inheritance, to no tradition ; bound by no law, and worshippers at no shrine : without meditation, without reverence, without patience, they utter, and would have us hear, their hasty and uncertain fancies. To what ' lyrical cries ' do they bid us listen : to what ' psychological moments ' do they invite our attention ! These have no habitual, nor constant, principles of thought ; no test, nor standard, of judgment : loose sentiment, and lawless imagination, are the signs to them of free and fearless genius. It is easy indeed for a man to be ' deep-versed in books, and shallow in himself, crude or intoxicate ' ; but that is not a common danger in these days : rather are the humble students of modern literature moved to exclaim, with Dr. Johnson ; ' I never desire to converse with a man, who has written more than he has read.'

In the second place : at one with our test by ancient greatness, is the test by our proper conscience. There are occasions, when we say, with a confidence beyond words, *This is right* : against text-book and precept, warning and exhortation, we know our work to be true. The pedant, with a mechanic reverence, in a blind fidelity, through a dull understanding, may quote against us his Aristotle, his Vitruvius, his Pope, his Reynolds : we know, that we are their dutiful sons, not he ; that what we try to do, in humility following our conscience and our light, is in the spirit and in the truth of what they did, following theirs. With the increase of knowledge, the growth and change of civility, the diverse forms and novel aspects of men and things, there comes a like alteration in the manners of literature : but it must be a rational development, not a mindless innovation ; the work of a loyalist, not of a rebel ; careful in spirit of art's constitutions, not indifferent to their violation. Hereditary virtues must be discernible, if the new art is to be legitimate : and they must be nurtured and tended well. As in the spiritual or interior life, the Church would have a man perfect himself by the help of approved rules and meditations, not superseding, but directing, his conscience : so in art, where also there is an interior life, the collective wisdom of the great masters must help to nourish and sustain that conscience, which cannot thrive wholly upon the desires and the intimations of its own genius. If we regard such men as Spenser, and as Sidney, in Elizabethan times ; or as Mr. Whitman in our own : we find not their greatness, nor their felicity, to lie in the attempt to compose English poetry in the antique metres of Greece and Rome ; nor in the attempt to rob English poetry of all metrical law. Yet Spenser, in that early enthusiasm of the English Renaissance, was certain that the new age, with its new learning and its new taste, demanded his innovation : Mr. Whitman is still more convinced, that Democracy, America, and many things beside, justify his bold adventure. See here the dangers of art, and its ironical revenges ! For Spenser's hapless innovation came of a false deference to antiquity : he misapprehended alike the needs of his own age, and the lessons of the great past. But when he came to himself, he showed a triumphant apprehension of both : and in the *Faery Queen*, the spirit of old romance, and the spirit of new times, met together without discord. And, to consider Mr. Whitman : is he not then most a poet, when, forgetting the imagined new needs of his time and country, he chaunts simple, heroical things, with a ' large utterance,' almost Homeric ? Let Sir Joshua sum up for us, in two weighty passages, the issues of the whole matter, upon both sides. First, for tradition : ' The habit of contemplating and brooding over the ideas of great geniuses, till you find yourself warmed by the contact, is the true method of forming an artist-like mind ; it is impossible, in the presence of those great men, to think or invent in a mean manner ; a state of mind is acquired that receives those ideas only, which relish of grandeur and simplicity.' Next, for originality : ' I should hope that it is not necessary to guard myself against any supposition of recommending an entire dependence upon former masters. I do not desire that you shall get other people to do your business, or to think for you ; I only wish you to consult with, to call in, as counsellors, men the most distinguished for their knowledge and experience, the result of which counsel must ultimately depend upon yourself. Such conduct in the commerce of life has never been considered as disgraceful, or in any respect to imply intellectual imbecility ; it is a sign rather of that true wisdom, which feels individual imperfection ; and is conscious to itself of how much collective observation is necessary to fill the immense extent, and to comprehend the infinite variety, of nature. I recommend neither self-dependence nor plagiarism.' He, who falls into neither of those criminal mistakes, is the perfect humanist : he reveres the past, he comprehends the present : he ' sees life steadily, and sees it whole.' The humanists, in any liberal sense of that term, are the catholics of art : well balanced and well proportioned in mind, they exaggerate nothing, and they ignore nothing ; but upon the facts of life, spiritual and material, they look with a discernment, which tries to realize them all at their true value. The worthiest, the most valuable, facts of life are the human emotions and the human passions, ' in widest commonalty spread,' yet touching, to all imaginable varieties of issue, each single soul. It is the aim of these essays to show, that Mr. Hardy is often of the humanists : that he may be of the classics.

His chosen method of expression is the novel : that method, which, since the days of Elizabeth and of the Stuarts, has more and more won for itself a high and serious consideration : so that it is commonly recognized in our times, as the characteristic method of presentation, for the high play of motives and adventures. I have insisted upon the unchanging identity of human emotions and of human passions, under all circumstances of time and place : and I see, in this universal triumph of the novel, no sign of a wholly new order of things for artistic treatment ; but a sign, that with an increased conflict and complexity in the old play of human life with life, art has established, by means of the novel, a new and lively convenience for giving to that play a form. Our fashionable talk, about our marvellous subtilty, analytic skill, psychological insight ; as though our forefathers in the arts had been fools and blind ; seems to compliment ourselves, upon the creation of a state of things, for which the whole great course of social history is responsible. It is the office of art, to disengage from the conflict and the turmoil of life the interior virtue, the informing truth, which compose the fine spirit of its age : and to do this, with no pettiness of parochial pride in the fashions and the achievements of its own age, but rather with an orderly power to connect what is, with what has been, looking out prophetically towards what will be. *La partie immortelle et vraiment humaine survit :* how small a part is that ! Yet the by-ways of the world, and the back-waters ; the rare nooks and corners of life, where the passions and the emotions play their freaks and phantasies : there is no reason, why the curiosity of art should not dwell upon these to fine purpose ; discovering, among so much quaintness, repulsion, or obscurity, the spirit that unites them to the general life. 'There is no excellent *Beauty*, that hath not some strangenesse in the proportion.' I can think of nothing, so beyond hope deformed, so past endurance dreadful, but art could show it to me, humanized, and brought within the pale of beauty. But for this kindly office of art, in art's romantic moments, is required a classic sense of scholarship : otherwise, this romantic delight in subtilties of situation, and in audacities of thought, will run riot, and produce those uncouth, clever pieces of extravagance, which charm the undisciplined. There are certain English writers, who in compliment, as it were, to republican France, appear to hold all French novelists for free and equal : when we have perused and weighed their adjectives in praise of living men, whose claims and charms are of to-day, we fall to wondering, what praises may remain for Balzac and for Flaubert. Nothing can cure this desire for novelty, corrupted into a disease, but contact with wide ranges of knowledge : a prolonged handling of the serene classics, until the beauty, the greatness, the goodness of them grow wonderful to us, and romantic ; fresh and living. Be it the *Iliad* or the *Agamemnon*, *Paradise Lost* or the *Ancient Mariner*, that we taste, and learn, and master ; still we are left with the one assured sense of having spent our time in a great society, in a good company : *Deus nobis haec otia fecit !* Clear of controversy, away from the noise and dust, happy among the immortals, we can study them under the light of our own day ; and only then shall we understand,

upon what matters of our own day to turn that living
light, and so find in them the soul of our living age.
Only when a delight in the classics has passed into
a dislike of contemporary art ; when a living love
of the classics has degenerated into an artificial habit
of esteem : does familiarity with the classics become
dangerous to the critics. In the study of novels,
that danger is never far away ; for novels, to be true
to life, must deal with its medley of matters in a
spirit of impartiality, which is often hard to bear :
and the protest of many a reader against the levity
or the seriousness, the sunlight or the twilight, the
conflict or the calm, which distresses him in a novel,
is often an unconscious protest against its truth to
his own experience ; and a longing for those older
books, whose old-fashioned charm of manner and
of matter has given him some respite and release.
That may not have been the office of those older
books in their own day : but, daring and romantic
then, they are classical and familiar now. The
novelist must lay his account with all that : remembering, that not in China only do men live backward and forward ; but that only in China do they
write books for the dead.

Much has been written about the English origins
of that great art, which Mr. Hardy pursues with so
eminent a zeal, and with so excellent a skill : erudite
dissertations, upon the sources of the *Morte d'Arthur* or
of the *Arcadia* ; upon the Elizabethan novel at large.
Much, again, has been written about that invention
of the dramatic spirit and form, whence in great

measure came the art of fiction. But these intricate matters may be with reverence dismissed : for the modern novel can find a point, in the long rolls of its pedigree, whence date all its more characteristic features. The desire to tell stories, the love of hearing them, are among the oldest things in the world : Homeric rhapsodists, and Eastern fabulists, and savage persons known to anthropology, witness to it. But the simple dramatic instinct is satisfied by almost any dramatic method : verse or prose, it is all one, so a story be told. The modern novelist would scarce recognize a brother artist at Ionian festivals, in Oriental bazaars, beside savage camp fires. His humanism would make him at home, his sympathies would go out to his surroundings : but not his conception of his own art. So, too, with the *Gesta Romanorum*, with Maundeville, with Boccaccio, with Malory, with More, with the Euphuist authors of pastoral, with the earlier writers of stirring history or travel, with the earlier essayists and disciples of Theophrastus, with the voluminous inventors of French romance : germs of the modern novel lie concealed in all these ; but not the most vital, nor the most fertile. Call it fanciful, if you will : I incline to think, that the modern English novelist, bent upon genealogical research, would do well to consider the three familiar names of Bunyan, Pepys, Defoe. It is true, that the *Pilgrim's Progress* was for long held low, plebeian, and inelegant, a kitchen book : but its marvellous power of direct narration by strong strokes, its living portraiture and steady movement, forced it upon the attention of all classes. Pepys came to light too late, to be the joy of innumerable wits and worthies, who would have tasted him with relish ; he has had, therefore, no part in the formation of the novelist's art, by the example of his infinite curiosity and vivacious style : but he is a most notable figure in the history of literature, by virtue of those qualities and of his use for them. A constant readiness to note the value of trifles in the art of life ; an appreciation of facts, of realities, of things, veritably seen and heard and done : few earlier writers, dealing with their own experience, have shown these powers in so great a degree. With the name of Defoe, we come to the first writer of English novels, in whom we can recognize and revere a modern master. He has had hard measure dealt out to him : he stood in the pillory of the law, and in the more cruel pillory of Pope : and, though Dr. Johnson ranked *Robinson Crusoe* with the masterpieces of Cervantes and of Bunyan, as one of the three books, which their reader could wish longer than they are ; for the most part, he has been abandoned to boys, and neglected by men. That he wrote two masterpieces, is indeed remembered : it is commonly forgotten, that he wrote many things of only less great merit. In praise of these three, Bunyan, Pepys, Defoe, it suffices to say, that their works ; in the cases of Bunyan and Defoe, both imaginative and real ; are beyond all reckoning more true to reality, than the narratives of the old, famous News-Writers : more true, that is, to the genius of persuasive narration, to the spirit of verisimilitude, to the powers of alert and faithful story-telling. It were beside the mark, to waste words upon the work of such less worthy writers, as Mrs. Behn or Mrs. Manley; though in these, and in many others, the modern novel may be descried, not always under the most happy conditions : between Defoe and Mr Hardy come all the greatest English novelists, with all their great allies.

Five years after the birth of Defoe, was born the great and terrible Swift : and that name carries forward our thoughts, with no considerable change or break, until we reach that second Renaissance, associated with the names of Wordsworth and of Coleridge. The century of the wits, the satirists, the essayists ; of stately common sense, of scholarly grace, of leisurely perfection ! Let me add, and ignore all ridicule from *les précieux ridicules*, a century of admirable poets, and of novelists unsurpassed. The English Revolution had established a solid peace and security at home ; all the foreign wars, the strife of parties, the national difficulties and dangers, were as nothing beside those ages of storm, which the country had already known : and the French Revolution was yet to come, with its long train of disturbing consequences. The world of English letters betook itself to the maintenance of sober reason. The very heterodox in faith, in philosophy, and in morals, prided themselves upon their sound sense, and had no airs of superior inspiration. Experience, verified facts, the ascertained contents of life, the clear prin-

B

ciples and powers of human nature : these were the plain arguments and matters, for the consideration of reasonable men. The roll of moralists, or of metaphysicians, illustrates this reliance of thought upon common sense, in very various ways : there were the elegant Shaftesbury, with his characteristics of Men, Manners, Opinions, Times ; Mandeville, with his Private Vices, Public Benefits ; the rhetorical commonplaces, uttered in no commonplace rhetoric, of St. John ; the mixed depravity and charm of Chesterfield ; Johnson's golden mean of wisdom ; the composed and Attic reasonings of Berkeley ; the Gallicized Scotch sceptic, Hume ; the moral father of political economy, Smith ; Butler, the champion of probability ; Burke, the Hooker of statesmen, upon whom at last fell the moral horror of the French Revolution, in all its lawlessness. Here is no lack of variety ; here are prelates and professors, statesmen and politicians, lights of the court and oracles of the coffee house : but in all, we note a desire to be sensible and reasonable ; to present, each his own views of truth, as the plain, sane statement of facts ; demanding, doubtless, care and labour from the student of truth ; yet not exceeding the grasp of any honest and educated man. We are far away from the breathless heights of German speculation. Neither was it an age of general and shallow culture ; the learned composed a somewhat close corporation : yet the simple citizen, and the plain tradesman, were apt to feel a respect for letters, an interest in them, comparatively rare in these more pretentious days. And the immediate precursors of the great eighteenth century novelists found their material for art among the busy places of their world : continuing, in a measure, the traditions of Elizabethan comedy, but imparting to them a greater seriousness and a greater grace, Addison and Steele brought to its perfection the English essay. Neither the fierce note of revolt in Swift, nor the more exquisite, if sometimes indecent, sensibility of Sterne, so directly suggested or improved a way for English fiction, as did those satires, sketches, pathetic or ironical masterpieces, which immortalized the memories of Addison and Steele. In these, the spirit of pure humour walks abroad, now touching to tears, now brightening with smiles, the sensitive and the observant : dwelling upon the kindly details of life, the little graces, fashions, absurdities, enchauntments, which go to its merry making ; as also upon the simple, grave, and eternal elements in human nature, which make of life so solemn a thing. Notably in Addison and in Steele, noticeably in their successors and imitators, an habit of interest in the common life prevailed : their lightness of air, that dainty felicity of phrase, witnessing less to any artificial survey of life, than to a power of seizing upon the main matters in hand, and of presenting them clearly and well, free from the encumbering mass of things. They made no pretensions to the novelist's art, but limited themselves to the design of the essay, as they conceived and brought to perfection that difficult form : the rich, massy, and sententious

Bacon, Montaigne the eloquent and the elusive, whilst they excelled Addison and Steele, beyond all reckoning, in genius of thought, were yet inferior to them in justice of design. In this rare quality lay their influence upon the art of the novelist: that just and clean design, exhibited in so many of their little narratives and incidents, cannot but have prompted others, of less delicate a concern for moral meditation, but of an equal turn for discerning the plots and plays of common life, to draw character, and to describe adventure, upon a more considerable scale. The literary annals of the last century swarm, indeed, with stories, romances, sketches and satires in prose, sprung from most various originals: but, setting aside these obscure products, we may fairly claim for the great essayists of the last century, that they did much to help and to inspire that characteristic art of England, the novel of common life.

We come to the great triumvirate of early English novelists; to Richardson, to Fielding, and to Smollett: now at last, we can delight, as Mrs. Sarah Battle at her whist delighted, in ' a clear fire, a clean hearth, and the rigour of the game.' Perhaps, they have few lovers left them now; tedious Richardson, hearty Fielding, gross Smollett! for tediousness should in these days be the tediousness of a problem in psychology; heartiness, that of a riotous and brutal pessimism; grossness, the grossness of a mock scientific curiosity. But from their lovers, who constantly converse with them, the great three, in a very English way, and upon a vastly lower level, have something of the inseparable love and reverence, which the three great tragic Greeks will always have. *Pamela, Clarissa, Sir Charles Grandison ; Tom Jones, Joseph Andrews, Amelia ; Humphrey Clinker, Peregrine Pickle, Roderick Random :* the names are redolent of joy and gladness. There is a tendency to accuse these books, and their partial prototypes, in French or Spanish literature, of inartistic methods : the digressions, the interpolations, the reflections, the leisurely pace, the dalliance with every passing thought and sentiment ; upon all this, we hear, the laws of art cry out. If so it be, the ' gentle ' readers of these books must lie under a very evil spell : for at the close of their reading, the delusion is strong upon them, that they have been present at a very miracle of art's working. All the wayward wanderings from the straight path, in the matter of epistolary episode, meditative diversion, irrelevant narrative, seem to have been necessary to the complete expression of the writer's mind : far from ignoring, or perverting, the true method of his art, it was with deliberation, that he thus conceived and followed his method. There are two kinds of old books, full of charm : the stories, which take the road, and put up at inns, and fall there into singular entanglements ; which resound with laughter, and bustle, and the voices of a medley world, yet with a strong hand keeping all in order : and there are the stories, with the tranquil air of certain old manor houses, where the genius of the place is gracious and strong, in book room and in still room and in oratory, a placid spirit perfected by long years. Richardson, Fielding, and Smollett, each in his way and measure, combine these charms : if you weary of Richardson's fine-drawn sentiment, until at last you could hang yourself, as said his friend the Doctor ; you will presently fall upon some scene of a vigour all the more impressive, for its lengthy prelude : if Fielding tire you with his rough and ready adventures, you will soon meet with some incomparable stroke of wit, or wisdom, or tender thought, all the more affecting by force of contrast. These writers determined the course of the English novel : they gave the word of command, that English novelists should thrive upon a generous spirit of humanity ; concerned for the little realities of life, but still more concerned for the great realities. So doing, they established it upon a firm footing : and gave examples of success in the new art found for prose, fashioned after the heart and mind of Shakespeare, the head of the new art found in his day for verse.

Signs were not wanting, that this too was the day of a new art, of a new spirit, for verse also : the impulse towards a truer simplicity, or a greater depth, had already begun to stir. Collins, Gray, Shenstone, Goldsmith, Percy, Warton, Cowper, Chatterton, Crabbe, Blake, Burns : between all these, we may find a closer similarity, than the fact that they preceded Wordsworth. As Gray to Goldsmith, as Chatterton to Crabbe, as Blake to Burns, so was Richardson to Fielding : but as Richardson and Fielding, despite all differences, were fellow workmen in the same cause, so too were those opposed poets. They provoked the spirit of reality once more : and, as the novelists went deeper than their predecessors the essayists, so these poets went nearer to the heart of things, than went Pope the admirable, and his lifeless imitators. Goldsmith, restoring comedy and pastoral romance to life, while sweetening the theme and metre of ' heroic ' verse ; Collins, with ' sweet entrancing voice ' and ' mingled measure ' ; Gray, bringing a lively culture, Italian, Celtic, classical, artistic, scientific, to the service of an over anxious Muse ; Cowper, pondering the quiet country ways with a mind as natural, but less quiet ; Crabbe, a master in ' real ' tragedy ; Chatterton the mediaeval dreamer, Blake the universal dreamer, and Burns the first ' magician ' of the North : here are mighty workings of the spirit, not without their influence upon the novel. For the unity of the arts, that neglected truth, is a most undeniable truth : and, with no foolish encroachment of one art upon another, either on the part of artist or of critic, it is easy to discern the mutual help of all arts to each other, and of each branch of one art to each other branch. For a time, the novel was composed with no great change of manner or of matter ; the delightful Miss Burney, first of the great English women, who have composed novels, did not vary from the essential character- istics of her predecessors, unless in a certain sprightli- ness of humour, commonly found among the letters and the memoirs of distinguished French women : but the general tone of literature was changing, in ways curious enough to observe. The school of sentiment, glorified in England by Richardson, was a dangerous school for those of smaller powers : the ' Man of Feeling,' and yet more the woman, exercised strange fascinations : even Lamb was under their spell, when he produced the fine tragedy, but the strained sentiment, of his *Rosamund Gray*. Mocked by the wholesome laughter of Goldsmith and of Fielding, it yet maintained a place : under various forms and influences, it was ever displaying its sickly affectations. ' Ossian ' had nothing to do with sentiment proper ; nor yet Rousseau : but all kinds of stuff about the gray ghost of the departed warrior, and the innocent delights of the noble savage, mingled with the proper concerns of sentiment and sensibility. The novel of extravagance in sentiment, whether accompanied by melodramatic effects, or merely left to its own melancholy moonshine, may be dismissed without regard to chronological precision. Writers of ability allowed themselves to use the novel of extravagance, for the expression of their ideas : and writers of no great merit have captivated, by their novels, writers of the highest excellence. Godwin, for an example of the first class, though less extravagant in his novels than dull, no longer rests upon them for his fame : Clara Reeve and Brockden Brown did little to deserve the admiration of Shelley and of Landor. Beginning with Walpole, the miscellaneous list continues with Mackenzie, Shelley, Lewis, Mrs. Radcliffe, Maturin ; with the writers of the Minerva Press, whimsically

dear to Macaulay ; with an array of feeble and spas-
modic works, echoes of German romance at its romantic
worst ; I am half disposed to end the list with the
names of *Guy Livingstone* and of *Pelham*, at the period
of muscular and of fashionable novels. I confess,
that so receptive a roll brings together, and ranges
in succession, names and works of an amazing variety :
but through them all runs a strain of extravagance,
due to some perversion or excess of mere sentiment,
enough to link them together, if not in every case
enough to deprive them of a certain merit. It may
be counted not the least of Peacock's good deeds,
that his pungent satire gave the death blow to the
more frantic follies of. the sentimental kind : to the
rhetoric doing duty for eloquence, to the silliness
masquerading as romance, to the meagrims dignified
with the name of despair, to the blood and thunder,
skull and crossbones, cypress and nightshade, of
spurious Goethes and of mock Byrons. From this
absurd outcome of the French Revolution in the
state, and of the English and German reformations
in literature, let us turn to the genuine tradition
once more.

Among the dead English novelists of our century,
there are seven great names : at the least, seven
names so far above mediocrity, that we can only
call them great. These are Scott, Miss Austen,
Dickens, Thackeray, Charlotte Brontë, Emily Brontë,
and George Eliot. Among lesser names, there are
Miss Ferrier, Miss Edgeworth, Mrs. Gaskell, Bulwer
in his happiest books, Reade and Trollope in two

or three masterpieces : and there are schools innumerable of particular novelists ; whose novels either
rank below the great novels in virtue of their local
or temporal limitations, or are not the chief results
of their writers' genius. Newman, Kingsley, and
Disraeli, as novelists, may be thought to come under
both heads. I began this rapid survey of the English
novel, with one possibly fanciful statement : I am
now forced to conclude it, with another. The modern
novel of to-day, in all its phases and developments,
seems in my judgment to begin with the work of
George Eliot : the more ancient novel, to end with
the work of Thackeray. Not that I see any violent
break with the past ; no sudden discovery of new
form or matter : the old is not obsolete and outworn, the new is not perfect and complete ; they
touch at countless points, and are not antagonistic :
rather I mean, that in reading Thackeray, I am led
to think about his predecessors ; in reading George
Eliot, I am led to think about her successors, and
in no slight degree, about Mr. Hardy ; whom I am
approaching in a leisurely and, it may be, in a too
leisurely, way.

All times of great development have increased
men's capacity of apprehension and of appreciation :
the last and most notable of such times was that of
the French Revolution. At the Italian Renaissance,
according to familiar definitions, there came about
a ' development of the individual,' followed by a
' discovery of the world and of man.' These ingenious phrases discover and disguise the truth in

almost equal measure : but upon the whole, they
are not to be condemned. They are very applicable to the French Revolution also : if it be well
kept in mind, that the same process of development
and of discovery has been in progress, since the most
primaeval days. But the age of the French Revolution had upon literature a marked influence : its
theoretic justifications, its appeals to passion and to
principle, its splendours and its terrors, all its vast
energy and impulse of spirit, culminating in the
supreme figure of Napoleon ; all that, from first to
last, served to quicken the creative powers of the
imagination. Upon some of the poets already named,
the Revolution acted, like a revelation ; Burns, the
Ayrshire peasant, felt the prouder for it : to Wordsworth and to Coleridge, in whom the tendencies of
these earlier poets were summed up and perfected,
the Revolution was the dawn of hope and joy in all
things. The tendencies of literature, apart from all
social and political events ; and the social and political
events, hopes, possibilities, of the Revolution ; combining with the natural genius of Wordsworth and
of Coleridge, produced the wonderful results, all
know : as all know, how by the same things was
affected the genius of Shelley and of Byron, in a less
perfect way. All of them, all writers of distinction
at the time, felt their sympathies widened and deep-
ened : nature, all that was meant by nature, in the
heart of man and in the visible world, became clearer
to them. ' The wonder and bloom of the world,'
came back : and Wordsworth turned for beauty

and for truth to homely men, and to natural scenes ;
whilst Coleridge, as though the old world's privilege
to dream were returned in all its freshness and its
fullness, turned to the ' magical nature ' of the world,
with its rare powers. A shepherd, a beanfield, a
spring in the hills, a cottage tragedy, strange histories
of enchaunted seas : out of these came a philosophy
and a poetry, hard at first sight to associate with the
heroism and the horror, with the waves and storms,
of insurgent France. Yet the association was real :
and even when Wordsworth and Coleridge were disappointed of their hopes in France, that freshness
and depth of thought remained. One year after
Wordsworth, one year before Coleridge, Scott was
born : and I have touched upon the two greater
poets, because they illustrate one side of the new
stir and impulse, which was to become, through Scott
the poet, so potent an influence upon Scott the novelist ;
whilst Scott the man shared nothing of the social and
political aspirations, in their case combined with it.

I can hardly forgive myself, if I say anything against
the last century ; so great is the debt of gratitude,
that I owe to its French and English literature : yet
the age, which ' slavishly bowed down to the word
of John Locke,' as Rosmini puts it, was an age of
singular narrowness, of singular self-sufficiency. In
nothing was this more shown, than in its attitude
towards the past : its cant word ' Gothick,' flung at
most things between the age of Charlemagne and the
age of Louis XIV. ; its contempt for the ' lifeless
imbecility ' of such national and poetical relics as

Chevy Chace; all the coarseness and the rudeness, that afflicted Gray; the serene elegance and airs, with which the gentlemen in fine wigs and dainty ruffles, smiling upon us from the canvases of Reynolds, fixed, settled, determined, and established, all things in heaven and earth : all this is apt to irritate us, who are ourselves, may be, not too conscious of our own fallibility. Scott, once and for all, confounded that smiling contempt, and displayed the riches of the past : drawn to the past by that instinct of sympathy, quick within the blood, which peoples the past with personal friends and foes. It is dangerous, in the present temper of many eminent persons, to profess an admiration of Scott : to whom Cardinal Newman, as a boy and as an old man, professed no less than ' a devotion.' Yet to err, if error it be, in the company of our English Plato, is better than to be exceeding wise in that of our English, and American, sophists : whose voices are somewhat high-pitched and discordant. In Scott, the antiquarian spirit awoke a passion, instead of a science ; it laid upon him a duty and a service of romantic patriotism, and was no mere minister to his curiosity : in the border legends and ballads, the pageantries of the middle age, the humours of his countryside, all the beauty and gallantry and pity in the world's chronicles, he found out the worth of life, past and present. It matters very little, that his style could be faulty, and his archaeology wrong : Shakespeare is not blameless in either respect : it matters very much that, like Shakespeare, Scott could marshall and control high actions and high passions upon the field of art. Here are *les bons clercs et les beaux chevaliers morts en bataille et en fortes guerres, les braves sergents d'armes et les hommes de parage.* Here are *les joueurs de harpe, les jongleurs et les rois du monde.* And, side by side with these, are the poor, with their tragedies and their comedies, full of that reality, which imagination gives : an host of men and women, without the frequent rudeness of Fielding's humble figures, and without the grotesqueness common in those of Dickens. Scott had something of the high office, which belonged to Homer, to Dante, to Shakespeare, and to Goethe : he seems to draw into his art a thousand matters of fact and thought and imagination, which lay loose and scattered before : he enlarged our sense of human life, by enlarging literature with fresh expressions of the 'fair humanities.' To him the novel owes a rank, in the history of literature, equal to the rank of the epic and of the drama : the work of Wordsworth, Coleridge, Keats, Shelley, Byron, greater though it be in itself, wrought no effect so great, no result so new. Each after his own way, those poets caught and, it may be, heightened and magnified in some things, the spirit of the old, imperishable poets : Scott taught the writers of stories in prose, all Europe over, to attempt things unattempted and undreamed of by their greatest predecessors.

In the books of Miss Austen, appears the most delicate genius, that has yet found expression in the English novel : an humour, which ripples gently through the scenes ; a patience, which never tires,

nor is tired : an exquisite touch, said Scott, denied
to him. Hers is a more fine and subtile manner,
than that of the eighteenth century humourists :
there is a modern note in its refinement of simplicity,
an accent of deeper truth. Yet she belongs rather
to the past, than to the present : that serenity and
sobriety are marks of a mind at rest in its enjoyment
of quiet humour, not busy with the solution of intricate moral and æsthetic questions. And even the
great name of Bronté carries nothing typically modern
in the mention : the two sisters wrought out their
masterpieces of passion in remote places, or among
strange circumstances : something primitive and
vehement stirs them, ·they have a northern inspiration. The fire and gloom of Elizabethan tragic
poets, the mystery and darkness of German romantic
rhapsodists, the flash and clearness also of the French,
go to compose their charm : their sincerity is too
direct, almost too childlike, to be modern. In Dickens
and in Thackeray, the old English novel took its
widest range : with how triumphant a success ! The
powers of wit and humour, the springs of tears and
pity, the comprehension of life in its greatness and
in its littleness, its loftiness and its absurdity : all
these are in Dickens and in Thackeray. Writers so
great have great faults : let us not speak of their
faults with easy condescension or contempt. The
desire of the artist for perfection is an excellent thing :
but I cannot understand, why your soldier and your
saint should be remembered for their victories, and
pardoned for their faults ; whilst your artist of a

thousand conquests must have ever rehearsed against
him the tale of his failures and of his faults.   There
is no such man, as a perfect artist : he knows it best,
whom the world holds most perfect.   Hold you your
peace about the ' cheap cynicism,' the egoism, the
personal intrusion, of Thackeray : I promise you
mine about the ' cheap pathos,' the declamation,
the fustian tragedy, of Dickens : let us give thanks
together for Esmond, Colonel Newcome, Beatrix,
and Becky Sharp ;   for David Copperfield, Mr.
Pickwick, Mr. Pecksniff, and Mrs. Gamp.   After
all, Shakespeare may have written *Titus Andronicus*.
The modern novel differs from its predecessors
mainly in this : that it is concerned, not with the
storm and stress of great, clear, passions and emotions,
but with the complication of them : the greatness
remains, the clearness is gone.   There is a sense of
entanglement: right and wrong, courage and cowardice,
duty and desire, are presented to us in confused
conflict.   Scientific law, irrevocable fate, inherited
impulse, thwarted and perverted emotions, distracted
and uncertain passions, take the place of the old simplicity : a simplicity, no doubt, of various degrees,
but in the main quite simple.   An early Italian artist
gives us his Moral Virtues, each a fair and stately
form, unmistakeable and complete : there is Forti-
tude, and that is Temperance : from a German artist
we have, here, Death the Skeleton, and there, Time
the Reaper.   It was a large, sane way of expression :
and that large, sane way, in spirit and in essence, may
be traced throughout literature also, up to modern

times. But in the troubled air of later days, obscure
with mists of doubt and difficulty, those lucid forms
have grown hard to discern, and dim : they move
against a background of shifting lights and colours.
Fielding and Thackeray may arrest their stories, to
say with the Cardinal de Retz : ' Permettez-moi, je
vous supplie, de faire un peu de réflexion sur la nature
de l'esprit de l'homme ' : but we no longer use set
phrase, or put forth a definite scheme : our work is
full of permeating influences, unseen forces, cross
currents, vague drifts and tendencies ; all obeying
some law, could we find it, and following some instinct,
could we detect it. The greatest modern novels
have about them a mysterious awe, like that of the
Æschylean drama : the Powers and Laws, almost
personified, of a Science, almost deified, hold the
actors in their grasp : and the actors, with their
rebellious dreams, revolts, desires, play a desperate
game. A vast deal of imposing nonsense is dealt out
to us, under the cover of these modern conceptions :
silly heroes posture in a fit of ' male green-sickness,'
unwholesome heroines display similar imaginations,
disease and delirium are pourtrayed with abnormal
gravity or delight. But from the weighty masterpieces of George Eliot, down to the daintiest trifle of
Mr. Henry James, works of singular power and
beauty have sprung from brains, that brood upon,
and imaginations, that dwell among, these problems
and questionings, bred of modern introspection.
Psychology, to use that ambitious term, supplies the
novelist with his studies and materials : not only the

free and open aspect of life itself.   It would be beyond
my purpose to discuss the foreign influences, that
have played upon the art of the English novelist : to
discriminate between the influence of Goethe and of
les Goncourt, of Stendhal and of M. de Maupassant,
of Balzac and of Count Tolstoi, of Flaubert and of
George Sand : it is done admirably, by skilled critics,
every week ; it is not necessary to my purpose of
dwelling, with what care and precision I may, upon
the works of an English novelist, who, continuing
the high traditions of his art, is faithful to the spirit
of his age ; but faithful also to the spirit of his country.

II

DESIGN AND COMPOSITION

In making mention of Mr. Hardy alone, as an eminent novelist of that modern kind, first raised to an high place by George Eliot, I do not forget his eminent fellows in the same field of art : nor do I forget those few brilliant writers of romance, who turn from anxious problems, to spirited adventures. But so great is the difficulty felt, and so great is the delicacy required, by critics of contemporary art, that the safer plan is to examine each notable writer by himself : and, in place of comparing to-day's artists with each other, to compare, contrast, and confront them, with the fine work of an established fame. That diligent and accomplished scholar, Dr. Birkbeck Hill, has of late pointed out to us time's many reversals of the verdicts, passed upon men of letters by their contemporary friends or foes : Shakespeare increases, Cowley decreases, Sterne stands firm, despite the prophetic censures of his day. Horace, with his parable of the horse's tail, long ago warned the world, how hard it is to fix the date, at which a writer receives the canonization of art, and becomes a classic : it is equally hard to determine the date, at which a writer, once noised and famous, ceases to find favour. Browning and Arnold died but a few years since ; yet

I cannot imagine that age to come, which will not esteem them, as great poets : Ascham and Habington, Drayton and Wotton, have now but few lovers ; yet to my own private taste, they very greatly relish. Upon the whole, sure and sound is the world's judgment, that these are classics, and those are not, these great, and those not great : but, chiefly honouring the classical and the great, let us recognize many degrees of merit and of fame. I dare not promise myself, since I have no voice in the decision, that Arnold and Browning, among the lately dead, Mr. Meredith and Mr. Hardy, among the yet living, will be held great and classic : but I have a right, upon a survey of literary annals, to feel sure, that favour, esteem, and consideration, in no slight degree will be always theirs. At the very least, there can be no presumption in the desire, and no great presumption in the attempt, to discuss those qualities of a living writer, which have won him the applause of his own day : though I desire not in panegyric to emulate the Alcalde of Corcuvion, who proclaimed Jeremy ' Baintham,' a Solon, a Plato, and a Lope de Vega.

It is to be borne in mind, that Mr. Hardy is no veteran in the service of good letters ; his first novel was published but twenty-one years since ; for aught we know, he may not have come to the plenitude of his powers : to say more upon this point were to risk an impertinence. With this fact of chronology in mind, to warn and to correct us, we may turn to Mr. Hardy's fifteen volumes. Thirteen of these are novels, of more or less elaborate design :

two are collections of short stories. For clearness'
sake, a classification of these fifteen volumes may
be tried, according to the dominant tone and nature
of the various groups, into which they fall with ease.
There seem to be three such groups : the *Tragic*,
the *Idyllic*, and a third ; for which I can find no
name, until one word be discovered to express in
combination the *comic*, the *ironic*, the *satiric*, the
romantic, the *extravagant* ; a spirit of mocking audacity,
and of serious laughter, animating a Pantagruel of
Psychology. The *Tragic* group comprises ; besides
Desperate Remedies, an early failure of much promise ;
the six books, upon which Mr. Hardy's readers love
to dwell : *The Return of the Native*, *The Woodlanders*,
Tess of the D'Urbervilles, *The Mayor of Casterbridge*,
Far from the Madding Crowd, and *A Pair of Blue Eyes*.
To these, may be added the finest of the *Wessex Tales*,
with other short stories, yet uncollected. The *Idyllic*
books are two : *Under the Greenwood Tree*, and, notwithstanding its greater dignity and sadness, *The
Trumpet Major*. To the third set, belong *The Hand
of Ethelberta*, *Two on a Tower*, *A Laodicean*, the short
stories called *A Group of Noble Dames*, and the *Romantic
Adventures of a Milkmaid*. No doubt, this classification is a little whimsical : all classifications, those
of the sciences excepted, must be so. I confess,
that the tragic novels contain purely idyllic passages ;
that the idyllic pair are not without their unhappy or
satiric touches ; that the remaining books, among
their engaging medley, exhibit simple tragedies and
simple idylls. But the dominant tone and nature of

the fifteen volumes warrant their careful reader, in making this triple division : a touch of innocent joy does but deepen the prevailing tragedy ; a stroke of grim tragedy does but add fresh zest to the sad laughter of the satirist ; a ripple of mockery, a breath from gloomier places, best serve to enhance the charm of idyllic scenes. ' Tragedy, comedy, history, pastoral, pastoral-comical, historical-pastoral, tragical-historical, tragical-comical-historical-pastoral ' ; thanks be to Polonius, for thus illustrating the necessity, the difficulty, and the frequent absurdity, of artistic classification. ' Blessed,' cried Hawthorne, ' blessed are all simple emotions, be they bright or dark : it is only the mixture of them that is infernal.' But his own miraculous charm comes of his concern for that mixture : and I doubt, whether Homer, the prince of simple and majestic art, does not most delight the world by the mingled emotions, both bright and dark, of Achilles and of Hector. With something in them of the beast, and something of the god, mortal men can know little of unmixed emotions. Mr. Hardy's moral treatment of these complexities, his artistic sincerity and truth, must be discussed elsewhere : at present, it is enough to say, that his stories, rightly or wrongly, blend darkness and light together ; that he mingles various proportions of either element, to produce various combinations ; and this, chiefly in the three manners already named.

The most appreciable mark of Mr. Hardy's power in design is the tenacity, with which his designs hold the memory : it resembles the power of architecture

to stamp there its great designs ; while music is
wont to leave but a vague sense of airy charm. That
flying, elusive, delight has its place in literature : but
only, I think, in verse. The genius of prose demands
a stricter beauty of design : graces it has, and delicate
adornments, and fit times for their introduction ;
but the genius of prose in general, and the genius of
narrative prose in especial, are averse from luxuriance
in these delicacies. M. de Maupassant declares his
hostility to those affectations in modern style, which
make of language a thing *bizarre, compliqué, nom-
breux, et chinois* : like affectations, in the construction of a story, are no less repugnant to the novelists
of lucidity and strength. To this matter of consistent and vigorous design might be applied a fine,
sententious, utterance of Mr. Pater : who himself,
by precept and by example, has so well insisted upon
the logical structure, necessary to good writing. ' The
perfection of culture is not rebellion but peace ; only
when it has realized a deep moral stillness has
it really reached its end.' Only when the artistic
teller of an imaginative story has passed through the
anxieties of choice, and determined his design ; when
he has realized that ' stillness ' and security of mind ;
can he hope to reach his end in peace of conscience.
He will not be enticed into divagations, pleasant by
themselves, but in the long run tiresome, because
distracting : he will eschew all matters by the way,
and confine himself to those, which serve his purpose
of exhibiting certain characters, under certain conditions and impulses, in their progress to certain

ends. He will know, when or whether to describe
the natural features of a country or place, and at
what length, and in what way : now, such a description is essential to a right understanding of his chosen
characters ; now, it is of the nature of a rare, justifiable,
digression. He will know, what variety of style is
in keeping with his final end and aim ; what, with his
immediate and subordinate business : nor will the
varieties employed in various passages be discordant
with that first and final end. If he have a dangerous
facility in pathos, or in humour ; a besetting desire
to use a certain kind of phrase or word, image or
illustration : he will constantly check himself, and
restrict the exercise of his facility to its proper occasions. He will know, that to give pleasure is the
end of his art ; but he will also know, that by doing
violence to the laws of his art, he will give pleasure
to many : and, in loyalty to his art and to his conscience,
he will choose rather to give a greater pleasure to
the few by his loyalty, than a less pleasure to the many
by his rebellion. Lastly ; to write down a commonplace, which some ' artists ' call a paradox ; the ideal
artist, and not least the novelist, will know with
Lessing, that truth is a necessary of the soul, and
may not be suppressed : but that pleasure, the end
of art, is not a necessary, and may be dispensed with
or foregone. To hold otherwise is, in the term of
Gregory XVI., a *deliramentum*.

The novelist's art, then, is a serious art : at the
present time, it is not easy to be a serious novelist
in the right way. The aim of a novel, as of all artistic

works, is pleasure : but pleasure is not another name for amusement, although it be clearly not another name for instruction. Yet the great majority of readers ' take up,' and ' glance at,' and ' look into,' and ' skim through,' and ' pass the time with,' novels : whilst a large number of the minority fall to upon them, with appetites eager for doctrine and for edification. Tasteless levity, if you will, and, beyond question, silly seriousness ! between these horrid extremes must the novelist find his golden mean. Again, these extremes have some reason upon their sides : the novelist need not resolve, neither to amuse at all, nor to instruct at all : yet some able novelists, with the gift of wit or humour, deny their gift, and turn to preaching ; others, with a capacity for artistic seriousness, in fear of being dull, elaborate painful jest books. To crown all, there is the incessant chatter of the theorists ; *sermo in circulis*, the talk of artistic groups and gatherings, the enthusiasms of pioneers, champions, innovators, reactionaries ; all the attendant bustle and hubbub, that are the delight of the artistic world, and the worry of the artist : all this has its effect, not a beneficial effect, upon any but strong and resolute workmen. Such a workman is Mr. Hardy : I will try to prove it, from his works.

I have said, that there is an architectural quality in the designs of Mr. Hardy ; it may be, in a measure, a result of some intimate acquaintance with architectural art, such as is manifested, even to excess, by the love of architectural topics and terms in many of his books. But, to supplement so literal an explanation, we can take it for granted, that the bent of his natural genius is towards a measured and spacious order of design : his books have a large and sweeping simplicity. Not only in the collective impression made by their definite outlines, but in the detailed effect of single, isolated, passages or pages, is this quality of adjustment felt. It is but seldom, that a reader can find so few, as five lines in these books, which would not suffer by detachment from their structural context. The keen epigram, the swift and brilliant saying, are rare : ' Love is a possible strength in an actual weakness ' is an example of that manner, in which Mr. Hardy is not wont to write : as is his sentence upon Grace Melbury, that she ' combined modern nerves with primitive emotions.' Both examples show a nicety, a felicity, in the art of making brief, neat, phrases : but Mr. Hardy prefers to build up his speech upon a statelier plan, and a larger scale ; making each word in the phrase, each phrase in the sentence, each sentence in the paragraph, each paragraph in the chapter, each chapter in the book, do its definite work : he is no spendthrift, nor miser, of language, and has no notion of careless, or of niggardly, dealing with his material. This fine economy in the use of words helps towards that general effect of gravity, seriousness, deliberation, which Mr. Hardy's work creates : you can no more miss a sentence, or give some hurried minutes to a chapter, than you can appreciate the proportions of a great Palladian building, if you omit to notice one of its orders. This unity of effect is, in my own judgment, the distinction of Mr. Hardy : that eminent quality, which I place at the head of his fine qualities, and which should constitute his securest claim to a lasting regard. It matters little, which of an author's books, out of the many admirable examples, be held by this man, or by that for his chief and master piece. Temperament, for the most part, rules our choice. So, without impugning another's right to make a different choice, I readily confess, that I can as little question the pre-eminence of *The Return of the Native*, among Mr. Hardy's works, as that of *King Lear*, among Shakespeare's plays. The naked facts of the story are few and plain. A great, waste tract of land, called Egdon Heath : Mrs. Yeobright, a widow, some degrees higher of rank than her neighbours, the peasantry ; a stern, loving, inflexible woman : her niece, Thomasin, married, against Mrs. Yeobright's will, to Damon Wildeve, a plausible, pitiful fellow, once an engineer, now a small inn keeper, pretty, shifty, clever, and young : Eustacia Vye, living on the heath with her grandfather, an old seaman, after a life at Budmouth, a fashionable watering place ; Eustacia is beautiful, fitful, imperious, discontented, and inexperienced ; she hates the great lonely heath, and makes an ideal of Budmouth ; and she has, half in boredom, half from self-deception and love of love, enslaved Wildeve : Clym Yeobright, the widow's only son, come home from a jeweller's business in Paris, out of a partly Quixotic, but wholly noble, disgust with selfish and low aims in life ; a gentle, affectionate youth, and hard as iron against all opposition to his fixed resolutions, in matters of sentiment and conduct : and Diggory Venn, an early suitor of Thomasin, once a farmer, now an itinerant ' reddleman,' and still her chivalrous defender. These are the six principal actors : I have given the most bald and meagre indications of their characters and lots : I will but add similar indications of the resulting tragedy. Clym intends, in a fit of revolt against ambition and worldliness, to begin some scheme of education, moral and mental, for the benefit of his peasant countrymen, to which his mother, in her pride of him, is hardly reconciled ; upon that blow, follows the far greater blow of the discovery, that Clym has fallen in love with, and means to marry, Eustacia ; who, finding in Clym a finer likeness to her ideal lover and hero, has given over Wildeve, and fallen in real love with his successor. They marry : Mrs. Yeobright and her son having a bitter reproach, one against the other. She in no way sanctions the marriage : and any early attempts at reconciliation are frustrated by misunderstandings. Clym, finding his eyesight fail him, takes to furze-cutting, like a labourer, for his living : he occupies a small cottage with Eustacia ; who learns to repent of her marriage, which has brought no realization of her vague hopes for some splendid or rapid scene of life ; and to renew her old capricious relations with Wildeve. Venn, Thomasin's unselfish lover, moves about the district, alert to discover anything, that nearly concerns her : through his agency, much of the drama is developed. Mrs.

Yeobright at last relents, in love for her only son, and sets out to visit him and his wife, upon a day of intense heat. Clym, tired with labour, is asleep in his room : his wife Eustacia, and his cousin's husband Wildeve, are discussing affairs, while he sleeps. Eustacia sees Mrs. Yeobright at the door : their eyes meet : Eustacia does not open the door, startled and afraid : the mother knocks again : it seems to rouse Clym : thinking, that Clym will open the door, Eustacia dismisses Wildeve by another way. Coming back, she finds Clym still sleeping, and his mother gone : she does not tell Clym : Mrs. Yeobright, worn out with suffering and physical weakness, is found by Clym, after his going out, at the point of death upon her way home. He accuses himself of killing his mother, and falls into a fever : upon recovery, he learns from casual talk with the folk of the place ; and from an explanation of certain words, spoken by his mother to a small boy upon the heath, as she lay down to die ; that Eustacia had seen her, had not opened the door to her, and had been with a man at the time. Exaggerating, in ignorance, her culpability, he upbraids her violently and wildly : she leaves him, and returns to her father's house. The story ends, in tragical misadventure, with the deaths of Eustacia and of Wildeve, one wild night, when he meant to drive her to Budmouth, whence she would go alone to France. Thomasin marries her loyal lover, Venn : Clym betakes himself, full of sorrowful experience, to his mission of simple preaching among the country folk.

This sketch I have given, with full intention, in a way that can interest no one, who does not know the book, and can but exasperate those, who do. Just so, might one sketch the rude outlines of a great Greek play ; Agamemnon, King of Mycenae, captain of the Greeks before Troy, was killed upon his triumphant return by his guilty wife, Clytemnestra, for the sake of her paramour, Ægisthus : just so, might one adumbrate the great arguments of a Shakespearian tragedy ; King Lear, deluded by the hypocrisies of his two elder daughters, and angered at the fearless sincerity of his youngest, divides his kingdom among the two, only to be driven mad by their heartless ingratitude ; whilst the spurned child, and one loyal friend, and a fool, are faithful to him in his miseries. There is much significance in the fact, that only great works of literary art can be thus crudely sketched, with any coherence at all : their bare, stark facts contain the heart of the whole matter ; whereas the power or charm of lesser works is inextricably bound up with their wayward incidents, their desultory graces, their fortunate distractions. After reading *The Return of the Native*, with a perfect relish of its details, still the simple truth of those bare facts, a girl's passionate caprice, a mother's hungry and jealous love, a son's agony of contrition, remains in the mind and in the memory, as the one thing borne in upon them, by the gradual evolution of the story. Now, this singleness and simplicity of effect are secured, only by an exquisite skill. To know, when an ornament, by its nature and place, will

minister to the attainment of a general unity and
simplicity in design, is the prerogative attribute of
genius : the merely clever workman, conscious that
he is weak in harmonious order and organization,
relies for his degree of success upon his happy turn
for disconnected and unessential ornament. ' The
elevation is poor, upon the whole ; but those mould-
ings are pretty ' : or, ' The characters are unnatural ;
but the descriptive passages are charming ' : criticisms of that nature are nothing else, than condemna-
tions of the thing criticized. They cannot be passed
upon the chief works of Mr. Hardy. *The Return of
the Native* opens with a chapter of descriptive writing,
to which I can find no just parallel, save certain periods
of Lucretius : those tremendous periods, where single
words seem to gather out of the deep, and to rever-
berate like the thunder. Presently, there is an
humourous, wild scene of country folk, round a bon-
fire on the hills, pourtrayed with an almost kindred
humour, grotesque and quaint. I might pass through
the book, noting the various contributions of Mr.
Hardy's knowledge and imagination, to Mr. Hardy's
purpose and design. They are all instinct with life,
they are all full of strength : but not one exceeds its
just limit, not one makes me forget its final end,
in its immediate excellence. The few tragical conclusions of the relentless logic are all in all : the
premises are remembered, chiefly because to those
great conclusions, they so surely led. Chiefly, but
not solely : where the whole is good, the parts are
good, and will therefore stand a scrutiny, each upon

its own merits : Mr. Hardy's novels are rich in good details, duly subordinate to his design. Were the temper of this age a severe temper, there would be profit, no less than pleasure, in lingering over some examples of such workmanship in details : but the temper of the age is not severe. ' Every thought I think is thought : and every word I write is writing.' Few authors of our day can make their own that fine, true, declaration of Cardinal Newman : the many seem to consider it too practical and prosaic a care, for the luxurious souls of artists to entertain. We have already pleaded, that the faults of great writers are to be forgiven them : ' Let not their frailties be remembered ; they were very great men ' : but no amount of virtue can cancel or transfigure a vice, no degree of general success can obliterate a partial failure. Where a living writer, with many faults and failures, yet deserves, upon a just reckoning, our praises, let him have them : but where a living writer gives us nothing but *peccata dulcia*, ingenious extravagances of lawless art, he is past pardon. It matters not at all, that great writers fall, now and then, into the same snare : they break away from it. I dwell upon Mr. Hardy's unity of design, because it is an excellence rarely desired now, and an excellence, which atones for a multitude of faults. Mr. Hardy's faults, as I seem to see them, are easily copied : but his severity, his austerity, his clearness and seriousness of conception, cannot be copied : they are his proper birthright, as an inheritor of the spirit of art.

For he is an inheritor, by pure descent and kinship :
not a *parvenu*, a *nouveau riche*, of literature : the praise
bestowed by Plutarch, upon the works raised up by
Pericles, the praise of being new and old, is applicable
here.   Nearly all Mr. Hardy's novels are concerned
with the sentiment of those changes, which are ever
coming over the worlds of society and of nature :
and with those enduring characteristics, which make
life, after all, so uniform and so unanimous.   He
dwells, in a dramatic meditation, upon the earth's
antiquity, the thought of ' the world's gray fathers,'
and in particular, upon certain tracts of land, with
which he has an intimacy ;   upon the human traditions of old time, upon the pageant of the past, upon
the relics of long gone powers and forces ;   gene-
alogies, rolls, tenures, heraldry ;   old names and old
houses lingering in decay, unconscious of their age ;
pagan impulses, the spirit of material and natural
religion, the wisdom and the simplicity, the blind and
groping thoughts, of a living peasantry still primitive ;
the antique works and ways of labour in woods and
fields, the sense of a sacred dignity inherent in such
things, in that immemorial need of man to till the
soil for his daily bread ;   meditation upon ' the drums
and tramplings ' of great armies, the fair forms of
vanished civilities, the heroism and the ambition,
the beauty and the splendour, long past away, while
still the old necessities remain, and still men go forth
to their work and to their labour, until the evening ;
meditation upon the slow, sure, end of all those even-
ings, in the darkness and the pains of death ;   medi-

tation upon the deep woods, under the black, starry,
nights, among the sounds of that solemn time, and
upon the generations of labourers in their graves ;
meditation upon their stern or generous virtues, their
patience, loving-kindness, and self-sacrifice ; upon
their humours and habits, the homely, pleasant,
features personal to each man of them ; upon the
great procession and continuance, above and beyond
these mortal lives, of universal laws : And there is
another side to his dramatic meditation : he loves
to contemplate the entrance of new social ways and
forms, into a world of old social preference and tradition ; to show, how there is waged, all the land over,
a conflict between street and field, factory and farm, or
between the instincts of blood and the capacities of
brain ; to note, how a little leaven of fresh learning
may work havoc among the weighty mass of ancient,
customary, thought ; to exhibit the mercurial influence of new things upon old, the frivolous fashion
and light vulgarity of the seaside town, in contrast
with the staid dignity and cumbrous strength of the
gray village, the significance discernible in the intrusion of the jaunty villa among barns and dwellings
and churches, old ' as the hills ' ; to build up, touch
by touch, stroke upon stroke, the tragedy of such
collision, the comedy of such contrast, the gentle
humour or the heartless satire of it all, watched and
recorded by an observant genius.

So considering Mr. Hardy's work, I cannot confine
my thought of him to the immediate interests of
to-day : I cannot but think of him, as of one, upon

whom has fallen a powerful spirit of great art : as
of one, who has received a vocation to do great things
for English literature. We have too many writers,
who seem unconscious of their English birth ; to
whom ' the glories of their blood and state,' as Englishmen, bring no exultation ; who care nothing for the
distinguishing genius of their land, without pride
in its achievements, joy at the thought of it, love for
its earth. Placid cosmopolitans ! but not artists :
art must always be national, in the sense, that men of
a certain nature, in certain places, at certain times,
must, partly from the compulsion of circumstances,
partly at the dictate of their own artistic sense, display
the virtues, common to the art of all times and places,
in particular manners. Mr. Hardy can lie under
no charge of insular arrogance : but he uses powers,
in which I see many affinities with the French genius
of our time, not in a French manner, but in an English ;
revealing his art in no provincial way, but rather producing books of which, at their best, it may be said :
' Here is work, done after the best English manner :
and its truth to nature, its truth to art, are universal.'
That is really higher praise than : ' Here is work,
which looks like an admirable translation from the
French.' This patriotic element of Mr. Hardy's
art, felt rather in the whole drift of his natural genius,
than in any written profession of faith, or declaration in words, will be more closely examined, when
we come to consider by themselves his treatment of
country folk, his portraits of men and women, his
delineation of his own Wessex.   At present, it is in the

design and composition of his novels, taken together, that I would try to make clear his classic manner of work. His interest in modern subtilties of emotion and of thought is an interest, which separates him, as a novelist, from the older novelists : I do not say, which sets him above them. But in the largeness of design, in the march and sweep of imagination, in the greatness of his greater themes, he has given to the novel a simple grandeur and impressiveness, the more impressive, for his pre-occupation with the concerns of modern thought. "The figures of Tess, of Henchard, of Winterborne, of Mrs. Yeobright, of Marty South, of Boldwood ; tragic, passionate figures ; move across the stage ' in all the pomp of exquisite distress,' with sorrows full of dignity : yet nearly all, if indeed not all, are thwarted and cast down by some sentiment or event, which gives rise to troubled questionings and to searchings of heart, inarticulate or unintelligible, apart from the promptings of modern mental science, and of modern emotional thought." There is no discord between the old passions, and the new touches which arouse them ; between the old emotions, and the new appeals which wake them : Chaucer and Shakespeare, Shakespeare and Wordsworth, Wordsworth and Browning, one does not clash with the other, despite the vast changes of thought and knowledge, which make each of them present the same play of life, in very different fashions. The little men, for all their quick cleverness, cannot charm us by their tricks and turns, into thinking of them quite seriously : what is novel in them, may

deserve some compliment, but not the manner of
its presentation. In Mr. Hardy's work, there is a
manner of presentation, which has about it something
Elizabethan, something Shakespearian ; or something
of later date, Jacobean and Caroline : His morality,
be it the appropriate sentiment of his rustic folks,
or the prevalent tone of his whole works, contains
echoes of those spacious and elaborate times. Browne's
rich solemnity of meditation upon death and change ;
the lyrical dirges of Webster, Beaumont, Shirley ; the
peculiar accent of Shakespeare's commoners and
clowns, so racy and so shrewd, experience talking,
as it were, in quips and cranks and jests, conceits
and saws and by-words ; much of all that recurs
to the mind of Mr. Hardy's readers, as the slow story
unfolds itself so surely. The increasing gravity,
noticeable in the best of Mr. Hardy's later books, in
The Woodlanders, *The Mayor of Casterbridge*, *Tess
of the D'Urbervilles*, is the same in spirit and in kind,
as the increasing gravity in Shakespeare's maturer
work. What *Romeo and Juliet* is to *King Lear*, that,
each in its lower degree of excellence, is *The Trumpet
Major* to *The Woodlanders*. This steady progress in
seriousness of presentation marks the laborious artist,
not content with the more facile beauty, but pressing
on towards its more august and difficult forms.
Gravitas, *auctoritas*, the pressure of spirit upon matter,
controlling and informing it ; the heightened sense
of what is meant by these loves, hates, joys, sorrows,
lives, deaths, so ready to the artist's hand, but too
great to be lightly treated ; the stronger mastery

over that rhythmical impulse, which finds fit words to express the almost inevitable impulse of passion : these are signs of an art still unsatisfied, still hungering after its ideal ; an art, ambitious of nothing less than continual progress, and ever anxious for its perfection. Progress in art is progress towards simplicity : at first, the sense of power over the world intoxicates the artist : these tragedies and comedies, things humourous and things fantastic, are at his mercy, to be handled, moulded, shaped, as pleases him : he makes experiments among the lives and souls of men, luxuriating in the emotions of a creator. But, ' it 's no' fish ye 're buying—it 's men's lives ' : until the literary artist have a sense of sacredness in his relation of men's lives, he remains trivial, inconsiderable : ' For soul is form, and doth the body make,' as the poet said, after Aristotle. The humourist begins, either in pettinesses or in extravagances : he must find his way to the natural heart of things. When Fielding tells us of Major Bath, with his eternal talk about the dignity of man ; how he is found, wrapped in a woman's bedgown, warming his sick sister's posset, and heartily ashamed of his detection : then Fielding changes from our boisterous entertainer to our generous friend, and that, through a triumph of humourous art.

Mr. Hardy is fast making us forget his extravagances in his realities, and the change is great. Extravagance of a sort he will always love, it inheres in his chosen materials : but he has abandoned artificiality for art. His earlier extravagance is an

extravagance, which delights in audacities of situation, and in exhibitions of temperament, rather startling
than brilliant : a certain touch of unpleasantness,
and taste of vulgarity, just felt by the distressed
reader, went near to spoiling some stories, otherwise
delightful. The satire seemed almost splenetic, the
humour little else than bad nature : the cynic's
wit was mordant, the jester's smile, a sardonic
wrinkling of the lips. *A Laodicean, The Hand of
Ethelberta* and *Two on a Tower*, I write it with
reluctance, contain much that fills me with admiration, but still more that fills me with annoy-
ance : I see the conscious schemes of them, their
spirit and design ; the superb audacity, in especial,
which directed the fates of Swithin, Viviette, and the
Bishop : but something unkind, an uncanny sort
of pleased and sly malevolence, looks out upon me
from many a page, and stops the laughter. Whimsi-
calities, incongruities, detected by the humourist in
the nature of things ; degradations, disgraces, dragged
by him to the light of day : these need give no offence.
Nor is there any essential matter of offence in the
play of a philosophical humour, the mocking of a
keen wit. But a reader, capable of enjoying the excel-
lences of Rabelais, Voltaire, Swift, Heine, Sterne,
may yet refuse to admire certain things in some of
Mr Hardy's books : although he can find in them
nothing coarse, indecent, bestial, irreverent, salacious,
in the varied fashions of those five great men. Reuben
the tranter had much truth upon his side, when he
disagreed with his wife's distaste for the ' musical

circumstances' of old Michael Mail : ' Well, now, that coarseness that 's so upsetting to Ann's feelings is to my mind a recommendation ; for it do always prove a story to be true. And for the same reason, I like a story with a bad moral. My sonnies, all true stories have a coarseness or a bad moral, depend upon 't. If the story-tellers could have got decency and good morals from true stories, who 'd ha' troubled to invent parables ? ' Gross facts and unwelcome conclusions may test our sincerity in facing life : with those, we have no quarrel. But Ethelberta's matrimonial schemes, or the talk of Lord Mountclere with his valet, or Captain de Stancy's first stolen sight of Paula in her gymnasium, or Lady Constantine's rather sickly affection, are not gross, great facts, nor do they conduct us by a logic of wholesome severity to unwelcome conclusions : they are merely what annoyances are to sorrows, or bad manners to natural roughness. Doubtless, it would be foolish to look for a ' high seriousness ' in works of deliberate extravagance : it is none the less distasteful, to come upon a somewhat mean unpleasantness, pervading books of so much power.

A like displeasing artificiality spoils the narrative in these books : though with a less jarring effect upon the reader. A favourite contrivance is the assemblage of several actors upon the scene, sometimes unconscious of each other's presence, or intention to be present ; sometimes against each other's will, in a grotesque contrast with each other. Thus, in *Despeate Remedies*, which foreshadowed faintly many of

Mr. Hardy's coming virtues and vices, we have the
singular nocturnal procession, ' at equi-distances of
about seventy yards,' of Æneas Manston, Miss Ald-
cliffe, Anne Seaway, and the detective officer : in
The Hand of Ethelberta, the juxtaposition at the Rouen
inn, of Ethelberta and her three suitors ; Lord Mountclere in the lower room, while Ladywell and Neigh,
each in an upper room, lean from their windows,
and hear his lordship's proposal : and we have also
the journey of Mr. Mountclere and Sol Chickerel,
to prevent, the one his brother's, the other his sister's,
marriage ; the journey of Christopher Julian, her
lover, and the butler, her father, each unknown to the
other, upon the same business ; the union of the two
parties, and their arrival together, five minutes too
late. In *A Pair of Blue Eyes*, which deserves Mr.
Stevenson's description, ' a worthy specimen of the
dramatic novel,' there are coincidences, contrasts,
oddities of circumstance, almost wholly natural and
justifiable, yet with a touch of a like extravagance :
Elfride, Stephen, and Knight, that tragic trio, in
various combinations, repeating the same scenes,
meeting under conditions of curious strangeness ;
until they meet at last, Elfride in her coffin, the wife of
neither ; and her two rival lovers, with their strained
old intimacy of master and pupil, travelling in the
train that carries her ; each having concealed from the
other his purpose of going down to find her, both
ignorant of her death. Mr. Hardy is too simple and
strong a master of his art, to insist always upon his
coincidences of time and place, or his repetitions of

incident and experience, with any forced emphasis :
but, now and then, some artificiality, an occasional
stiffness and eccentricity of mechanical contrivance,
makes itself felt. Had the novelist done no more
than write the books, which contain such faults of
taste and artificialities of device, he would be no more
than a writer of great cleverness.

It is to be observed, that Mr. Hardy's sureness of
heart and hand deserts him, or in a measure deserts
him, only when he deserts Wessex and its people, or
when he deals with Wessex people, uncharacteristic
of Wessex. In fidelity to nature, his men and women
of what is called good society, or of what is called
education, compared with his Wessex folk, are like
Lady Blarney and Miss Carolina Wilhelmina Amelia
Skeggs, by the side of Dr. Primrose. Every novelist
of peculiar excellence in rendering the note, the *cachet*,
of certain classes and places, seems to lose something
of his skill in venturing outside them : Dickens, for a
familiar example, abandoned the great medley of
' middle and lower ' classes in the town, at his peril.
Mr. Hardy is fond of pourtraying the troubles, that
come from the infusion of a little experience, a little
education, dazzling and disquieting, into the old, placid,
homely village lives : or of showing the effect upon
new, vigorous mind and blood, of contact with hoar,
' effete ' antiquity. Grace Melbury, Eustacia Vye,
Ethelberta Petherwin, Stephen Smith, Bathsheba Ever-
dene, even Matilda Johnson, produced upon their
families or their neighbours the same effect : the
feeling of uncomfortable inferiority, the fear of being

' scorned ' by these elegant and accomplished persons, with their book learning and their polished airs.   Paula Power, again, heiress of a railway king, has an irresistible longing for the ancient splendour of the de Stancy line, whose castle she inhabits : Edred Fitzpiers, the very contemptible young doctor, last representative of an old house, fascinates farmer Melbury, against his will and sense of justice, into a preference for him above Winterborne, his farmer rival for the hand of Grace, so elevated by her fine schooling above the rustic level : the discovery, that Tess is a D'Urberville, has its profound charm for the very radical and modern Angel Clare.   Endless is the chain of thought, that these things prolong :   what ponderings upon necessity, upon assertions of the old blood, upon the revenges and the ironies of time and fate !   But Mr. Hardy himself, no less than his own creatures, seems at times perplexed by it all :   and to lose his clearness of sight, with gazing at the revolution of the wheel.

' It was at Rome, on the 15th of October, 1764, as I sat musing amidst the ruins of the Capitol, while the barefooted friars were singing vespers in the temple of Jupiter, that the idea of writing the decline and fall of the city first started to my mind.'   So confesses the luminous Gibbon :   and Goldsmith meditates, how

> ' In those domes, where Caesars once bore sway,
> Defaced by time, and tottering in decay,
> There in the ruin, heedless of the dead,
> The shelter-seeking peasant builds his shed ' ;

and Rabelais, in solemn speculation, thinks that

' plusieurs sont aujourd'huy empereurs, rois, ducs, princes et papes en la terre, lesquelz sont descenduz de quelques porteurs de rogatons et de costrets. Comme, au rebours, plusieurs sont gueux de l'hostiaire, souffre- teux et miserables, lesquelz sont descenduz de sang et ligne de grands rois et empereurs.' It is all trite and obvious, certainly ; the commonplace of moralists : but I find something far from commonplace in the spectacle of a writer, brooding over the ancient history of his native soil, and far back into the ages without history : and then surveying it with his own eyes, acre by acre, hill and vale by hill and vale, and marking the permanence and the change, the growth and the decay, the sublime in it and the ridiculous, the laughter in it and the tears. Little wonder is it, if Mr. Hardy should sometimes reflect the confusion of the change, rather than the calm of the endurance. But with any such defects, I have done, preferring to speak of triumphs and successes.

From long and frequent converse with the works of any favourite author, we often grow to thinking of them under some symbol or image ; to see them summed up and expressed in some one composite scene of our own making : this is my ' vision ' of Mr. Hardy's works. A rolling down country, crossed by a Roman road : here, a gray standing stone, of what sacrificial, ritual origin, I can but guess ; there, a grassy barrow, with its great bones, its red brown jars, its rude gold ornaments, still safe in earth : a broad sky burning with stars : and a solitary man. It is of no use to turn away, and to think of the village farms and cottages, with their antique ways and looks ; of the deep woods, the fall of the woodman's axe, the stir of the wind in the branches ; of the rustic feasts and festivals, when the home-brewed drink goes round, to the loosening of tongues and wits ; of the hot meadows, fragrant hayfields, cool dairies, and blazing gardens ; of shining cart horses under the chestnut trees, and cows called in at milking time : they are characteristic scenes, but not the one characteristic scene. That is the great down by night, with its dead in their ancient graves, and its lonely living figure : it brings before my thought a pageant of Scandinavian warriors, Roman soldiers and Stoics, watchers upon Chaldaean plains, laborious Saxon peasants, Celtic priests in the moonlight ; and vast periods of early time, that chill the pondering mind. And the sentiment of a sacred dignity in pastoral, rural, labours, is prominent here : the lonely figure recalls the spirit of Virgil in his *Georgics*, of Giotto's shepherds with their flocks, of Wordsworth and of Millet : of Arnold's *Resignation*, of Arnold's *Scholar-Gipsy*. How much experience must the ' clown,' the ' common labourer,' have amassed from the earth, the downs, the fields, with their *vasta silentia*, their *otia dia* ! Like Claudian's old Veronese, the man has lived close to his mother earth, not hurried hither and thither :

> ' *Erret, et extremos alter scrutetur Iberos :*
> *Plus habet hic vitae : plus habet ille viae.*'

Painful, such a life must be ; not without its heaviness and its weight : but not ignoble, its very offences

in our more civilized eyes being animal, not bestial.
Sordid and gross, savage and repulsive, such a life
can be : but not utterly grovelling and inhuman, at
its worst : at its best, full of grandeur and high virtues.
Mr. Meredith's Master Gammon embodied, to the
anxious minds at Queen Anne's Farm, ' the grand
primæval quality of unchangeableness ' : Hawthorne's
Silas Foster gave a like healthy lesson to his trans-
cendental pupils in agriculture : and the labouring
man, whom I see by night upon the downs, at his
patient watch, is the incarnate emblem of Mr. Hardy's
books.

This is no more than an imaginative summary, by
the help of concrete symbols, of the finer and the
deeper impressions made upon the mind, by Mr.
Hardy's best work : a sense of awe, in the presence of
a landscape filled with immemorial signs of age ; a
sense of tranquillity in the presence of human toil, so
bound up and associated with the venerable needs of
human life.   But Mr. Hardy is no mere patron of the
dignity and the honour of labour, standing at heart a
little aloof from its realities ; content to admire its
historical and monumental aspects ; satisfied with
blessing its nobility from a distance.   How near and
dear to him is the labouring life of Wessex, I hope
to show presently : now I will rather indicate, with
what stir and movement of strong passions he animates it all.   ' He rides well his horse of the night,'
said Emerson of Hawthorne, after one of his long,
unbroken silences : take away the tinge of unhealthy
restraint, at which the sentence hints, and you have a

marked feature of Mr. Hardy's ' heroes.' They are
strong, generous, and capable of ' a wise passiveness ' :
and their part is the part of Jacob serving Laban for
love of Rachel. Giles Winterborne, John Loveday,
the Reddleman, Gabriel Oak : how well do they
contrast with those worldlier lovers, men with the
spirit, now of a tarnished Lovelace, now of a gilded
Branghton ; men of imperfect gentilities, and of in-
complete refinements ! With the trials, overcome or
not, of these flighty creatures, we have little sympathy :
but when Winterborne dies his gracious death, we are
present at the passing of a martyr :

> ' Nothing is here for tears, nothing to wail,
> Or knock the breast ; no weakness, no contempt,
> Dispraise, or blame ; nothing but well and fair,
> And what may quiet us in a death so noble.'

We have the same exaltation of heart, when the
Trumpet Major's ringing step is heard, as he leaves
his lost love to his unworthy brother, in the disguise
of a brave gaiety, going off ' to blow his trumpet, till
silenced for ever upon one of the bloody battlefields
of Spain.' And the Reddleman, that guardian angel
of a grim colour, moves about ' haggard Egdon ' with
a loyal care for Thomasin, which even the winning of
her seems hardly to reward. And Shepherd Oak is
of the same strong make, patient and true. These
men endure dumb agonies and silent pangs : they
have a pagan majesty of mien, these Wessex country
folk, with their slow speech and ancient dialect.
Against these, are set the figures of plausible scamps
and braggarts, vulgar and mean in their flashy tricks

of accomplishment : Sergeant Troy, who has at least a martial bearing ; Fitzpiers, the tinsel gallant and spurious gentleman ; Wildeve, the dangling, pretty fellow ; Bob Loveday, with his stupid insincerity and shallowness ; even Jim Hayward, so skilled in the diplomacy of love. And the plays are played out among the most appropriate scenes : be it woodland or moorland, sheepfold or dairy farm, seacoast or inland, market town or hamlet, Mr. Hardy knows what the nature of things will bring about in each case. He has, what Hawthorne had, a gift of sight into the spirit of place : a most rare gift. With a few words, he makes us smell the damp woods ; catch the change in the wind's voice, as it travels through each kind of tree ; know the foldings of the hills by heart, and by instinct, what lies beyond them ; recognize each tree, by the noise of its snapping twigs, or the rustle of its dead leaves underfoot ; keep the path through the heath at night, by the feel of its worn herbage ; remember, how the ash and the beech, more than other trees, hold the early dripping fog : a few words, and we can swear to the occupations of a dozen labourers, though in their Sunday dress, and without their implements ; distinguish upon the road the farmer, whose negotiations at market have prospered, from him, who has not hit things off to his mind ; is it not to be read in the complexion ? As the naturalist with a bone, so Mr. Hardy with a word can construct for us the whole manner of a man, the whole aspect of a place. Not the looks of definite objects only, but their surrounding and intervening atmospheres, become plain to us ; the blue mists, or dusty gold lights, or thin gray breaths of air : once familiarized with one of his places, we know all about it.   If we step out of doors in Little Hintock, or upon Egdon, or at Casterbridge, in some dream or fancy of our own, we know our way ; we know, according to season, what the wind will be doing with the cottage chimney smoke by nightfall, or what apples will be upon the grass by morning, or what prices are current at the corn exchange, or what likelihood there be of a fair lambing time.   But if we search Mr. Hardy's books, to discover why we know this so surely, we are hard put to it for a reason : so delicate has been his manner, so natural and unobtrusive his ' mental tactility,' that we have learned it all from his pages, as we should learn it by experience : our certainty and familiarity have grown upon us.   It is in a very different manner, that M. Zola instructs us : ' Those are the facts,' he seems to say, ' catalogued and scheduled ; you may rely upon their technical accuracy ; and you may take it for truth, that I have omitted nothing and added nothing ' : with the result, if I may quote my humble experience, that I remember little, but his fine violations of his own laws.   *Quelle magnifique carrière il a mal courue !* and how thankful must he be, that he is not living under Theban law.

This subtile fidelity to nature makes it difficult to light upon separable passages, by way of example : detach a phrase, a scene, a dialogue, and it cries out against you for the mutilation, like the trees of Virgil and of Dante.   I have already spoken of Mr. Hardy's almost architectural feeling for constructive unity :

E.

but constructive unity of design may be the cold result of a servile respect for laws and canons, the correctness of a pedantic humanist : the subtile fidelity, the living congruity, which we have just considered, show us that from such pedantry and coldness, Mr. Hardy is free. Each of his greater books, the books of high and simple intention, has its orderly movement towards its end predestined : there is no wantoning with chance attractions by the way : phrase and scene and dialogue, incident and narrative and meditation, like the members of a body, do their part in their several places, for the general and common good. A curious effect is produced by the patient elaboration of story and of style, in these novels : it brings a strange conviction home to the reader, a comfortable assurance. Line upon line, as characters unfold, and passions wake, and motives meet or cross, the reader's mind falls into step with the writer's : to vary the figure, I might say that the reader answers the writer's call, as one instrument another, by sympathy. But so quietly do the fine actors perform their allotted parts ; without strut and blare and fustian, but in the plain beauty of all natures, faithful to themselves ; that when they have done, we seem to have assisted at the progress of a story within our actual experience : romance ? we ask ourselves ; psychology ? or what is the name for this spirit of simple truth ? After all, critical terms are poor enough : and this rich play of passions and emotions, with its ancient elements, in their modern combinations, deserves no poorer name than truth.

In dwelling upon a few results of Mr. Hardy's style,

I recognize the inexhaustible amount of positions, from which style may be considered, and of lights, under which it may be viewed. Yet all is said, if we are content to say, that scholarship is the only arbiter of style : scholarship, the adroit urbanity of an artist, which passes judgment upon his aims and inspirations. In any living sense of the term, scholarship is a natural good breeding in the arts of humane life, quickened and trained by discipline : it implies a sense of the absurd, the impossible : it may show itself in a thousand forms, and always with becoming grace :

'*Mille habet ornatus, mille decenter habet.*'

Pedantry and illiteracy, it holds in equal abhorrence ; all lack of urbanity, all failure in courtesy, all marks of the clown and of the fop, are hateful to scholarship : whilst it is tolerant of infinite variety. The scholar thinks with Pope's friend : ' my Lord has so bad a taste, as to like all that is good ' : he has his preferences, but no prejudices. Among authors and books and styles, he has his more intimate friends and favourites : but he is convinced, that the good of all ages and of all kinds are more like each other, than they are like their bad contemporaries. From Thucydides' *Reflections on the Revolution in Corcyra*, we pass to Burke's *Reflections on the Revolution in France*, with no sensible discomfort, or surprise of complete change. The style of Mr. Hardy is a deliberate and a grave style : his thought falls into phrases and paragraphs of a Latin massiveness. Rarely can it be called supple, agile, brilliant : the sentences do not flash out with a bright play of wit and fancy, in the manner of some delightful modern writers.   Rather, Mr. Hardy culti- vates a sustained equability, like that of the Roman writers : he gives us the comfortable sense of dealing with realities.   Of each page, and paragraph, and sentence, we can say, that we know the reason of its existence : the measured expressions, one with another, each contributing its just service, compose an organic whole.   There is no hurry : none of that haste to be concise and tense, which makes a cluster of excited epigrams do the work of many rich and thoughtful pages.   The genius, which gets at the ultimate sim- plicity of things, their vitality, their reality, knows with what care of expression, at what expense of space, in what tone and key, to communicate its apprehensions of each several thing : and, the thing communicated rightly, the reader accepts it rightly, without any immediate sensation of wonder or surprise.   That sensation is felt, when the story is over : then comes the rush of emotion, as the accumulated truth and beauty, which in detail we have quietly accepted, come home to us in their unity and their entirety.   *Tantae molis erat*, we say, so great a labour and a toil were wanted, to build up this one human soul in strength and truth, to work out these fates of a few men and women, to make real the pity and the glory of it all : meditating upon the evolution or construction of the work, we have no lack of enthusiasm and of delight. Much, doubtless, of the dignity of the work comes from its occupation with dignified natures : with men and women conscious, in a deep and fearless way, of

the great, commanding verities, life and death, love
and hate ; beings of a pagan resignation, almost of a
sombre pride, at the thought of fate and of fatality ;
creatures unskilled in the culture of light emotions,
vagrant impressions, the cross purposes and chance
hints of those, whose nerves are over sensitive, whose
minds are over flexible. To say this, is to say that
Mr. Hardy's form is proper to his subject : for there
is evidence in plenty, that his work is full of conscious
pains, of forethought, and of elaboration.

The scholarly workmanship of Mr. Hardy recalls
to me the large manner of our early masters in English
prose : those masters of the rich phrase, the elaborate
cadence, the liberal and golden eloquence. Many a
passage in these novels, where the writer has gathered
up his powers for a prolonged triumph over the difficulties of a great occasion, seems to belong in spirit
to those writers of ' might and majesty,' whom Landor
loved ; to whom Edward Irving paid allegiance, in
periods equal to their own : ' I cannot learn to think,
as they have done, which is the gift of God : but I
can teach myself to think as disinterestedly, and to
express as honestly what I think and feel. They are
my models of men : of Englishmen, and of authors.
My conscience could find none so worthy, and the
world hath acknowledged none worthier. They were
the fountains of my English idiom : they taught me
forms for expressing my feelings : they showed me
the construction of sentences, and the majestic flow
of continuous discourse.' Examine some of Mr.
Hardy's heightened passages, knit together and com-

pact, instinct with a passion strongly controlled : and
then turn to those old classics of our tongue. You
will find the same air of delighted mastery, the same
sense of royal command over a rich language, the same
exercise of unwearied powers throughout great reaches
of thought and feeling. Sometimes, the resemblance
is of a lesser kind ; an echo of some choice, particular
style, just caught and recognized : thus, is not Burton
audible here ? These were among the things but
darkly known to Angel Clare, before his farming life :
' the seasons in their moods, morning and evening,
night and noon in their temperaments, winds in their
several dispositions, trees, waters, and clouds, shades
and silences, *ignes fatui*, constellations, and the voices
of inanimate things.' Down to the touch of Latin,
that roll call of great natural facts, where the writer's
mind and ear can be felt luxuriating in the richness
of sense and sound together, is in the full and flowing
manner of Burton : whom Mr. Hardy further resembles, in that he too is *vere Saturnius*.

For the most part, Mr. Hardy delights in the immense resources of our traditional speech : without
wandering into new paths, he knows, how much
strength and beauty spring from the simplest words,
well chosen and well consorted by the scholar's dis-
crimination. Perhaps, it is not sufficiently remembered by some readers, that scholarship and erudition
are no less concerned with simple things, than with
recondite and abstruse : that what charms them, in a
writer's sure and lucid style, so full of grace and ease,
is quite as much a result of knowledge, as it is a natural

gift. It is a truth best learned, by study of the classical
French prose writers : of Pascal and Voltaire, Fénelon
and Rousseau, Massillon and Bossuet. A clear conception of the thing to be set down in words, the quite
simple and appropriate words, produces wonders.
Modern English is in some danger of losing that
powerful charm, by its hatred of simplicity : but our
old writers, even the forgotten among them, are seldom
without it. I take down the first book, ready to my
hand : it is a version of Herodian, ' Done from the
Greek by a Gentleman at Oxford,' 1698. Commodus,
we read, was very beautiful : ' His Eyes were languish-
ing, and yet had a particular sort of lustre : His Hair
was curled, and yellow, resembling Flame, when he
walked in the Sun ; which made some Men fansie
he was powdered with Dust of Gold.' Here, the
writer has not a free hand ; he is translating : but
the singular charm of the sentence is due to the trans-
lator's satisfaction with simple words, full of force and
grace, dexterously assorted. Mr. Hardy abounds in
such fine simplicities : and, whilst his happy turns
and phrases do not startle us into a surprised delight,
disproportionate to their importance, they fill us with
a continual pleasure. ' The sad science of renuncia-
tion ' : Pascal could not better that. ' They sat in a
rigid reticence, that was almost a third personality ' :
it is as good as Browning's ' one and one, with a
shadowy third.' ' Her touch upon your hand was as
soft as wind ' : Fletcher might have imagined it, or
Herrick. ' The shearers reclined against each other
as at suppers in the early ages of the world ' : it is

said in the most delicate manner of Hawthorne. ' The occasional heave of the wind became the sigh of some immense sad soul, conterminous with the universe in space, and with history in time ': Senancour wrote so, at the height of his mournful wisdom. There is no cleverness, sought after and hard won, in these perfect sentences : they are right, by some natural magic of their own, as Virgil's and as Dante's words are right : and, again in the way of those masters, it is scholarship, with its disciplined joy in the simple and the severe, that helped the writer to capture the beauty of this natural magic. In his greater books, the four or five tragedies upon which, surely, his fame will rest, Mr. Hardy preserves, with scarce a lapse into less austere a style, the accent of stateliness and of solemnity, unsoftened and unrelieved by the gentler spirit of sympathy, so frequent a companion of the delicately austere. And now, to more literal matters.

Verbal criticism has its antagonists : before, then, I venture upon some verbal criticism, I may in brief touch upon the controversy. Pope spent some of his glorious wit upon the verbal critics :

' Each wight, who reads not, and but scans and spells,
    Each Word-catcher, that lives on syllables ' :

And Pope, whom Hazlitt echoed, is still, in my belated judgment, an authority upon points of the kind. But so too is Ascham : ' They be not wise, that say, *what care I for Man's Words and Utterance, if his Matter, and Reasons be good?* . . . Ye know not, what Hurt

ye do to Learning, that care not for Words, but for
Matter ; and so make a Divorce betwixt the Tongue
and the Heart.' And, to provide one more champion,
let us hear Landor : ' There are those, who would persuade us, that verbal criticism is unfair, and that few
poems can resist it. The truth of the latter assertion
by no means establishes the former : all good criticism hath its foundation on verbal.' Pope was too
brilliant a master of words, and too brilliant a verbal
critic, to condemn all such criticism : he did but mean
to condemn the petulant pedantry, which is wholly
enslaved to the letter.

Upon points of construction, I have one charge,
and only one, to bring against the style of Mr. Hardy :
he, like Miss Burney, is an inveterate patron of ' the
split infinitive ' : an usage, which deserves the severest
censures of purist and precisian. This excepted, Mr.
Hardy writes a style of grammatical nicety : nervous
and sound. I may add, that his style is unaided by
his stops : among recent novelists, Dickens alone,
whose knowledge of the last century novelists was
thorough, has preserved their perfect punctuation.
Against his vocabulary, here and there, has been
brought a charge of undue parade and pomp, in the
use of erudite terms : a fondness for the expressions
of physical sciences, the phraseology of the arts, and
the like. Before coming to a consideration of the
charge, in Mr. Hardy's case, some older critics may
help us : Flaubert and Baudelaire and Gautier, Henne-
quin and M. Zola and M. Mallarmé, with all their
colleagues or opponents, may sometimes be set aside,

and suffer us to hear Quintilian or Ben Jonson,
Cicero or Dryden.

Here is a little wisdom from the *Discoveries* : ' Some
words are to be culled out for ornament and colour,
as we gather Flowers to strow Houses, or make Gar-
lands ; but they are better when they grow to our
stile ; as in a Meadow, where though the meer grass
and greenness delights ; yet the variety of Flowers
doth heighten and beautifie. Marry, we must not
play or riot too much with them, as in Paranomasies.'
Again : ' Words borrowed of Antiquity do lend a kind
of Majesty to stile, and are not without their delight
sometimes. For they have the Authority of Years,
and out of their intermission do win to themselves a
kind of grace-like newness. But the oldest of the
present, and newest of the past Language, is the best.'
Once more : ' You are not to cast a Ring for the per-
fumed Terms of the Time, as Accommodation, Complement, Spirit, &c. But use them properly in their
place.' Dryden also, whose *Prefaces* are among the
masterpieces of our criticism and of our prose, warns
the writer against ' a too curious election of words.'
And Quintilian, protesting against the abuse of rhetoric,
denounces those who, ' seduced by glittering show,
and shrinking from common ways of speech, encom-
pass all that they have to say with floods of verbosity ' :
and Cicero, who ' writes Roman,' is no less anxious
to avoid the *emblema vermiculatum*, intricate mosaic
work in words.

Now, there is no lack in England of flourishing
eccentrics, who devote a passionate diligence to the

construction of such work : I would, Pantagruel had
by the throat these professors of strange speech. They
suffer, many of them, from the delusion, that they
are very French : emulating, with pathetic zeal for
the impossible, certain French graces, and still more,
certain French follies, which cannot survive trans-
plantation. ' French folly,' wrote Voltaire in English,
' is pleasanter than English madness ' : *pleasanter* :
that is precisely true : English writers play the fool
but awkwardly. But there are others, who do not
offer violence to the genius of the English tongue ;
yet whose writing contains words and phrases, not
wholly acceptable at first sight : writers, who have
the desire strong upon them, to find the exact expression for their thought ; though the quest should lead
them to explore the vocabularies of the sciences, the
arts, the metaphysics. Such an one, Mr. Hardy
would seem to be : simple and severe, we have already
found him ; we have now to consider him, as a lover
of learned technicalities, for occasional use.

In the first place, it is to be remembered, that art
requires self-denial : a beautiful, rich word, a learned,
weighty phrase, excellent in themselves, may be at
war with their humbler context : it is the sin of ' the
purple patch.' The artist, then, must decide each
case by itself ; and determine, whether the harmonious
tone of his work would be spoiled by a brilliance
borrowed from another range and another rank of
style : or, again, by fetching from antiquity, or from
' modernity,' words and phrases fallen into unjust
neglect, or delayed upon their way to common use.

If he decide to insert among his pedestrian words some word of poetry, to take a metaphor from scientific theory, to ' snatch a fearful joy ' by any such bold transgression from the common way ; he must be very sure, that the possible success is worth the certain risk.   Thus, Mr. Pater, writing in all the strength of his fine scholarship, inclines to hold, that contemporary prose might well absorb and naturalize the larger terms of modern science : those expressions, which are but as ' resident aliens ' in our literary language.   Mr. Pater can do it : but can lesser men be safely urged to so delicate a task ?   For to take the case of contemporary science and metaphysic : it requires a prophetic gift, to know which, of all the many phrases in the air just now, will endure and will always be intelligible.   *Substance, accident, subject-matter ;* these have endured and are intelligible ; men use the terms, who know nothing of their first significance.   But were I, airily and confidently, to use the term *holenmerian* or *nullibist*, I should deserve a grave rebuke : even *pineal gland*, or *conarion*, are not precisely popular expressions, to be used at random.   Certainly, there are some terms, in which modern science expresses very plausible views, and in very simple language : *natural selection, survival of the fittest :* so great is the intellectual stir, the mental animation, connoted by these phrases, that no future age will be at a loss to comprehend them : whatever may be the fate of the hypotheses, which gave them birth.   Again : certain words, expressing facts about which there is no question, are universally understood :

certain others are not. Thus *perpendicular*, *axis*, *vertebrate*, are universally understood ; *binomial*, *agnation*, *atavism*, are not : *dynamic*, *crystallization*, *segment*, require little or no apology ; *quaternion*, *polarization*, *kinetic*, require a good deal. It is clear, that all these terms cannot be used, by the mere man of letters, with equal readiness : in each case, the exact thing signified by the term, the propriety of its employment *here* and *now*, its intrinsic force or beauty, must be separately studied. These terms, as many writers use them, are not so won for literature, as to have lost all harshness of the schools : they are obtrusive, impertinent, glaring. Like the foolish among the Ciceronians of the Renaissance, like the foolish among the Euphuists, so too the foolish affecters of the scientific phrase are in our day mistaking elaborate precision for meritorious pains : and bringing into discredit the more scholarly labourers in the same field. There must always be much learning in a writer's mind, of which he can never make a direct use : but it is not wasted, although it be not displayed. The knowledge, with the train of thought that follows it, strengthens and fertilizes the mind by its silent influence : and when the writer writes, not from the plethoric abundance of his knowledge, but from the strength of his thought, it is clearly seen, how the half may be greater than the whole. ' Le pédantisme,' writes M. Renan, ' l'ostentation du savoir, le soin de ne négliger aucun de ses avantages, sont tellement devenus la règle de certaines écoles, qu'on n'y admet plus l'écrivain sobre qui, selon la maxime de nos vieux maîtres de Port-Royal, sait se borner, ne fait jamais profession de science, et dans un livre ne donne pas le quart des recherches que ce livre a coûtées. L'élégance, la modestie, la politesse, l'atticisme passent maintenant pour des manières de gens arriérés.'

The practice of Mr. Hardy is much akin to that of George Eliot: though she, indeed, had the more simple interest, of a moral kind, in the hints and suggestions supplied by scientific metaphor : Mr. Hardy is rather impassive, and concerned for accuracy of description. I may give sundry examples of his ' learned ' language : *static, momentum, thesmothete, zenithal, nadiral, monochromatic, isometric, mechanized friendship, photosphere, untenable redemptive theolatry, pink nebulosity, yellow luminosity*. These are fair examples : and Mr. Hardy's readers, who remember, or who discover, the various contexts, will agree that those words and phrases are not felicitous in themselves, or necessary to their surroundings. To take some passages : ' The oat-harvest began, and all the men were a-field under a monochromatic Lammas sky, amid the trembling air and the short shadows of noon.' ' Under the thatched roofs her mind's eye beheld relaxed tendons and flaccid muscles, spread out in the darkness beneath coverlets made of little purple patchwork squares, and undergoing a bracing process at the hands of sleep for renewed labour on the morrow, as soon as a hint of pink nebulosity appeared on Hambledon Hill.' Or this, a somewhat different kind of example : ' Viewed sideways, the closing-line of her lips formed, with almost geometric precision, the

curve so well known in the arts of design as the cima-
recta, or ogee. The sight of such a flexible bend as
that on grim Egdon was quite an apparition. It was
felt at once that that mouth did not come over from
Sleswig with a band of Saxon pirates whose lips met
like the two halves of a muffin. One had fancied
that such lip-curves were mostly lurking underground
in the south as fragments of forgotten marbles. So
fine were the lines of her lips that, though full, each
corner of her mouth was as clearly cut as the point of
a spear.' Or, again, ' the wet cobwebs, that hung like
movable diaphragms, on each blade and bough.'

It is not difficult to imagine Mr. Hardy's intention
in using the terms *monochromatic, pink nebulosity,
cima-recta or ogee,* and *diaphragms* : they represent
attempts to give in words the greatest possible effect
of reality and exactitude. What was in Mr. Hardy's
mind, or before his eyes, was not a rosy mist, or a red
haze, or a ruddy glow, or a faint purple cloud, nor
yet a morning flush : it was something *pink*, and something *nebulous* ; a *pink nebulosity* therefore. And even
that is not the perfect truth : to rival the delicacy of
nature herself, with her tender gradations, it must be
a hint of pink nebulosity. There, at last, is the very
thing itself. Were Mr. Hardy engaged upon a description of morning twilight, in an Apuleian vein, the
phrase would do mighty well : yet, as Keats confessed,
' scenery is fine, but human nature is finer ' : our
thoughts are busy with the picture of those tired
labouring men and women, under their ' coverlets made
of little purple patchwork squares.' We know them

so well : Tess, too, upon her lonely walk at that strange hour, and her thoughts of those low cottage rooms, with their homely memories and associations, fill our minds and hold our affections.   Then, upon all this simple emotion, comes the *hint of pink nebulosity*, to the disturbance and the confusion of our pleasure.   Elsewhere, the phrase may pass, may even charm : here, it is an offence.   So too, *monochromatic* conflicts with *Lammas* : the words are oil and vinegar, refusing to mix. And, whilst the Saxon pirates, the two halves of a muffin, the broken marbles hid away in the South, the spear point, are one and all harmonious and agreeable with the third scene : the *cima-recta, or ogee*, is an intrusion.   Just so, when we are looking down with Angel and 'Liza-Lu upon the towers of Winchester, waiting for his wife, her sister, to die a shameful death : it is incongruous with the solemnity, the naked horror, of it all, to be told that the prominent buildings showed, ' as in an isometric drawing.'   It may be so : I have looked down upon the old city, some hundred times, from the same height, without realizing the fact : and at so culminating a moment, at the dark close of the great, simple tragedy, the mention of so professional and technical a detail affronts the reader.   Not so did Dante, at the height of his great arguments, mar their intensity and plainness : then he used, not learned terms, but the simplest and the homeliest possible.   Such phrases as these, that I have ventured to disapprove, set side by side with the phrases, that I took leave to praise, carry their own condemnation.

Mr. Stevenson has well said : ' What sort of English

word I use is a matter of the very slightest moment to me, so long as I can get the meaning close, and so long as the word is in the key of what I am writing. This question of key is—I am afraid it is really incommunicable. A good example of a key perfectly held, perhaps as good as I can name, is the Church of England Prayer Book. There does not seem to me one word in the whole of that, which is not of near æsthetic kin to all the rest.' Upon the same occasion, Mr. Stevenson also said, of Mr. Hardy : ' I have seen sentences of his, that I don't think could be bettered in any writer or in any language.' All Mr. Hardy's readers have seen the same : but it was when Mr. Hardy had observed . the sound principle of Mr. Stevenson's other saying. For the most part, his vocabulary, simple or learned, is employed with scrupulous care : and, if I have taken upon myself to point out a few cases of dubious success, it is because untempered panegyric is no less impertinent, than absurd.

With certain chief characteristics of Mr. Hardy's design and composition, the following essays will deal : with his presentation of the Wessex country, with his sympathetic skill in setting forth the country folk, with his manner of showing the natures and passions of some men and women in particular, their simplicity and their complexity ; with his view of those vexed, great questions about art and morals, artistic sincerity and moral truth. These considerations will exhibit the psychological, modern character of Mr. Hardy's novels : his love of making clear the difficult play of

F

motives and of characters, among scenes where all looks placid, taciturn, or dull. For the present, I have been content to dwell rather upon the general qualities common to all his books, in matter and in manner; though more prominent, both good and bad, in some books than in others. In especial, I have tried to suggest, what must haunt the minds of all his readers, who care for the great traditions of English letters : his affinity with the great makers of English literature. George Sand or Count Tolstoi, Flaubert or Balzac ; to these, and to many others, we may discern resemblances in Mr. Hardy : resemblances and contrasts ; the result, now of conscious or unconscious influence, now of chance and of co-incidence. No writer escapes, or should desire to escape, the influences of his age : but it is not merely by recording them, that he will live : it is by showing that in them, which is of no time or country, but old as the human race. Partial success in that endeavour marks a writer for a humanist ; perfect success, for a classic : the humanist may be recognized by his contemporaries ; the classic must have faith in himself, whilst his contemporaries can have no more than hope on his account. If Mr. Hardy have deserved the perfect success, he will command it also : when, matters not at all.

III

WESSEX

In a *Study from Euripides*, Mr. Pater tells us, how
Theseus destroyed ' that delightful creature, the
Centaur,' and warred with the Amazons also : and
how ' they exerted the prerogative of poetic protest,
and survive thereby.' That is a thing to muse upon :
Art the Preserver ! Art, gathering up the wonders
and the powers, no longer living of themselves ; but
henceforth to live only in Art : which has a natural
office of piety towards the past. Mr. Hardy has done
this service to a great region of England, to Wessex :
for so, with characteristic love of reality, he calls the
land of his inventions ; by no imaginary name, but
by a name of famous age and meaning. It is not
with any mere desire to make an open secret of his
choice, that he has given an ancient name to the
country, where the people of his imagination live :
Wessex is full of significance, and no outworn appella-
tion of antiquity, without a living force. In calling
the land of his birth and of his art after its ancient
name, the Land of the West Saxons, Mr. Hardy would
have us feel the sentiment of historical continuity
from those old times to ours ; the storms of violent
fortune, the slow touches of change, which have left
their trace upon the land, whilst leaving it at heart

the same : Wessex, the Land of the West Saxons, preceded by Romans and by Celts, followed by Danes and by Normans. In Mr. Hardy's books, all that succession of races, their fusion and confusion, are brought before the mind : with a scientific severity, and with an artistic beauty, to which there is no parallel in English literature. Many an English writer has a *Patavinitas* of his own ; a touch of native patriotism upon his ways of speech and habits of thought : but none have quite that cast of mind, that bent of imagination, which make Mr. Hardy's concern for Wessex so singular and rare a power in art. An ardent zeal, antiquarian and patriotic, for some county, district, or place, is common enough ; but it is rarely directed by a spirit of art : a romantic love of some country side, rich in memories and legends, is common also ; but it is rarely combined with the spirit of science. Mr. Hardy has all the zeal, say, of the old county historians, and all the romance of Scott, minstrel of the Border : the study of these Wessex books excites two passions, the intellectual love of science, and the emotional love of beauty.

This concentration of Mr. Hardy's art upon the varieties of one great theme, Wessex and its people, has provoked, now and again, complaints from readers, to whom Wessex is not infinitely interesting : give us Wessex to-day, they entreat, but let it be Japan to-morrow. For my own part, I would apply, to the art of literature, what Thomas à Kempis wrote, concerning the art of religion : *qui multum peregrinantur raro sanctificantur :* much pilgrimage rarely sanctifies.

Our modern journeys to the shrines of ' local colour,'
the wide world through, result in little fine art : they
allow no leisure for patient meditation upon the nature
of the men and things selected, nor for confident
familiarity with them. But that art, which meditates
at home, and whose longest travels are of the mind,
is the conquering art. Yet hasty and restless art is
fashionable : and, as young labourers upon the soil
swarm into distant towns for alien labour, so young
labourers at the arts fly abroad for foreign themes of
art. Certainly, art should not be parochial, provincial :
but the art, which sketches the round world with an
airy ease, is worse than the most untravelled and un-
adventurous art. One is moved to wonder, when
these Ariels of modern art will cease to put a girdle
round the globe, and will begin to think. It is not,
that we want art to show signs of effort and of labour :
we want art to be the result of great effort and of long
labour, whilst wearing a look of spontaneous creation.
Sir Joshua Reynolds, said Hazlitt, ' being asked how
long it had taken him to do a certain picture, made
answer : " All his life." ' That fine artist, Mr.
Whistler, once made a similar reply. A single sojourn
in Italy, very brief, affected Chaucer, Milton, Gray,
during the whole course of their lives and studies. It
matters nothing, whether a work of art be produced
with painful care, or with a breathless and delighted
speed : so it be the outcome of thought, a designed,
composed, and meditated work. Mr. Hardy's way
of work, to judge by his choice of matter, and by the
perfection to which it is wrought, is the way of elabora-

tion ; a cautious, anxious way. If the monotony, the unity, the sameness, of all his work, have for some readers so powerful a charm, it is for this reason : that, content to labour in one rich field, he shows us the wealth of human nature. Wessex, one part of a small island, is his ground ; and of Wessex, he takes one part in especial, the county of Dorset : he has rarely left it, throughout fifteen books. He has studied it in his maturity of mind ; he has loved it with the fervour of a patriot ; he has understood it with the instinct of a child : it is his own. As Wordsworth would have the poet find his mystery in a ' primrose by the river's brim ' ; as Shelley would have him watch the sun upon ' the yellow bees in the ivy bloom,' to some high Platonic end : so Mr. Hardy has pondered the looks and the ways, the histories and the associations, the places and the people, of his native region. He has done it with that patient contemplation, which is so English a thing : that satisfaction with experiences, few perhaps, and monotonous, yet deep and strong, which is sometimes corrupted into stolidity. But Mr. Hardy, like Hawthorne of Salem, has the gift of vision, to penetrate beneath the familiar surface, and to surprise us with ever fresh manifestations of the riches there : to reveal varieties of human nature, infinitely unlike each other at heart, yet all sharing the same birthright, in that Wessex has set on them all its seal, as born there, bred there, moulded upon a Wessex plan. No lover of Hawthorne can quite reconcile himself to the *Marble Faun*, with its Italian colour and Roman interest : that gray New

England of the Puritans was Hawthorne's very own. Old America, the ruined cities of Yucatan : what a fascination is in that unrealized antiquity ! what a charm in the thought of Aztecs and of Incas ! And there are the days of Spanish domination : New Orleans, the glory of the South, aristocratic and decaying ; old Spanish kings, Charles or Philip, with their Viceroys in New Spain ; all the slow impressiveness of Castile, corrupt and haughty, in a conquered land, itself to be conquered by the modern American ; Mr. Cable has told that story : then, too, there is the *Grand Monarque*, with the nobles of France ; Canada, and the Jesuit missions ; Quebec and Montreal, Montcalm and Wolfe ; that is another aspect of American romance in history. But Hawthorne did not touch these moving themes of art : a child of the Puritans, he made art out of their memories. Yet his attachment to the past was not only the loving attachment of an antiquary, an humourist, who delights in the thought of what is ancient or fantastic, venerable or quaint : no Antony à Wood, no Lamb. Hawthorne had a deeper sentiment than that genial, cordial, reverence and habit of affection : he had, in his own phrase, ' a mere sensuous sympathy of dust for dust ' ; dull, fallen Salem ! so mean, so chilly, so commonplace ; yet, in that town were done the sins, and the benefactions, of his forefathers : ancestral Hawthornes, with their sad raiment, and gloomy creed, walked those streets, breathed that keen air, gave their dust to those grim church-yards. Again ; to take a living writer, at the outset, surely, of a great career ; Mr.

Barrie has been content to spend the same loving pains upon a little community of Scotch folk, dear to him for home's sake : until he has given us some scenes of truth and beauty, for which he should be honoured by all, who know in part the sorrow and splendour of the world. A clinging to home, old memories, old associations, is the mark of fine natures : like Scott in Italy, like the exiled Jacobite, who

> ' Heard on Lavernia Scargill's whispering trees,
> And pined by Arno for his lovelier Tees ' :

So too, it is permitted us to think, would Mr. Hardy long for his Wessex folk, and beseech the divinity of Domiduca, should occasion lead him to write about another people. It is these writers, men with love for their place of patient work, whom we trust : they have reached the truth, hard to reach, and undiscerned by the passers by. Through these writers, we come to learn, how every place, dull though it be to us, and of no account, is like Bunyan's Valley of Humiliation : ' Though Christian had the hard hap to meet here with Apollyon, and to enter with him into a brisk encounter, yet I must tell you, that in former times men have met with angels here, have found pearls here, and have in this place found the words of life.'

Mr. Hardy's Wessex is not a region of strict boundaries : it touches Exeter, Bristol, Salisbury, Winchester : but, for our present purposes, it may be considered, as equivalent to the County of Dorset. Critics have already identified Mr. Hardy's localities with their originals ; a map of them has been published :

and most careful readers could assign to each novel, with no great labour, its corresponding scenery and actual home. It is impossible, not to feel some regret at this publicity : innocent as it is, it yet savours of intrusion. From pointing out the originals of places, it is but a short step to pointing out the originals of persons : let us rest content, in their lifetimes, with what our novelists tell us. Granted, that Mr. Hardy's Casterbridge is Dorchester ; his Melchester, Salisbury ; his Sherton Abbas, Sherborne : Mr. Hardy has not pledged himself to the literal fidelity of a guidebook. Nothing is gained, by a minute comparison of the real places, with their imagined counterparts : it is better, to dwell upon the general characteristics of the county, which Mr. Hardy reproduces, than to linger upon the details, which he combines, transposes, and employs, to suit his immediate ends.

No place ; I had almost said, in the world ; but certainly, no place in the greater part of it, is dissociated from history : and few parts of England seem more saturated with historical memories, more stratified by the successive passages of historic time, than Dorsetshire. Mr. Hardy appears well suited, by natural tendencies of his mind, to such a region : for no novelist has a greater appreciation of historic, and even of prehistoric, records. All nature is in his eyes, what it was in Bacon's : a field for the conquests of science. Thus, he tells how, to Swithin the young astronomer, in the southern region of stars, ' space, being less the historic haunt of human thought than overhead at home, seemed to be pervaded with a more lonely loneli-

ness.' The sentence is full of suggestions : it illustrates Mr. Hardy's somewhat rigid and impassive
attitude towards the history of man ; natural science
is the true history, and man is but a natural product.
Thus, whilst he is fond of conjuring up the long pageant
of human history, those Celts and Romans, those
Normans and Danes, it is often in a hard and marble
manner : without the spiritual imagination of Bossuet,
but rather with the cold splendour of Gibbon. Yet
the artist in Mr. Hardy can overpower the man of
science : he can dwell upon the human history of
Wessex with an evident emotion. Dorset looks ' a
very old, aged ' county : a home of venerable tradition, symbolized by its lonely barrows, its weathered
towers, its homely streets. Its old towns, Roman in
plan, Georgian in architecture, combine the virtues
of nice precision, severe regularity, and comfortable
cleanness ; the ages have met and mingled, to result
in a grave, decorous, compromise. The whole region,
its towns, villages, woodlands, pastures, heaths, downs,
and people, affect their student in this singular way :
an impress of many ages and of many influences is
stamped upon them. Dorset has a character, distinct
from its neighbours : Cornwall and Devon, with their
Atlantic seaboard, their Elizabethan romance, their
vague memories of Mediterranean commerce, all the
wild medley of tradition and of myth, are of another
spirit : nor are Somerset, Wiltshire, and Hampshire,
of one character with Dorset ; which seems to have
kept by itself, primitive and quaint in its own way.
Here, each influence, military from the Romans,

ecclesiastic from the Saxons, feudal from the Normans, has sunk deeply into the land : whilst the aboriginal character has received each influence in a particular fashion. There are barrows, camps, rings, all over the district, of which the learned cannot determine the origin and date : one race may have succeeded to its predecessor's works, and changed them for its own needs : until the mounds, raised by human hands, have come to look like nature's work. That is an inverse symbol, of the immaterial results of ancient history, upon this tract and people : get past the confused traces, blent and crossed, of historic ancestry, and you reach the primitive pagan stock. To read aright this living palimpsest, requires a disciplined skill and a long familiarity : Mr. Hardy, who is thus qualified, lets no hint or trace escape him. ' They are the representatives of antiquity,' he says of the Dorset folk : ' Many of these labourers about here bear corrupted Norman names ; many are the descendants of the squires in the last century, and their faces even now strongly resemble the portraits in the old manor-houses. Many are, must be, the descendants of the Romans, who lived here in great pomp and state for four hundred years. I have seen faces here that are duplicates of those fine faces I saw at Fiesole, where also I picked up Roman coins, the counterpart of those we find here so often. They even use Latin words here, which have survived everything.' The old town of Casterbridge ' announced old Rome in every street, alley, and precinct. It looked Roman, bespoke the art of Rome, concealed

dead men of Rome.   It was impossible to dig more than
a foot or two deep about the town fields and gardens
without coming upon some tall soldier or other of the
Empire, who had lain there in his silent unobtrusive
rest for a space of fifteen hundred years.   He was
mostly found lying on his side, in an oval scoop in the
chalk, like a chicken in its shell ; his knees drawn up
to his chest ; sometimes with the remains of his spear
against his arm ; a fibula or brooch of bronze on his
heart or forehead ; an urn at his knee, a jar at his
breast, a bottle at his mouth ; and mystified conjecture pouring down upon him from the eyes of Casterbridge street boys and men, who had turned a moment
to gaze at the familiar spectacle as they passed by.'
There, just without the town on the south road, is the
vast Amphitheatre : where, so old people affirmed,
' at certain moments in the summer time, in broad
daylight, persons sitting with a book, or dozing in the
arena, had, on lifting their eyes, beheld the slopes
lined with a gazing legion of Hadrian's soldiery, as
if watching the gladiatorial combat ; and had heard
the roar of their excited voices ; that the scene would
remain but a moment, like a lightning flash, and then
disappear.'   In that grim place met the Mayor of
Casterbridge and his wife, sold long years before :
and when she died, she was buried in ' the still-used
burial-ground of the old Roman-British city, whose
curious feature was this, its continuity as a place of
sepulture.   Mrs. Henchard's dust mingled with the
dust of women who lay ornamented with glass hair-
pins and amber necklaces, and men who held in their

mouths coins of Hadrian, Postumus, and the Constantines.' This Roman feeling pervades the countryside : a wanderer, of the impressionable kind, would hardly be startled, to descry a cohort glittering upon the white, straight road ;[1] to come upon the paved villa, in all its Italian elegance, the home of some high official ; to find the builders at work upon those massy walls. He too, like the peasant by the Loire, ' pâlit de la grandeur des ossements romains ! ' And, just as the Roman Empire seems very present with the Wessex wayfarer, so too seems the Roman Church : from Wimborne in the east, to Sherborne in the west, that august presence still rules the land, a mighty memory. Saint Aldhelm, famous scholar and bishop, crosses the downs, leaning upon his ashen staff : Saint Osmund, Count of Séez, builds his cathedral church of Old Sarum, and compiles the Sarum Use : Saint Cuthburga presides at Wimborne, Saint Edward lies at Shaftesbury, Saint Stephen Harding learns of the Sherborne Benedictines. It is no mere dream of the early ages, an indulgence of gentle sentiment : it is enough to go through the land of Wessex, noting the names of its villages, the remnants of its religious houses, the proud beauty of its churches and of its minsters ; if you would realize, not the fancies, but the facts, that make those times so great, and ours, so

---

[1] Since writing this, I have read with pleasure a sentence in *The Wrecker* of Mr. Stevenson and Mr. Lloyd Osbourne, about Stalbridge Minster, their Dorset town : ' The town was of Roman foundation ; and as I looked out that afternoon from the low windows of the inn, I should scarcely have been surprised to see a centurion coming up the street with a fatigue draft of legionaries.'

full of their memories. Old episcopal and abbatial
places, long since stripped of their honour, keep something magisterial about them, something sacrosanct
and austere : the sense of a'comely order surrounding
the throne, the cloister, centres of light and strength :
a grace seems to go out of the ancient stones, built up
after a plan so consecrated. Much comes of living
beside them.

Like Sir John Durbeyfield, Mr. Hardy is proud
of the many brave and goodly ' skellintons,' that lie in
his native Wessex : ' dear, delightful Wessex, whose
statuesque dynasties are even now only just beginning
to feel the shaking of the new and strange spirit
without, like that which entered the lonely valley of
Ezekiel's vision, and made the dry bones move, where
the honest squires, tradesmen, clerks, and people
still praise the Lord with one voice for His best of all
possible worlds.'

Tess of the D'Urbervilles is a long tragedy, upon the
striving of that modern spirit, among the ancient
Wessex places : how ancient in spirit, perhaps Mr.
Hardy alone knows. Some of his *Noble Dames* excepted, his story of *The Trumpet Major* deals with
older matters, than any other of his stories : and yet,
those villagers on the alert to welcome Bonaparte,
are no more primitive, than are the villagers described
in *Tess*. Here is a long passage, in which Mr. Hardy
dwells upon some moving thoughts, very apt for
quotation at this point.

' They sheared in the great barn, called for the
nonce the Shearing-barn, which on ground-plan re-

sembled a church with transepts. It not only emulated the form of the neighbouring church of the parish, but vied with it in antiquity. Whether the barn had ever formed one of a group of conventual buildings nobody seemed to be aware ; no trace of such surroundings remained. The vast porches at the sides, lofty enough to admit a wagon laden to its highest with corn in the sheaf, were spanned by heavy-pointed arches of stone, broadly and boldly cut, whose very simplicity was the origin of a grandeur not apparent in erections where more ornament has been attempted. The dusky, filmed, chestnut roof, braced and tied in by huge collars, curves, and diagonals, was far nobler in design, because more wealthy in material, than nine-tenths of those in our modern churches. Along each side wall was a range of striding buttresses, throwing deep shadows on the spaces between them, which were perforated by lancet openings, combining in their proportions the precise requirements both of beauty and ventilation.

' One could say about this barn, what could hardly be said of either the church or the castle, akin to it in age and style, that the purpose which had dictated its original erection was the same with that to which it was still applied. Unlike and superior to either of those two typical remnants of mediævalism, the old barn embodied practices which had suffered no mutilation at the hands of time. Here at least the spirit of the ancient builders was at one with the spirit of the modern beholder. Standing before this abraded pile, the eye regarded its present usage, the mind dwelt upon its past history, with a satisfied sense of functional continuity throughout—a feeling almost of gratitude, and quite of pride, at the permanence of the idea which had heaped it up. The fact that four centuries had neither proved it to be founded on a mistake, inspired any hatred of its purpose, nor given rise to any reaction that had battered it down, invested this simple grey effort of old minds, with a repose, if not a grandeur, which a too curious reflection was apt to disturb in its ecclesiastical and military compeers. For once mediævalism and modernism had a common standpoint. The lanceolate windows, the time-eaten arch-stones and chamfers, the orientation of the axis, the misty chestnut work of the rafters, referred to no exploded fortifying art or worn-out religious creed. The defence and salvation of the body by daily bread is still a study, a religion, and a desire.

' To-day the large side doors were thrown open towards the sun to admit a bountiful light to the immediate spot of the shearers' operations, which was the wood threshing-floor in the centre, formed of thick oak, black with age and polished by the beating of flails for many generations, till it had grown as slippery and as rich in hue as the state-room floors of an Elizabethan mansion. Here the shearers knelt, the sun slanting in upon their bleached shirts, tanned arms, and the polished shears they flourished, causing them to bristle with a thousand rays strong enough to blind a weak-eyed man. Beneath them a captive sheep lay panting, increasing the rapidity of its pants as misgiving merged in terror, till it quivered like the hot landscape outside.

'This picture of to-day in its frame of four hundred years ago did not produce that marked contrast between ancient and modern which is implied by the contrast of date. In comparison with cities, Weatherbury was immutable. The citizen's *Then* is the rustic's *Now*. In London, twenty or thirty years ago are old times; in Paris ten years, or five; in Weatherbury three or four score years were included in the mere present, and nothing less than a century set a mark on its face or tone. Five decades hardly modified the cut of a gaiter, the embroidery of a smock frock, by the breadth of a hair. Ten generations failed to alter the turn of a single phrase. In these Wessex nooks the busy outsider's ancient times are only old; his old times are still new; his present is futurity.

'So the barn was natural to the shearers, and the shearers were in harmony with the barn.'

Certainly, at Cerne Abbas or at Abbotsbury, the sight of those old granaries, where bundles of straw protrude through noble windows, calls up the same thoughts, with which the scholar looks upon Virgil's very plough, still furrowing the earth of Italy: as does Mr. Hardy's picture of the calves, sheltered under old arches, who cooled 'their thirsty tongues by licking the quaint Norman carving, which glistened with the moisture.' In Wessex, one feels it hardly behind the age, to travel with no road book, but the *Itinerary* of Antoninus, or at the least, of Leland: and to

use no book of husbandry, but the *Five Hundred Points*
of Tusser.   Each spirit of change, each breath of new
doctrine, ' comes slowly up this way ' : here time is
slow, and almost drowsy : and here, all distances are
great.   Tess, after her calamity, seeks out a refuge
in another tract of her county : ' It was not quite so
far off as could have been wished ; but it was probably far enough, her radius of movement and repute
having been so small.   To persons of limited spheres,
miles are as geographical degrees, parishes as counties,
counties as provinces and kingdoms.'   There is but
the faintest touch of caricature in the following talk of
Wessex labourers.   Cainy Ball was asked, what,
besides his Mistress Bathsheba and Sergeant Troy,
he saw in Bath.

' " Great glass windows to the shops, and great
clouds in the sky, full of rain, and old wooden trees
in the country round."

' " You stun-poll !   What will ye say next ? " said
Coggan.

' " Let en alone," interposed Joseph Poorgrass.
" The boy's maning is that the sky and earth in the
kingdom of Bath is not altogether different from ours
here.   'Tis for our good to gain knowledge of strange
cities, and as such the boy's words should be suffered,
so to speak it."

' " And the people of Bath," continued Cain, " never
need to light their fires except as a luxury, for the
water springs up out of the earth ready boiled for
use."

' " 'Tis true as the light," testified Matthew

Moon. " I 've heard other navigators say the same
thing."

' " They drink nothing else there," said Cain, " and
seem to enjoy it, to see how they swaller it down."

' " Well, it seems a barbarous practice enough to
us, but I daresay the natives think nothing of it," said
Matthew.

' " And don't victuals spring up as well as drink ? "
asked Coggan, twirling his eye.

' " No—I own to a blot there in Bath—a true blot.
God didn't provide 'em with victuals as well as drink,
and 'twas a drawback I couldn't get over at all."

' " Well, 'tis a curious place, to say the least,"
observed Moon, " and it must be a curious people
that live therein." '

This mixture of natural ignorance and shrewd
humour, the one heightening the other, is faithful to
fact : a like concentration of knowledge, and of interest,
upon one small place, marks your true Dorset labourer.
Upon the top of a great hill, close by the sea, stands
a Chapel of Saint Catharine, according to ancient
custom : ruinous, but arrested in its decay. A venerable man, whose face, like that of Dame Martin,
' showed itself worn and rutted, like an old highway,
by the passage of years,' replied to the question of a
pilgrim, when was the Chapel ruined ? by the emphatic words : ' There 's not a man can say that, but
his lordship, who keeps the records and the writings :
not a man. But it 's been as 'tis, ever since I were
a boy.' The conviction, that local history could only
be known to local scholars, or dignitaries, is charac-

teristic, and delightful. Customs, dialect, all the
traditions fast rooted in the soil, flourish for centuries
in one place, while they seem outlandish to the people
of another, within a day's walk. ' When Abbotsbury
people came to Poole,' said Mr. Gosse, the late eminent
naturalist, in a posthumous paper, Poole folk were
amused at a peculiarity in the Abbotsbury speech :
the two places are not more than thirty miles apart.
One comes to understand the attitude towards public
affairs of the Dorset Clubmen, in the days of the great
War : ' a plague on both your houses ! '

There is much virtue and significance, for many
reasons, in names : a fine use of them, with sympathy and imagination, a memory and an ear alive to
their rich meanings and associations, have been held
to mark great poets. Arnold found in them true
spiritual analogies to the temper of their bestowers
and employers. ' As the Saxon names of places, with
the pleasant wholesome smack of the soil in them,—
Weathersfield, Thaxted, Shalford,—are to the Celtic
names of places, with their penetrating, lofty beauty,
—Velindra, Tyntagel, Caernarvon,—so is the homely
realism of German and Norse nature to the fairy-like
loveliness of Celtic nature.' Dorset names, a whole
roll call of them, illustrate the kinds of historical influence, that have affected the country ; and also the
kindly, homely sentiment, which has led Mr. Hardy
to adopt so many of them, for the names of his places
and of his people.

There are the Latin names, with all sorts of ecclesiastical and other flavours about them : Toller Porcorum,

Toller Fratrum, Ryme Intrinsica, Cerne Abbas, Milton Abbas, Melbury Abbas, Bradford Abbas, Winterbourne Abbas, Compton Abbas, Blandford Forum, Whitechurch Canonicorum, Lyme Regis, Bere Regis, Minterne Magna, Fontmell Magna. There are the names, which preserve the memory of veneration paid to certain Saints ; not the phantom Saints of Celtic Wales and Cornwall, but Saints familiar throughout Christendom : Sydling St. Nicholas, St. Martin's Town, Frome St. Quentin, St. Margaret's Marsh, Stanton St. Gabriel, Melbury Osmund, Fifehead Magdalen. There are the names, which recur again and again, sometimes with that neighbourly air of community, telling an historic tale : Tarrant Gunville, Tarrant Launceston, Tarrant Rushton, Tarrant Crawford, Tarrant Rawston, Tarrant Keynston, Tarrant Hinton, Hinton Martell, Hinton Parva, Hinton St. Mary, Gussage St. Michael, Gussage St. Andrew, Gussage All Saints, Melbury Osmund, Melbury Bubb, Melbury Sampford, Melbury Abbas, Winterbourne Abbas, Houghton Winterbourne, Winterbourne Whitechurch, Stickland Winterbourne, Winterbourne Kingston, Winterbourne Zelstone, Winterbourne Clenstone. Finally, to conclude this pardonable indulgence in the manner of Walt Whitman, there are the names, some richly romantic, some comfortably rural, which seem to demand celebration in prose or verse : Winford Eagle, Compton Vallance, Lytchett Matravers, Langton Matravers, Worth Matravers, Purse Caundle, Marsh Caundle, Caundle Bishop, Corfe Mullen, Stower Provost, Iwerne Minster,

Wootton Glanville, Hazelbury Bryan, Sutton Pointz, Owre Moigne, and all the countless ' barrows.' Mr. Hardy's readers will recognize some of these : and others, which he has either taken or adapted ; Fitzpaine, which suggests Edred Fitzpiers ; Charmouth, which recalls Mrs. Charmond ; and the Chickerels, made famous in the name of those good workmen, Sol and Dan.

It would take years to discover, how much history is hidden away in these names : what memories of old houses, what stories of Catholic devotion, what records of Norman pride, what monuments of Saxon labour : and, earlier than all, what dim traces of Celtic worship, civility, and war. Antiquaries give their lives to the discovery of these things : archæological bodies discuss them ; as did that meeting at Coomb Castle, to which went Ethelberta upon her donkey. But there is no life in the results of these researches ; none, in the collections of museums : and the writers of imagination, who might devote themselves to the animation of this buried past, so rich, so romantic, so real, are busy with Morbihan or Dinapur. Almost alone, Mr. Hardy has cared for the ' Past and Present ' of an English county : finding in it a field of art, upon which he can work, with all his science, all his imagination. He gives us no hint, by any flagging or repetition of old work, that he tires of his Wessex, or that he has done all things possible with it : more than Herrick did for his Devon fields, Crabbe for his eastern coasts and fens, Burns for his Ayrshire streams and ploughlands, Wordsworth for his Cumbrian lakes and moun-

tains, the Brontés for their Yorkshire moors, has Mr.
Hardy done for Wessex. It need hardly be said, that
I make here no comparisons between the work of
those writers, and that of Mr. Hardy, in point of
literary merit : I do but say, that Mr. Hardy, more
than any other English author, has demonstrated the
value of a single, little region, as a field of art ; and,
by implication, the rich value of many fields un-
noticed or unvisited.

It may be an idle fancy, yet I think that it is not,
to see in this close and long attention to the characteristics, very various, but all noted, of one locality,
a spirit and an energy parallel to those, which prompt
in our day the students of anthropology. One may
mark, how the books of that science, so gravely im-
partial and impassive in their collection of facts, are
more full of pathetic, of sympathetic, human interest,
than are most novels : Those records, unsparing and
unadorned, of primitive races and of savage tribes,
apart from all initial or complementary theories about
them, touch us very nearly, wakening ' the sense of
tears in mortal things.' Reading these books, one
cries out with Newman :

> ' O man, strange composite of heaven and earth !
> Majesty dwarfed to baseness ! fragrant flower
> Running to poisonous seed ! and seeming worth
> Cloking corruption ! weakness mastering power !
> Who never art so near to crime and shame,
> As when thou hast achieved some deed of name.'

In the brooding woods, or in the busy streets, there
are times when, if one consider the lives of men, all

the pity and all the pride, there rises from the heart
no word, but the constant word of Saint John : *Filioli !
filioli !*   Little children find infinite pleasure and pain
in the most trivial things : nothing is too common,
too ugly, too dull, to become the centre and masterpiece of their play, their work of imagination. They
have means

> ' To see a world in a grain of sand,
>   And a heaven in a wild flower ;
> Hold infinity in the palm of your hand,
>   And eternity in an hour.'

Children, with their instinctive glorification of all
things round them ; men of scholarship and science,
with their patient attention to the least signs and vestiges of human nature ; artists, with their necessity of
piercing through its piteous littleness to find its true
greatness : all these are allies and friends. Doubtless, the writers, who find their happiness in the
recital of conspicuous and shining deeds ; blades
flashing, trumpets sounding, the savour of the sea
in the nostrils, or the surge of the wind in the ears ;
these writers, who

> ' Chase brave employments with a naked sword
> Throughout the world,'

do us fine and heartening service : but I find the
greater beauty, and the greater strength, in the writers,
who meditate more common things : things of no
stir and show, the old and wonted experiences of men.
It is curious to consider, how much there is in life,
which has never found a place in art : for an example,

we might take the various forms of industry and
labour; not to produce technical treatises upon
them, diversified with narrative; but to bring out
the human features in the forms of human work.
Every man, who has a work of his own, a daily business with art, or trade, or the public service, knows
how strong has been the influence of that business
upon his character; how it has affected his views
of life, and his principles of conduct. Yet the novelists,
detaching men from their common interests, present
them, for the most part, under the sudden storms of
passion, or in rare and subtile difficulties: and the
reader neither knows, nor can gather, anything of the
actors' habitual selves. It is an admirable method,
rightly used: but not a method for common use. The
whole story of *Tess* might have been told in a few
pages, each electric as a flash of lightning; so too
might have been told the stories of *Adam Bede*, or of
Wuthering Heights: they would have stricken and
have blinded us, with rending agony. Now, they fill
us with an emotion, which is no rapid pang, but a
gradual appeal to the charity of intellect: we have
watched life, slowly and fully lived, among the Dorset
valleys, the Midland fields, the Yorkshire moors; the
trivialities, businesses, experiences, set before us with
so skilful a choice, have made the eventful tragic acts,
an hundredfold more tragic. The stroke of sentiment, the touch upon the nerves of sensibility, how
easily are these effected! But the gradual evolution
of a tragedy, by dwelling with art upon the forces and
necessities, which surround the actors in their daily

life, demands of the artist a deeper mind. Sudden
death, grievous calamity, or signal joy, the heroic
points and rare heights of life, are imaginable with no
great effort : still easier is it, to practise a mechanic
and unimaginative fidelity, in transcribing every
detail of life : Mr. Hardy can fill his books with the
breath of life, yet he asks no excessive help from rare
accidents of romance, nor places all his reliance upon
the witness of his senses. The anthropologist knows,
that in rude customs and in savage rites may lurk a
soul of pure spiritual desire : the grossness and the
brutality do not blind him to the human sense of
need and reverence and adoration, corrupted or concealed beneath them. Just so, Mr. Hardy and the
novelists resembling him, undeterred by any look of
triviality or of insignificance, discern dominant emotions and potent passions, behind the use and wont
of every day. It is to be noted, that in his finest
books, Mr. Hardy contrives some special touch of
rare romance or strangeness : but never, as the great
and palmary excellence of his story. In *The Woodlanders*, there is Melbury's vow to Winterborne's
father, his dead friend : in *The Mayor of Casterbridge*,
there is Michael Henchard's sale of his wife : in *Tess of
the D'Urbervilles*, there is the murder of Alec D'Urberville, the enchaunted walk, the solemn morning hour
at Stonehenge, the sad end of all at Wintoncester.
But while these touches of rare romance or strangeness, each in its degree, are very strongly felt, they
are not felt with a sudden thrill : they are of one kind
with all the touches of quieter experience throughout

the work : and *The Return of the Native* has its profound charm for, at the least, one reader, by reason
of that uniform simplicity ; which is so impressive, as
to overpower the mind with a sense of high romance,
in Dante's way. So wonderful a thing is common
life, considered by the artist or the priest.

Each of Mr. Hardy's books takes us into a most
definite sphere, and naturalizes us among a most
living people : we carry away the conviction, that
we have dwelt in the woodlands, under the greenwood
tree, by country market places, upon waste heaths, at
dairy farms, and among sheepfolds. It is a real
accession of knowledge, extension of sympathy, en-
richment of experience : we have not been burdened
with useful information, yet there is nothing vague
about our thoughts and recollections. In this simple
love for simple, ancient, varieties of life, Mr. Hardy
has the manner of early poets. Literature holds
nothing more delightful, than Homer's account of
daily life : now it is the business of seafaring, now of
festival, now of gardening, now of artists' work, and
now of hunters' : there is an innocent, healthy pleasure
in the reading of it, as there must have been in the
composing. Virgil has not lost that pleasure ; but
he has mingled with it melancholy : and Mr. Hardy
is too meditative an artist, to find nothing but a natural
joy in his contemplations. Now and again, as in
Under the Greenwood Tree, he yields himself to the
Arcadian sentiment, though with strict veracity of
description : but for the most part, it is through the
homely features of his pastoral scenes, that he makes

his most poignant emotions felt. To take a slight example : Giles Winterborne drove home from Sherton to Little Hintock, Grace Melbury, just done with her fine school : he has loved her all his life, and he is no more than a woodlander, a man of orchards, a ' rustic.'

' " Don't Brownley's farm-buildings look strange to you, now they have been moved bodily from the hollow where the old ones stood to the top of the hill ? "

' She admitted that they did, though she should not have seen any difference in them if he had not pointed it out.

' " They had a good crop of bitter-sweets, they couldn't grind them all "—nodding towards an orchard where some heaps of apples had been left lying ever since the ingathering.

' She said " Yes," but looking at another orchard.

' " Why, you are looking at John-apple trees ! you know bitter-sweets—you used to well enough ? "

' " I am afraid I have forgotten, and it is getting too dark to distinguish."

' Winterborne did not continue.'

Here is very simple talk : but this matter of the bitter-sweets and the John-apples does in a few words the work of many pages. One feels the not unworthy limitation of the man's interests to the fruits of the earth and their seasons : the girl's thoughts, busy with the delicate, cultured ways of her late life : the distance between the two. It excites a long train of reflections about life : and when sorrow falls upon Grace, and she finds in Giles, his very simplicity and

homeliness, a saving strength, the incident comes
back to mind. Finally, when he dies in serving Grace,
Marty South, who has loved him with resolute silence,
gives him a farewell of praise, which leaves us among
the woods and orchards, with a strange sense of endurance and of peace.

' " She entered the churchyard, going to a secluded
corner behind the bushes, where rose the unadorned
stone that marked the last bed of Giles Winterborne.
As this solitary and silent girl stood there in the moonlight, a straight slim figure, clothed in a plaitless gown,
the contours of womanhood so undeveloped as to be
scarcely perceptible, the marks of poverty and toil
effaced by the misty hour, she touched sublimity at
points, and looked almost like a being who had rejected with indifference the attribute of sex for the
loftier quality of abstract humanism. She stooped
down and cleared away the withered flowers that
Grace and herself had laid there the previous week,
and put her fresh ones in their place.

' " Now, my own, own love," she whispered, " you
are mine, and on'y mine ; for she has forgot 'ee at
last, although for her you died. But I—whenever
I get up I 'll think of 'ee, and whenever I lie down I 'll
think of 'ee. Whenever I plant the young larches
I 'll think that none can plant as you planted ; and
whenever I split a gad, and whenever I turn the cider
wring, I 'll say none could do it like you. If ever I
forget your name let me forget home and heaven !
. . . But no, no, my love, I never can forget 'ee ; for
you was a good man, and did good things ! " ' '

None but a great artist could have closed his work
thus perfectly : with that passionate simplicity of
speech, straight from the heart of a noble woman,
whose silent and austere suffering, as she went about
her woodland labour, had given so grave a beauty to
the tragic play. Without the woodland talk and
work and air, made real to us, touch by touch, we
should have missed the pathos of that final scene.
In like manner, without the elaborate, slow pourtraiture of Egdon Heath, we should have missed some
depths of tragedy in Eustacia, Yeobright, and his
mother : without the detailed dairy work and field
work of Tess, we should have missed the glow of
her love, the strength of her endurance : the artist
has felt the fulness of life, and made us feel it ; with
what force and what conviction, they best know, who
best know Wessex. It is no small task, to set whole
spheres of life and work in a light so true, that all
must own its truth. Patience and loving study alone
can do it : no brilliant epigram, nor biting phrase,
can make us understand the slowly prevailing, gently
lingering, charm of all those rural lives and ways. It
is the province of a deeper art : an art, patient, studious,
and sure : an art without those graces could but
pourtray the country in its mean dulness, or in the
violence of its incivility. 'In sleep,' writes Mr.
Hardy, 'there come to the surface buried genealogical facts, ancestral curves, dead men's traits, which
the mobility of daytime animation screens and overwhelms.' The 'sleep' of Wessex, its air of long
repose, in which ancient memories assert their claims

to life, is never far from Mr. Hardy's mind, when he dwells upon the present stir and business of Wessex : he writes of the labourers, who work there to-day ; and the reader is left with thoughts of patriarchal days : from the faithful pourtraiture of a secluded village, a lonely farm, the reader gains that range and height of contemplation, whence the life of long and battling ages wears in part that look of still life, which it must wholly wear for eternal eyes.

Through his concentration upon this kingdom of Wessex, where he rules alone, now that its poet is dead, Mr. Hardy has been able to write out of the abundance of his heart : love of Wessex has urged him to the knowledge of Wessex. Not the calm curiosity of a stranger, among the old castles of France or churches of Italy ; but the warm love of one at home, among the old sights and sounds, ' old ' in another way, is the moving principle of his Wessex books. But he is the least sentimental of writers : he never lets sentiment take art into captivity. Examine those passages, in which Mr. Hardy, like the Welsh preacher with his *hwyl*, gives a play to all the powers of his thought and style, that he may compose a worthy praise of some Wessex greatness : you will find no verbiage, nor effusion of sentiment. He writes with emotion, but not in agitation : he has learned much of Virgil's secret ; the art of being stately in passion, with a natural instinct of fine manners, in the presence of fine things ; yet with swells and storms of emotion, beneath the austere solemnity.

Egdon Heath never fails to rouse a kind of personal

pride in Mr. Hardy : he dwells upon the beauty of its
desolate wastes, with the glow of a lover : No Carew
nor Crashaw, Cowley nor Donne, exercised more ingenious an art for passion's sake, than this restrained
writer exercises on behalf of his ' great, inviolate
place.' He would not for the world, that haggard
Egdon should blossom as the rose : he, a writer little
given to quotation, quotes Domesday Book and Leland,
in proof of Egdon's wildness from ancient times.
' The untamable, Israelitish thing that Egdon now
was it always had been.' It is older than the sea.
' Who can say of a particular sea that it is old ?   Distilled by the sun, kneaded by the moon, it is renewed
in a year, in a day, or in an hour.   The sea changed,
the fields changed, the rivers, the villages, and the
people changed, yet Egdon remained.' These sentences are in that masterpiece of almost Roman
grandeur, the first chapter of *The Return of the Native*.
But Egdon's praise is not forgotten in other of Mr.
Hardy's books.   When Tess and Angel Clare took
the milk cans to the station, ' in the diminishing daylight they went along the level roadway, through the
meads, which stretched away into gray miles, and
were backed in the extreme edge of distance by
the swarthy abrupt slopes of Egdon Heath.   On its
summit stood clumps and stretches of fir-trees, whose
notched tips appeared like battlemented towers crowning black-fronted castles of enchantment.' Clare, in
his remorse, went to find Tess at Sandbourne, a
fashionable watering-place.   ' An out-lying eastern
tract of the enormous Egdon Waste was close at hand,

yet on the very verge of that tawny piece of antiquity such a glittering novelty as this pleasure city had chosen to spring up. Within the space of a mile from its outskirts every irregularity of the soil was pre-historic, every channel an undisturbed British track-way; not a sod having been turned there since the days of the Caesars. Yet the exotic had grown here, suddenly as the prophet's gourd; and had drawn hither Tess.' Rhoda Brook and her boy, in that grim story of *The Withered Arm*, lived at ' a lonely spot high above the water meads, and not far from the border of Egdon Heath, whose dark countenance was visible in the distance as they drew nigh to home.' Rhoda, with Gertrude Lodge of the withered arm, together sought out Conjuror Trendle ' in the heart of Egdon.' On their mysterious errand, ' they hardly spoke to each other, and immediately set out on their climb into the interior of this solemn country, which stood high above the rich alluvial soil they had left an hour before. It was a long walk; thick clouds made the atmosphere dark, though it was as yet only early afternoon; and the wind howled dismally over the hills of the heath—not improbably the same heath which had witnessed the agony of the Wessex King Ina, presented to after-ages as Lear.' When Gertrude made her journey to Casterbridge, to win leave of the hangman to touch with her arm his dead victim's neck, she rode over Egdon: and Mr. Hardy takes occasion to tell, how ' Enclosure Acts had not taken effect,' even at that not remote date. ' Gertrude, therefore, rode along with no other obstacles than the

H

prickly furze bushes, the mats of heather, the white
water-courses, and the natural steeps and declivities
of the ground ' : And again, when Elizabeth-Jane
and Donald Farfrae went in search of her stepfather,
Henchard, late Mayor of Casterbridge, they heard
news of him in Egdon. They drove ' across that
ancient country whose surface never had been stirred
to a finger's depth, save by the scratchings of rabbits,
since brushed by the feet of the earliest tribes. The
tumuli these had left behind them, dun and shagged
with heather, jutted roundly into the sky from the
hill above, as though they were the full breasts of
Diana Multimammia supinely extended there.' It
might be thought, that at certain times Mr. Hardy's
way of writing has certain qualities of Egdon : the
rigid, sombre, air of its soil, its combination of vast-
ness and compression, are matched by Mr. Hardy's
close, reticent, and weighty style.

It is hard to express that singular quality of Mr.
Hardy's writing, when he deals with the aspects of
Wessex : that quality, by virtue of which the reader
sees the very landscape in its exact truth : although
Mr. Hardy is neither an ' impressionist,' nor a ' word-
painter,' nor a maker of ' prose poems.' He has well
recognized the part really played by the natural scenes
of a landscape, in the daily life of those among them :
he never makes the mistake of describing the scenery
of his stories, as though it were fresh and new to
his people. Few things are more curious, than the
effect of trying to imagine, that the roads, the fields,
the woods, familiar to us from childhood, are now

seen by us for the first time : the landscape changes, and all is new, touched with fresh colours, seen under a strange light ; the homeliness of the old place has gone. Most novelists are not at home among the places of their imagination : from first to last, they describe their woods and fields, not as long familiarity makes them appear, but as they appear to unaccustomed eyes : there is no heart in them. But Mr. Hardy has the art of impressing upon us so strong a sense of familiarity with his scenes, that we read of Wessex, and we think of our own homes, far away and far different though they may be. To one, familiar with Wales, the rural aspects of Dorset are scarcely less foreign, than those of Limousin or of Lombardy : yet, by virtue of that sense for the humanity in a landscape, Mr. Hardy's woods and valleys, fields and farms, take him back to the wilds of Merioneth. Once more, here is the classic power of the humanist : that power to touch all hearts and minds, not by vague generalities common to all the world, but by the evocation, from special things, of a general truth.

Certainly, there is no lack of special things, peculiar to Wessex : among them is the genius of their cele-brator. All men of ' sense and sensibility ' feel the spirit of the country, at large and in particular : few can express it in forms of art, though many try. There is no half truth more dangerous to art, than the half truth, that many men are poets, merely ' lacking the accomplishment of verse ' : singers, who ' die with all their music in them.' This injudicious kindliness

is often extended to all manner of potential artists :
yet in art, unlike ethics, work is not valued by the
nature of its intention, but of its performance. Rhetorical description, and servile enumeration, and bold
caricature, are ways of treating country things, not
too difficult for many a gushing, stolid, or unscrupu-
lous writer : but art has nothing to do with all that.
Even so good and pleasant a writer, as was the late
Mr. Jefferies, could but touch country life and country
looks, with complete felicity, in essays and in disquisitions : the constructive powers were denied him.
That Mr. Hardy, so concerned for all manifestations
of the liberal arts and human sciences, so wrought
upon by the spirit of local patriotism, so abounding in
mental curiosity, should have so firm an hold upon
his art, and pay so loyal an obedience to its laws, is a
notable triumph for the lovers of severe beauty. The
severity, I had nearly said, the hardness, of his ideal
has preserved him. If we have looked upon Mr.
Hardy's Wessex country, before we have read his
books ; in reading them, we are filled with astonish-
ment at the simplicity of his dramatic power : what
our eyes saw, what our fancy made, of those various
landscapes, is proven so poor and shadowy, beside
the wonderful truth, as it is in Mr. Hardy. There
are the pasture valleys : ' delightful meadows and
rich lands,' so an old writer describes those of the
Stour ; Spenser's ' Stour with terrible aspect ' : and
most Dorset valleys deserve the description. But
we cannot seize upon their points of singularity, their
peculiar charms : to us, all are great valleys of green

fields, where the air is full of gold dust, and the grass
gleams with warm light. They lie deep below ranges
of high downs, on whose sides the chalk shows in
white scars : a long, white road leads through them,
bordered with white strips of wooded pasture, set
with flowers among the tangled thickets : rough
horses, with black, shaggy manes, browse leisurely
along, under green oak trees : no one is in sight, but
some young boy, with large eyes and grave face, in
charge of a brindled cow, armed with a fading branch.
The downs give place to wooded hills : wooded hills,
waving ranges and circles of them, with a blue, soft
mist glowing upon their massed boughs, in the heat
and sun : and there are stretches of woodland on
either hand, where the woodmen are at work, among
the fallen, stripped trees, the stacked hurdles, piled
spars, and bound faggots. Presently, the valley
narrows down by steep slopes ; the road falls away
towards a nestling village, between high banks, upon
which great beech trees stand, their branches sweeping low across the way : in the hollow lies a dreamy
cluster of little houses, their thatch-eaves rounded
over the windows, and drooping between them, dis-
persed round the gray church ; behind them are the
meadows, deep in rich grass, yellow with blossoms ;
fields full of sheep, very white in the blinding sun ;
and uplands climbing to the sky, patched with heather,
shadowed with beech and fir. Then, there are the
clear rivers, in which the dark rushes bend to the
breeze : rivers, winding never far from the way, and
bridged by old, stout arches of gray stone. And there

are the two kinds of desolate country : the gray, green downlands, rolling away in easy undulations ; and the brown, dark heaths, that look so stiff and menacing, with their hillocks topped by fir clumps : both, so silent and so still, that time seems at a pause upon them. Something in this way, does the unilluminated writer describe the ' Dorsetian fields ' of Drayton, the ' pure Dorsetian downs ' of Thomson ; sometimes he may catch a little of Tom Warton's pretty sentiment, or the pensive elegance of Bowles. But the masters cover him with confusion : only a Coleridge can tell,

> ' How exquisite the scents
> Snatched from yon bean-field ! and the world so hushed !
> The stilly murmur of the distant sea
> Tells us of silence ' :

or how,

> ' The dell,
> Bathed by the mist, is fresh and delicate
> As vernal cornfield, or the unripe flax,
> When, through its half-transparent stalks, at eve,
> The level sunshine glimmers with green light.'

As Coleridge knew to fit his musings to his Somerset dell, expressing perfectly the sentiment of meditation in a lonely village place, an English village place : so Mr. Hardy knows to fit his invention and his imagination to the Wessex scenes. He may have followed ' the white roads up athirt the hills,' all Dorset through, with no conscious plans of art to come ; have so entered the long, straggling villages, talked with the folk there, and watched the labourers and the gossips ; have so gone by the fields in seedtime or harvest,

summer or winter, letting no sign of life escape him ;
have so visited ancient houses, fallen from their
manorial honours, barrows eloquent of old Britain,
camps eloquent of old Rome ; so too, have turned his
thoughts upon the elder antiquity of the earth itself,
and upon earth's changes witnessed by the same calm
stars : into the private history of Mr. Hardy's art, I
have no right to enquire : but I enjoy the right to
praise its works, for truth, and strength, and beauty.

It may be thought, that there is enough, and to
spare, of a meditative quality in these rural books :
surely, summer suns might have shone in them more
brightly, and winter winds blown through them more
freshly ! there is but one *Under the Greenwood Tree.*
But that is only a first thought, and not of the best :
Chaucer and Walton, Herrick and Burns, can always
give us their less premeditated delights.   Mr. Hardy,
almost alone, but for certain resemblances to Wordsworth and to Crabbe, has pondered the country, and
brought thought to bear upon it.   And his stories,
learned though they be, do not seem to have come
from the silence of a library, fragrant with old books :
they seem to have come of long meditations in the
open air ; art shaping into form, science moulding
into thought, pure influences of earth and sky.   Seldom
do trains of grave thoughts, arrays of learned remem-
brances, and musters of happy images, more often
crowd upon the brain, than in a spell of undirected
musing out of doors.   Our own house is our familiar
friend, we are upon intimate and equal terms with it :
there are the backs of our books ; a glance across the

shelves, and we fall into some accustomed, literary, mood. But the universe, which has no rights, nor powers, inside our library, makes good its full claim upon us in the open air : we are children again, and prehistoric men, and wondering creatures : we cannot help meditating, waywardly and dreamily, upon the gravest matters. Then, nature prompts us with all manner of felicitous suggestions : and, whatever art or learning be ours, it is quickened into life, and responds to the inspiration of nature, with all its might. The final form, the last graces, are achieved at home, by long and patient care : but the work will not have lost the character of its original conception, that share in ' the first integrity of things.' It is so, that Lucretius must have composed his ' mighty line ' : and it is this impression, that Mr. Hardy's greater books leave with their readers. This meditative quality, full of nature's own deepening power upon us, forms the large and wholesome atmosphere of Mr. Hardy's finer novels : he deals with perversities of conduct, sentiment, and situation ; but the air is never tainted, never loses its clearness, never stagnates. In his less austere stories, there is no such sense of an healthy atmosphere : breaths of malice vitiate the air around them ; and Mephistopheles infects their world, with horrid cleverness.

There is one aspect of Mr. Hardy's devotion to Wessex, upon which I must again touch : its example, in an English writer, of that spirit, which animates the *félibrige* of Provence, the Celtic gatherings of Brittany, the *Eisteddfod* of Wales. In one way, the late Mr. Barnes, by writing in Dorset dialect, more closely resembled those confraternities of provincial patriots in art : but Mr. Hardy has done the greater service, by the greater dignity and range of his work. He shows, how to write of provincial ways without provincialism : rather, how to write of them in the most liberal spirit. Among the misfortunes of Ireland, not the least has been the note of provinciality in her literature : Carleton and Banim could not overpass their limitations of tone and culture. Wessex, a less distressful country, has in Mr. Hardy an ardent lover and a stern chronicler. He laughs at Wessex, he is unsparing of Wessex, he delights in Wessex : with all the world round him, and all history behind him, he is content to find ' infinite riches in a little room,' and he cleaves to Wessex. It is an example of voluntary attachment upon an artist's part, to be commended and emulated : for in losing the ties and bonds of home, art in these days is losing its strength. *Spartam nactus es : hanc exorna.* Mr. Hardy has his Sparta : its ancient ways will long boast their grave adornment and orderly display at his hands, in a great province of art's kingdom.

IV

COUNTRY FOLK

' John Hewet was a well-set man of about five and twenty; Sarah Drew might be rather called comely than beautiful, and was about the same age : They had pass'd thro' the various labours of the year together with the greatest satisfaction ; if she milk'd, 'twas his morning and evening care to bring the cows to her hand : it was but last fair that he bought her a present of green silk for her straw hat, and the posie on her silver ring was of his choosing. Their love was the talk of the whole neighbourhood ; for scandal never affirm'd that they had any other views than the lawful possession of each other in marriage. It was that very morning that he had obtain'd the consent of her parents, and it was but till the next week that they were to wait to be happy. Perhaps in the intervals of their work they were now talking of the wedding cloaths, and John was suiting several sorts of poppys and field flowers to her complection, to chuse her a knot for the wedding-day.

' While they were thus busied (it was on the last of July between three and four in the afternoon) the clouds grew black, and such a storm of lightning and thunder ensued, that all the labourers made the best of their way to what shelter the trees and hedges

122

afforded. Sarah was frightned, and fell down in a
swoon on a heap of barley. John, who never separated from her, sate down by her side, having raked
together two or three heaps the better to secure her
from the storm. Immediately there was heard so
loud a crack, as if heaven had split asunder ; every
one was solicitous for the safety of his neighbour, and
called to one another throughout the field. No answer
being return'd to those who called to our Lovers, they
stept to the place where they lay ; they perceived the
barley all in a smoak, and then spy'd the faithful
pair ; John with one arm about Sarah's neck, and
the other held over her, as to skreen her from the
lightning.

' They were both struck dead in this tender posture.
Sarah's left eyebrow was sing'd, and there appear'd a
black spot on her breast ; her lover was all over black,
but not the least signs of life were found in either.
Attended by their melancholy companions, they were
convey'd to the town, and the next day interr'd in
Stanton-Harcourt Church-yard.'

This letter by Gay, which Thackeray has immortalized in another version, enshrines with so great a
grace one view of country life, that I have set it down
here : innocent, comely labourers ; pretty, serious
ways of love in the fields ; glimpses of the fair, that
last fair at the busy, homely town ; the kindly concern
of the neighbours ; then, the angry storm bursting
over that hot hayfield, the storm so grand a visitation :
all this makes of John Hewet and Sarah Drew, typical
figures, whom we can see now in the fields, with no

harsh presentiment of poverty or of coarseness to come :
they lie dead, those English country lovers, in all the
significant beauty of Cleobis and Bito. It is a story,
of which one loves to think, when challenged to think
well of country life, in face of certain horrors and
brutalities, undeniably there : as in Madame Dar-
mesteter's *The New Arcadia*, or Mrs. Woods' *A
Village Tragedy*. It helps us, this true idyll of the
last century, to believe that much vaunted sentiment
about the country is born from more than love of a
pretty insincerity ; Strephon sighing to Chloe in the
shade, Damon piping to Phyllis among the flocks ;
those nymphs and swains, whom French and English
art made so delightful, an hundred years ago ; giving
them, for all their coats and gowns of another mode,
something of Apollo's glory and something of the
Muses' grace. The apparent monotony of rural
ways, viewed by spectators used to streets crowded
with strange faces, inclines a writer to people his
fields and villages with primitive virtues, or with primitive vices, but hardly with both. ' To make men
moral something more is requisite than to turn them
out to grass ' : wrote George Eliot, in protest against
the superstition about blameless Arcadians. But
from George Eliot's protest to M. Zola's practice, the
descent is long and difficult : *la bête humaine* is no
more real than the Arcadian, nor Hodge than Strephon.
No long acquaintance with country folk is wanted, to
persuade us that every Sabine labourer is not hardy,
not every Breton poetical, not every Russian patient.
Though ' rustics ' be to some men as undistinguishable,

as ' silly sheep,' the shepherd can distinguish a world
of difference between silly face and face.

Mr. Hardy has given us some ten groups of country
folk ; the farm hands, woodlanders, shepherds,
dairy-maids, furze cutters, carriers, nondescript
labourers, servants, cottagers, who form the main
populace of his Wessex scenes. Unessential, in
many cases, to the conduct of the mere narrative,
they and the landscape around them yet serve to
emphasize the force of that narrative : far from being
picturesque accessories, they form the chorus, whose
office is to insist upon the stable moralities, the tried
wisdom and experience, with which the fortunes of
the chief actors are in contrast. Young and old,
prudent and foolish, consciously or unconsciously,
they come to represent a body of sentiment and
opinion, the growth of rustic times : their proverbs,
witticisms, anecdotes, comments, are all sententious.
Thus, as a Greek chorus, with its leisurely, appropriate utterances, sometimes full of an exasperating
sobriety, stands round about the two or three passionate souls in travail ; so these aged patriarchs, half-
witted clowns, shrewd workmen, village butts and
wits and characters, move through the Wessex scenes,
where Henchard or Eustacia or Tess is acting and
suffering, with grotesque, stolid, or pathetic commen-
taries. But they never lose their reality, their hold
upon life and truth, in the creator's hands : not one
of them is set up, a puppet of the stage, to drawl bucolic
commonplaces in a dialect, or to pass the bounds of
nature in savagery, and whimsicality, and uncouthness.

As we read, it is borne in upon us, that in this peasant talk we have the spiritual history of a country side : feudalism and Catholicism and Protestantism, law and education and tradition, changes in agriculture and commerce and tenure, in traffic and society and living, all these have worked and wrought upon the people, and here is the issue : *this* and *this* is their view of life ; *thus* and *thus* they think and act ; *here* is a survival, and *there* a desire ; *here* a spirit of conservation, and *there* a sign of decay, and *there* again a look of progress. Poor laws and school boards, the Established Church and the Dissenting Mission, the extension of the franchise and the condition of the labourer, matters for grave enquiry and debate among men of social studies, though you may read Mr. Hardy's books without noticing them there, are there none the less : not discussed in set form, often not so much as mentioned, admirably kept back from intrusion, they are yet to be recognised and felt. Not only what the peasants are, but also the causes of their being that, are implied in Mr. Hardy's artistic treatment of them : he deals with men, hard to understand and to pourtray ; but mere ghosts and caricatures of men unless pourtrayed with understanding. In literature, no less than in life, they resent patronage : the rustic, whose office in a book is that of a gargoyle upon a tower, to look quaint and to spout, takes revenge by becoming very wearisome.

The country life has received two chief kinds of celebration in English literature : the academic, so to call it, and the popular. There are the writers, who

derive from Cicero and the younger Pliny ; who
talks of Cincinnatus and of Diocletian in their retreats ;
who quote *Corycius senex* and *Angulus ille* ; men of
gracious minds and manners, half courtly and half
cloistral. Such are Evelyn and Bacon, Cowley and
Temple, Marvell and Vaughan, Spenser and Milton :
Lord Falkland with his friends at Tew, Dr. More in
the gardens of Cambridge, even Pope in his grotto
and Thomson by his peaches, wear this air of cultured pleasure and of conscious virtue. Plato and
Epicurus and Saint Benedict, turned mightily Cice-
ronian, preside over this company : a company high-
born, well-read, often devout and grave, often profound
and passionate. Of a piece with these academics of
country life are the dainty votarists of pastoral : men
of whom Shenstone is the type, men for whom the
lawns and fields have a pleasant, cleanly look of
innocence and peace, not felt at heart, but relished
upon the surface. They might sing in Addison's
delightful chorus, with no suspicion of its gentle
raillery :

> ' O how fresh the morning air !
> Charming fresh the morning air !
> When the Zephirs and the heifers
> Their odoriferous breath compare,
> Their odoriferous breath compare.'

But all these aspects of country life come from the
graceful inspirations of culture : that love of a decent
ritual for daily life, beyond its positive necessities,
which gives a charm to Colleges and to Inns of Court,
where old habits linger still. It is pleasant to walk

along a formal terrace, with worn gray steps and balustrade, holding an Aldine classic, less for study than for company : to look out, with comfortable joy, across the flourishing landscape : to taste the solitude, the dignity, the peace, of a country day. The Golden Age, embellished to a courtly, cloistral perfection, with finer music than pastoral reeds, and daintier fare than acorns and spring water, returns at such a time : at this happy distance, the town seems vile. Theocritus and Ronsard are good to read in a sunny kind of dream ; *Comus*, and *L'Allegro*, and *Il Penseroso* are pure delights : but ' the swinkt hedger ' rouses less lively interest in rural toil, than literary interest in old English.

The writers, who compose pictures out of their sentimental impressions, are very much our benefactors : ' sit by my side, and let the world slip : we shall ne'er be younger,' is sometimes the invitation to a wise indulgence. But there are other writers, whose treatment of country life is not so decorative : men, who feel a strong drawing towards the earth and its tillers, from mere love of life, or sympathy with men ; because both emotions are most felt among the scenes of men's oldest and earthiest occupations. No metaphorical truth is so true, Lucretius be our witness, as is the Motherhood of Earth : I do not understand the temptation to worship the sun : but I understand very thoroughly the temptation to worship the earth ; not with a vague, pantheistic emotion, but with a personal love for the sensible ground under my feet. The thought, that the earth

is doubly sacred; both blessed and cursed; is a
thought past fathoming. And all needs of men, that
have an immediate connection with the mysterious
earth, have themselves a share in the mystery, the
primaeval sacredness. One may stand before a steam
engine, in shameful, yet unashamed, ignorance of its
construction: but in presence of the ploughman,
shepherd, gardener, reaper, sower, woodman, and of
their implements and operations, he has a longing to
comprehend those venerable crafts, which speak so
movingly of men's natural needs. The smell of the
dark earth, ruddy original of Adam, as the share
breaks into it, seems fragrant with the first breath of
mornings in the early world:

> ' Come, sons of summer, by whose toil,
> We are the lords of wine and oil;
> By whose tough labours and rough hands,
> We rip up first, then reap our lands.
> Crowned with the ears of corn, now come,
> And to the pipe sing harvest home.'

Indeed, I have a fellow feeling with Triptolemus
Yellowley, whose taste was all for the rustical parts
of Latin literature. The lust of labour, glad and sad
together, of labour for our daily bread, seems glorified
by an ancient sanction, in the case of agriculture:
whatever be its conditions now, once upon a time the
tilling and preparing of the ground was the most
natural, simple, and imperious necessity of men.
Akin to it are the pastoral arts and sciences, all dealings with the earth and the earth's tribes, all Virgil's
themes of husbandry. Such pictures of the early

I

world, as that in Lucretius, charm us by the romance inseparable from simple and dignified things : the old poets did wisely, in their ignorance, to fill the early world with innocent tribes of men ; to discover them at peace. So, one loves to think, it should have been : that laborious burden of daily work lies more gently upon our shoulders, when we consider the golden days of Arcadia and the Hesperides, those lands and blessed fields of Kennaquhair. Demeter and Persephone, Dionysus and the Mighty Mother, were divinities not hard to love, for they were very good to men : and other gods also :

> ' *O montana Pales !   O pastoralis Apollo,*
> *Et nemorum Silvane potens !* '

It is this ' pagan ' sentiment, the sentiment of homely villagers, which makes many readers desire the triumph of those anthropologists, who maintain a great attribution of divinity to woods and fields : readers, for whom Mr. Frazer's *The Golden Bough* has a magical charm. Without putting our faith in Rousseau, nor even in Count Tolstoi ; but with a firm faith in the growing civilities of the world ; we may still find, in country labour, the memory and the type of men's ancient business with nature. It is restful, among the bewildering commerce of life, to reflect upon those hard, yet wholesome, relations between man and the earth : the natural sacrament of ' daily bread,' to which is related, for innumerable men, another, and a more than natural mystery :

' Car sur la fleur des pains et sur la fleur des vins,
Fruit de la force humaine en tous lieux répartie,
Dieu moissonne, et vendange, et dispose à ses fins
La Chair et le Sang pour le calice et l'hostie ! '

But if this reverence towards the earth, and towards work upon it, is to be fruitful in literature, writers must not only be full of sentiment : they must be full of science. In literature, the place of experiment is taken by curiosity : by a desire to come at the heart of life, in its various forms and manifestations. With all allowance for the vague emotions, indefinite wants, and discontinuous thoughts, which throng the mind of a man at his work ; yet it is not in these, but in the material details of his work, that its power and significance for art reside : in the actual things, to be seen and handled, which the man uses ; among which he lives ; of which he is the master or the servant ; with which his senses have grown familiar, as with sunrise and with sunset. The Saints are pictured with the instruments of their glorious and crowning passions ; the swords and spears, which were not their weapons and companions ; but which are appropriate to them now, since the blows and thrusts of cruel steel in fierce hands made it suddenly clear, that their lives were battles, their deaths victories, themselves soldiers. Take what class of men you will : there will be always found some concrete thing, to be the symbol of their histories. In the case of peasantry, labourers at rural work, so intimate is the relationship between the workman and the work, that the least thing about them seems to have its significance, and to be ; rude,

poor thing that it is ! eloquent with appeals to our
sympathy, and charged with sentiment.   Remember
Mr. Secretary Pepys, and the old shepherd, whom he
held in talk upon the downs : a very famous scene.
The old man's little boy read the Bible to him : and
the old man blessed the boy : ' the most like one
of the old patriarchs that ever I saw in my life, and it
brought those thoughts of the old age of the world in
my mind for two or three days after.   We took notice
of his woollen knit stockings with two colours mixed,
and of his shoes shod with iron, both at the toe and
heels, and with great nails in the soles of his feet,
which was mighty pretty ; and taking notice of them,
" Why," says the poor man, " the downes you see
are full of stones, and we are faine to shoe ourselves
thus ; and these," says he, " will make the stones fly
till they ring before me." '   Then Mr. Pepys, good
gossip, gave the old man ' something,' tried to cast
stones with his horn crook, heard about the shepherd's
pride in his dog, about the number of his flock, about
his wages : and so, on to other pretty diversions.   We
could deny ourselves much fine talk about Humanity
and Man, for the sake of more personal, loving knowledge about the ways of men : about the touching
circumstance, the significant furniture and garniture,
of their laborious lives.   There is much wisdom for
daily life, to be learned from that most natural devotion of the Church, the devotion to holy relics ; piteous,
or marvellous, or homely, memorials of the sacred
dead : for there is something venerable in most
things, that speak of a man's personality.   They are

the winning writers, who know the truth of these
lines :

> ' Momentous to himself, as I to me,
> Hath each man been that ever woman bore ;
> Once in a lightning-flash of sympathy,
> I *felt* this truth, an instant, and no more.'

If this truth were felt, not for an instant, but for a
lifetime, by more writers, literature would boast of
fewer egoists and of better novelists.

Mr. Hardy's books, one and all, shew this consuming devotion to the old records, and to the living details,
of men : in especial, to those of labouring men, in
constant occupation with the earth, its living things,
and its things that give life. *Corn and wine and oil :
beasts and much cattle : the fruits of the earth in due
season : fields white to harvest :* he gives loving study
to men busied with all such things. But he pursues
them far beyond the fields and farms of their labour :
he knows them, not by sight alone, but by heart. The
Wessex traveller, the traveller in any rural part, is ever
alert with wonder, to see the wealth of obscure histories all round him. There are worn implements of
toil, rusty ploughs and harrows, lying alone in the
field ; they look immeasurably old, old as the heaped
graves of warriors, among which they rest : what
hands once grew hard with handling them, hands
mortified long since ! Here is a lonely, mean house,
built some forty years ago, standing back from the
road ; too commonplace and dull to hold the attention long : but the story of its successive inmates,
their labours and achievements, failures and desires,

the secret truths of the plays played out in the dreary place, might prove a masterpiece of life, and yield matter for a masterpiece of art.   Here is a milestone, crusted with gold lichen, or a signpost, coated with green moss, both long past their work : one meditates upon times, when they were new, and upon the travellers from village to village, who quickened or slackened their pace on reading them : what sort of men were those, before they went *per iter tenebricosum* ?   And the long, straggling villages ; barely picturesque, may be, save for the gray church, and all the decent associations of that ; some cottages, indeed, whose walls are thick, and their thatched roofs down to the ground among the tall flowers ; but more still with plain, slate roofs, and walls of crude, bad bricks : the long, straggling villages rouse thoughts in plenty, thoughts of infinite variety.   An old labourer passes by, trudging upon his ' ragged staff,' and gives me a gruff greeting : and I am suddenly aware, that to know this man's life, all spent within a circuit of twenty miles, I would be content never again to read one querulous French diarist ; to remain, in Baudelaire's despite, ' lecteur paisible et bucolique.'

For here too is the greatness of life, and here the littleness ; here, among the Wessex labourers, so easily caricatured, so hardly comprehended : Gray has said it all in verses, with which we are familiar to the verge of contempt.   ' The pale artisan ' is an estimable person, with good, strong virtues, and bad, weak vices, of his own : but, giving him all the good will in the world, we need not exalt him at the cost of

' clodhoppers ' and ' bumpkins.' It is a distinction
of Mr. Hardy, that he is honest in these matters : even
George Eliot could yield to the temptation of making
rustic characteristics, the foil to her own humour.
And Mr. Hardy has paid the penalty of honest work,
the penalty of misunderstanding : to the master of
Wessex ways and works have been applied the epithets,
theatrical and artificial, unimaginative and dull.

These charges were plausibly brought, by a reader
not conversant with Mr. Hardy's whole work : by
one, who should light at random upon some page of
rustic talk. ' How grotesque and strained are these
phrases ! ' he might think : ' how wandering and
aimless, the whole drift of talk. This is not the
manner of *Shirley*, of *Silas Marner* : there is no swift
brilliance of pourtraiture, no delicious play of humour ;
all is desultory, awkward, slow.' It were plausibly
concluded, by one unversed in Mr. Hardy's art : to
readers comfortably at home among his works, such
conclusions seem quite false. For they have learned to
see in Mr. Hardy an artist, obedient to the commands
of his art, and therefore resigned to the limitations,
content with the capabilities, of his materials: an artist,
like those, whom Mr. William Morris loves to praise ;
the artists, whose use of wood and stone and brick was
guided by the various natures of the various places,
where they had a call to exercise their art. A fen
country, a down country, a hill country, makes each its
own demands upon the designer of buildings : his
pride it is, to respect the universal laws of art, whilst
respecting the genius of place and circumstance, in the

application of them.   Mr. Hardy appreciates the nature
of the soil, in which he works, upon which he builds :
he knows it for Wessex, not Northumbria, West Saxon,
not East Anglian : his ground plan, structure, ornament are designed to harmonize with the definite
features of the land.   Men and women, he insists upon
it, are natural growths of the soil ; children of earth,
with a particular seal of that common lineage set upon
them, according to their lot of birth-place and local
origin : ' racy of the soil,' with him, is a phrase of
most exact and literal a meaning.   He dwells upon
the very externals of such ' raciness,' its visible and
concrete symbols, with an insistence almost excessive.   Thus, he speaks of dress : ' A person on a
heath in raiment of modern cut and colour has more
or less an anomalous look.   We seem to want the
oldest and simplest human clothing where the clothing
of the earth is so primitive.'   Again, in another place :
' When in the midst of the field, a dark spot on an
area of brown, there crossed her path a moving figure,
whom it was as difficult to distinguish from the earth
he trod as the caterpillar from his leaf, by reason of the
excellent match between his clothes and the clods.
He was one of a dying-out generation who retained
the principle, nearly unlearnt now, that a man's
habiliments should be in harmony with his environ-
ments.'   These are very literal applications of a great
artistic principle : yet, since Carlyle has taught us to
moralize upon clothes, we may well see in these sentences a suggestion of Mr. Hardy's general manner,
in dealing with country folk, and with country things.

It is not enough to know them, cut off from their circumstances, isolated and singled out : their circumstances, material and spiritual, must be mastered, before any attempt to present the men themselves. For the men are not prodigal of their own natures : they do not deal in the ' synthetic ' phrase, the ' decisive ' word, the clinching epigram : they are leisurely, discursive, roundabout : you cannot pierce through to their real selves, in the course of a brief acquaintance. Yet, they leave with their foreign hearers an impression of strong character : these are men, it must be, in touch with the facts of life, men of experience, and of original thoughts about that experience ; but without that quick versatility of expression, which enables far shallower men to play with a dozen philosophies in a dozen phrases : these children of the soil deal with the rich and rugged depths of their own minds, as they deal with the earth in view of harvest to come. They have no sophisticated fear of a moral sentence, or of a general principle : there is no safeguarding of themselves against the imputation of talking platitudes and truisms. The simple sentences of proverbial wisdom come, the fruit of a laborious experience, from these work folk, as like simple sentences came from early Ionian sages : old saws, well warranted from Aryan times. They waste no words in pure love for the game of talk, without any ulterior purpose : lumbering, cumbrous, they can often be : deliberately trivial, consciously fooling with phrases, they never are. Their set discussions upon the affairs of labour, or of life ; very much the same thing, to some of them ; may be rambling, and slow, and full of iteration : but they are not the less weighty for that.   They feel towards each other, not by the virtue of condescension learned from experience, but by an instinct of nature, what Herbert felt towards his poor parishioners : ' it is some relief for a poor body to be but heard with patience.'   One by one, gravely and slowly, they adduce their anecdotes in illustration of the theme, they elaborate their solid thoughts about it, they bring to light the ripe produce of their labouring minds.   No haunt of sad-cultured men hears so sturdy a debate upon life, as I chanced to hear at a Wessex wayside inn.   Many men were of many minds : until a well weathered labourer, whose great scythe leant against the wall beside him, closed the session with these words : *'Tis none too easy a matter, is life : take it gentle or take it rough.*   There followed, from all the company, a solemn shaking of heads, a pathetic thumping of knees, and a luxurious draining of two-handled pint cups.   Schopenhauer and Leopardi leave no such conviction, as that rustic sentence left : but it is one thing to recognize the depths of character in these folks ; and another, to comprehend the conditions and experiences of life, which go to its various formations.   Let us remember the talk, upon a memorable day, of the Mellstock quire.

' " Yes ; Geoffrey Day is a clever man if ever there was one.   Never says anything : not he."

' " Never."

' " You might live wi' that man, my sonnies, a

hundred years, and never know there was anything in him."

' " Ay ; one o' these up-country London ink-bottle fellers would call Geoffrey a fool."

' " Ye would never find out what 's in that man : never. Silent ? Ah, he is silent ! He can keep silence well. That man's silence is wonderful to listen to." '

That poor creature, the ' up-country London ink-bottle feller,' can do his best to describe rustics : he will hardly, without infinite pains, attain to the interpretation of them. But Mr. Hardy has all the powers required for both description and interpretation of his own countrymen : in his books, the rustic folk are perfectly alive. He knows what lies behind the silence of the shrewd, the sullenness of the stupid ; the blessings or the blows of fortune, which have moulded character ; the countless details of work, which have marked the workman's mind and hand : all the contents of his Wessex country. The views of life, of society, of religion, views multifarious and odd, entertained there, are familiar to him : but his knowledge is not a source of power alone ; it is a source of beauty too. In a paper upon ' The Philosophic and Historic Basis of State Intervention,' Mr. D. G. Ritchie, speaking of a prejudice against that intervention, observes : ' This view of the State as an alien and hostile power is admirably expressed in one of Thomas Hardy's *Wessex Tales*.' He alludes to that pleasant tale of the young Methodist preacher, and of the gentle smuggler, his landlady. Mr. Hardy

may have been led to write it, by the romantic legends
of smuggling upon the Dorset coast ; or by a desire
to exhibit, slightly and humourously, the view of
which Mr. Ritchie speaks ; or by the quaint problem
presented in the preacher's love for so lawless a sweet-
heart.   The one thing of importance is the skill, with
which the writer of a story, containing matter apt
for quotation in a grave, sociological essay, turns
that matter into art.   For there is no obtrusion of
knowledge in these novels :   no pages, which read
like the results of a scientific enquiry, undertaken for
its own sake, and forced into a story.   But the social
state of Wessex folk must be known, if you would
know the forces, which direct the story of their lives ;
high romance and rare comedy, and all things bright
or dark, in those lives, depend for their effect, in
literature as in life, upon the background against
which, upon the atmosphere in which, they appear
and are.
' These things are life :
And life, some think, is worthy of the Muse.'

In *The Woodlanders* and in *Tess of the D'Urbervilles*,
Mr. Hardy avails himself, with admirable effect, of a
peculiar mode in tenures : the system of ' liviers.'   In
the woodland story, Winterborne's tragic calamity in
love, and heroism in death, are intensified, and in part
occasioned, by his necessity of leaving his house : a
necessity caused by the fall of an old man's frail life,
brought about through his rustic superstition ; and
by the offended dignity of a capricious woman.   In
the later story, the final defeat of Tess is greatly

assured by the same necessity, which casts her and
her mother and her mother's children at the mercy
of the world, leaving Tess to the temptation of helping
them by a surrender to Alec D'Urberville. Inter-
woven thus with the fabric of the story, these facts
of rural life quicken wonderfully our living interest :
sudden death is a common device among the novelists :
but the sudden deaths of old South and of poor ' Sir
John,' involving plain, legal consequences of so tragic
and pitiful an issue, are more moving than a score of
less practical misfortunes. All the changes and
chances of village life, migrations and depopulations ;
the terms of rural service, matters of fact about wage
and hire ; the variations in local prosperity, affairs of
parchment and of record : all these become critical
turns in a romance, at Mr. Hardy's bidding. Through
the writer's sense of the piteous, human interest in
such things, we see the contrast between Tess and
Marian at Talbothays, the dairy farm in the rich
pasture land, where they lived and moved like pagan
nymphs of Arcady or Sicily ; Tess and Marian at
Flintcomb Ash, that gaunt, hard place, where they
bent over their weary work, ' like some early Italian
conception of the two Marys.' The contrast is brought
home to us, an actual bitterness and desolation to
think upon. The fortunes of John Inglesant's anxious
soul, the valourous and gentle spirit of Alan Breck,
the consuming selfishness of Sir Willoughby, compose
no more passionate and stirring histories, than do these
homely affairs of Wessex folk : provincials, but of the
centre also, when pourtrayed by the art of an humanist.

I have used the terms, ' country folk,' or ' labourers,'
or ' work folk,' or ' peasantry,' without precision :
these Wessex people, of whom Mr. Hardy writes,
include all varieties of class ; farmers and their hinds,
tradesmen in villages and market towns, gamekeepers
and millers, inn-keepers and servants. They vary
in degree from respectability to vagabondage : but
all have this in common, that they live under rural
conditions of life, and are scarcely affected by the life
of towns at all. The most flourishing of them, wealthy
farmers and merchants, are more akin to their de-
pendants, than to their immediate superiors ; parsons
and squires, whose rusticity, however great, is tempered with remnants of urbanity. These Wessex
folk are of the country alone : their towns are of the
country also. At Casterbridge, the chief of them,
' The farmer's boy could sit under his barley mow and
pitch a stone into the office window of the town clerk ;
reapers at work among the sheaves nodded to acquaint-
ances standing on the pavement corner ; the red-
robed judge, when he condemned a sheep-stealer,
pronounced sentence to the tune of Baa, floated in
from the remainder of the flock browsing hard by ;
and at executions the waiting crowd stood in a meadow
immediately before the drop, out of which the cows
had been temporarily driven to give the spectators
room.' The eastern purlieu of Casterbridge is
Dummerford : ' Here wheat ricks overhung the old
Roman street, and thrust their eaves against the church
tower ; green-thatched barns, with doorways as high
as the gates of Solomon's Temple, opened directly

upon the main thoroughfare. Barns indeed were so
numerous as to alternate with every half dozen houses
along the way. Here lived burgesses who daily
walked the fallow ; shepherds in an intramural squeeze.
A street of farmers' homesteads—a street ruled by a
mayor and corporation, yet echoing with the thump of
the flail, the flutter of the winnowing-fan, and the
purr of the milk into the pails—a street which had
nothing urban in it whatever—this was the Dummerford end of Casterbridge.' Under this single term,
then, Country Folk, is comprehended all the miscellaneous populace of Wessex, as men attached to the
soil, in the various ranks of a rustic hierarchy.

It must strike with force upon the mind of Mr.
Hardy's reader, that these folk, in rural towns, or rural
villages, are a Shakespearian folk : the very people of
that England, merry and old, which we are wont to
lament for dead ; gone with the maypole and with
the morrice, if not with the Mass. It is true, that the
dreary genius of Protestantism, the grim genius of
Puritanism, have wrought their will upon our national
life, to the souring of our tempers, and to the sadden-
ing of our souls : but it is a point for consideration,
whether those abhorrent Powers have wrought a
complete work. In England, as elsewhere, one can
discern two historical aspects of country life : the
joyous and the sullen, the happy and the oppressed.
There are the joyous, happy folk, with their carols
ringing on a night of stars and frost ; there are the
sullen, oppressed folk, with their rhymes of revolt and
discontent : the simple peasantry, all dance and song

and feast; the 'little people,' near neighbours of
Death: the 'pretty country folks'; and the ugly
country serfs.   Here is an honest *Jacques Bonhomme*:
his children may be of the *Jacquerie*.   Upon the one
side, we see the beauty of Catholic faith, of homely
pleasures, of fair work: upon the other side, there is
the cry of the poor, the peasant risings, the angry,
blind despair of men turned to brutes.   In the days,
for which Bishop Corbet sang his dirge, days of the
faeries, days of the Catholics,

> ' When *Tom* came home from Labour,
>   Or *Ciss* to Milking rose;
> Then merrily went their Tabor,
>   And nimbly went their Toes ':

Hobbes, it seems, made a comparison less insolent
than his wish, in comparing the Catholic Church and
the Faery Kingdom.   But, while merry songs are many
to quote, so too are the dismal rhymes, telling of misery
and want.   Here is a doleful screed, from one of the
old Penny Books, by ' our loving Friend Poor Tom.'

> ' Attend, ye gentlemen all,
>   A story oft proves true;
> For the poor suffer hunger and cold,
>   Which makes them look pitiful blue.
>
> It was writ in an evening bright,
>   When Bacchus began to be ruddy,
> And Luna began to give light,
>   Poor Tom fell into a study,
>
> Which vexed his brain right sore,
>   To see how oppression doth thrive,
> And conscience is kick'd out of door,
>   Such cruelty now is alive.'

In the same collection, mixed up with Dr. Faustus and Friar Bacon, Parismus and Angelica, Argalus and Parthenia, Sir Bevis and Don Belianis, all the broken fragments of scholarly and courtly reading, come down to the kitchen and the cottage, is an idyll of perfect simplicity and charm : the story of Honest John and Loving Kate. By the side of Sir Roger de Coverley and his adoring tenants may be set the sad fortunes of ' sweet Auburn.' It would be instructive, again, to compare the experiences of these lettered ecclesiastics at various times and places : Hooker of Bishop's Bourne, Herrick of Dean Prior, Herbert and Norris of Bemerton, Newton of Olney, White of Selborne, Crabbe of Belvoir, Sydney Smith of Combe Florey, Brontë of Haworth, Hawker of Morwenstow, Newman of Littlemore, Manning of Lavington, Keble of Hursley, Kingsley of Eversley. Their varieties of sentiment about country folk would be endless : yet, in our rough way, we think of all their rural flocks as ' the common people,' as ' rustics ' : just as we think of all the labourers upon one farm, as ' Hodge,' indistinguishable members of ' the agricultural class.' The changes of time, notably the great changes of the sixteenth and seventeenth centuries in faith and law, have changed the externals of country folk, to an incalculable degree : but their interior life, the life of thought and sentiment, has been more perdurable. In Wessex, or in any such districts, as those of which Dr. Jessopp and Dr. Atkinson have written well, the past survives : there are the railway and the steam plough, but there are the traditions and the habits of long ago, no less.

K

Read a page of rustic talk in Mr. Hardy, and you will think of Shakespeare : listen to an hour of rustic talk in Wessex, and you will think of Mr. Hardy. The common folk of Shakespeare are less serious and slow, more farcical and ready : their stupidity is lighter, their wit brisker. Mr. Hardy's men have learned, without loving it, Seneca's lesson : *non est viri timere sudorem*. They can less lightly throw off the burden of work : the village revels of the old day are gone, and only the ale house is left to loosen slow tongues, and to relax tired limbs. Yet when they speak, it is in a Shakespearian humour : from Shallow and Silence, to Mistress Quickly and Doll, from Lance and Lancelot, to Costard and Touchstone, we hear the old tones, taste the old wit, take the old humour, until we are ready to swear by that impressive phrase, the continuity of history. Let us compare two scenes : here is one beyond our praise.

'*Shallow*. O, the mad days that I have spent ! and to see how many of mine old acquaintance are dead !
Silence. We shall all follow, cousin.
Shallow. Certain, 'tis certain ; very sure, very sure : death, as the Psalmist saith, is common to all : all shall die. How a good yoke of bullocks at Stamford fair ?
Silence. Truly, cousin, I was not there.
Shallow. Death is certain. Is old Double of your town living yet ?
Silence. Dead, Sir.
Shallow. Dead ! See, see ! He drew a good bow ; and dead ! he shot a fine shoot : John of Gaunt loved him well, and betted much money on his head. Dead ! he would have clapped i' the clout at twelve score ; and carried you a forehand shaft a fourteen and fourteen and a half, that it would

have done a man's heart good to see. How a score of ewes now?

Silence. Thereafter as they be: a score of good ewes may be worth ten pounds.

Shallow. And is old Double dead?'

One comes to understand, why Hurrell Froude would bind together *Hamlet* and the *Georgics.* Here is another scene of tragic comedy, from Mr. Hardy: the gossips' commentary on death in general, and on Mrs. Henchard's death in particular.

' " And she was as white as marble-stone," said Mrs. Cuxsom. " And likewise such a thoughtful woman too—ah, poor soul!—that a' minded every little thing that wanted tending. ' Yes,' says she, ' when I 'm gone, and my last breath 's blowed, look in the top drawer o' the chest in the back room by the window, and you 'll find all my coffin clothes ; a piece of flannel—that 's to put under me, and the little piece is to put under my head ; and my new stockings for my feet—they are folded alongside, and all my other things. And there 's four ounce pennies, the heaviest I could find, a-tied up in bits of linen, for weights—two for my right eye and two for my left,' she said. ' And when you 've used them, and my eyes don't open no more, bury the pennies, good souls, and don't ye go spending 'em, for I shouldn't like it. And open the windows as soon as I 'm carried out, and make it as cheerful as you can for my Elizabeth Jane.' "

' " Ah, poor heart ! "

' " Well, and Martha did it, and buried the ounce pennies in the garden. But if you 'll believe words, that man, Christopher Coney, went and dug 'em up, and spent 'em, at the King of Prussia. ' Faith,' he said, ' why should death deprive life of fourpence ? Death 's not of such good report that we should respect 'en to that extent,' says he."

' " 'Twas a cannibal deed ! " deprecated her listeners.

' " Gad, then, I won't quite ha'e it," said Solomon Longways. " I say it to-day, and 'tis a Sunday morning, and I wouldn't speak wrongfully for a silver sixpence at such a time. I don't see no harm in it. To respect the dead is sound doxology ; and I wouldn't sell skellintons—leastways respectable skellintons—to be varnished for 'natomies, except I run out o' work. But money is scarce and throats get dry. Why *should* death deprive life of fourpence ? I say there was no treason in it."

' " Well, poor soul ; she 's helpless to hinder that or anything now," answered Mother Cuxsom. " And all her shining keys will be took from her, and her cupboards opened ; and things a' didn't wish seen, anybody will see ; and her little wishes and ways will all be as nothing ! " '

One might compare the talk of the workmen in the Luxellian vault, with that of Hamlet and the grave-diggers : the fine, rich foolishness of Joseph Poorgrass, that enchaunting character, with the fantastic tongue of many a Shakespearian fool : the difference, great indeed, is not merely the difference in abstract genius between Shakespeare and Mr. Hardy ; but also between the dramatic art, and the narrative. Yet we are led to the conclusion, that both men gave each his proper genius to the artistic treatment of characters, essentially the same. The old conditions of Elizabethan life before modern modes of travel and modern necessities of industry changed them, are not changed past recognition in Wessex, that ' outstep ' land : there are the same strong influences of locality, the same forces of conservation and endurance. And town life, country life, are not separate, nor causes of separation, for Wessex is not given over to urban trades and interests : so that Shakespeare's medley of people, from justices to clowns, is matched by Mr. Hardy's Wessex populace. The changes of time are duly considered ; he has laid his account with them : and the result is the discovery of a people, presented by a living artist in all the truth of their actual life, as it veritably is : yet a people, whom facts, not fancies, compel us to call Shakespearian.

It is to be observed, that these Wessex folk display their thoughts and humours most racily and richly, when talk turns upon the more common emotions : birth and death, and the two or three intermediate affairs of moment. But their talk is not wont to be prettily poetical, nor full of a simple elevation : it is shrewd, rude, of an earthy and material savour. In *Under the Greenwood Tree*, a tale of rural lovers, there is not a sentence of fine, bold, rushing oratory. True it is, as Tibullus put it, ' Love is gone into the country, and is learning the country speech ' ; at Mellstock, Love keeps his senses, and indulges in no romance of an operatic kind. Only the few characters of deep

and silent passion, Henchard or Marty South, break
sometimes into a natural eloquence, untutored save
by the dignity of emotion. The rest use quaintnesses
of speech, more coarse, gross, or irreverent of sound,
than they are by design : rough crudities or rare
felicities of phrase, which are grounded upon the facts
of life. These men have not made the grand tour of
culture, nor come home to themselves, dissipated by
variety of appreciation, surfeited with the taste of too
many fine interests : a neat phrase, of good literary
form, it delights them to hit on or to hear. ' More
know Tom Fool than Tom Fool knows,' said John
Hostler of the Old Fox in Weatherbury : and rejoiced
Michael the milkman with so choice a bit of wording.

' " More know Tom Fool—what rambling old
canticle is it you say, Hostler ? " enquired the milkman, lifting his ear. " Let's have it again—a good
saying well spit out is a Christmas fire to my withered
heart. More know Tom Fool——'

' " Than Tom Fool knows," said the hostler.

' " Ah ! That's the very feeling I 've feeled over
and over again, hostler, though not in such gifted
language. 'Tis a thought I 've had in me more or
less for years, and never could lick into shape !—
O—ho—ho—ho ! Splendid ! " . . .'

We are hastily inclined to think it caricature : yet
our own feeling towards some new dainty phrase in
literature is of a piece with Michael's rapture over the
scrap of sententious proverb, heard for the first time. ⁋

For men of wide culture, able to range at ease
through the literatures, the histories, the sciences of

long gone times, danger lies upon the side of vague
and dreamy thought, in which nothing, not truth itself,
is at a stay : ' the flowing philosophers,' to whom life
is a drifting and a change ; votaries of aesthetics, to
whom it is a pageant. But the danger for these
labouring men, fast rooted in the soil, lies upon the
side of mental immobility : the spirit is clogged with
earth, no less than braced by its contact ; and the
natural virtue of life in the open air, among the woods
and fields, may be corrupted into a stagnation of the
faculties. These are points for consideration, in any
estimate of rural thought about matters spiritual.
' Howe can he get wisdome that holdeth the plough,
and hee that hath pleasure in the goade, and in driving
oxen, and is occupied in their labours, and talketh but
of the breede of bullocks ? ' *Ecclesiasticus* asks the
question ; and, though it was said of Dr. Johnson
that he would ' learn to talk of *runts*,' with a man who
talked of them, he did not believe in the supreme
wisdom of country men and country minds. There
will always be two classes of rustic men : those, whose
stolidity requires the quickening influence of direct
education ; and those, whose lack of direct knowledge
is supplied by the indirect education of nature, in
somewhat a Wordsworthian way, or in that of Thoreau.
Sons of Jabal and Triptolemus, for good and bad they
are of the earth, earthy.

In Mr. Hardy's books, rustic religion is represented,
as ' fetichistic ' : a primitive superstition about places
and things, persons and practices, of a pagan original,
and only disguised under a Christian nomenclature.

' God is in ' this and that : God, or devils, certainly
great Powers.   Some Wessex folk still ' seek unto
them that have familiar spirits, and unto wizards that
peep, and that mutter.'   Dairyman Crick felt desperate,
when the butter would not come at churning.

' " 'Tis years since I went to Conjuror Trendle's
son in Egdon—years," said the Dairyman bitterly.
" And he was nothing to what his father had been.
I have said fifty times, if I have said once, that I don't
believe in him.   And I don't believe in him.   But I
shall have to go to him if he 's alive.   Oh, yes, I shall
have to go to him, if this sort of thing continnys ! "

' Even Mr. Clare began to feel tragical at the dairyman's desperation.

' " Conjuror Fall, t'other side of Casterbridge, that
they used to call ' Wide-O,' was a very good man when
I was a boy," said Jonathan Kail.   " But he 's rotten
as touch-wood by now."

' " My grandfather used to go to Conjuror Myn-
terne, out at Owlscombe, and a clever man a' were, so
I 've heard grandfather say," continued Mr. Crick.
" But there 's no such genuine folk about nowadays ! " '

To Conjuror Trendle went Rhoda Brook and
Gertrude Lodge : to Conjuror Fall went the Mayor
of Casterbridge : Susan Nonsuch made a waxen image
of Eustacia, murmuring the Lord's Prayer backwards
thrice, stuck it full of pins, and watched it waste in
the fire : Bathsheba, with her handmaid Liddy, tried
divination by the Bible and key : Mrs. Durbeyfield refused to let that grimy volume, the *Complete Fortune-
Teller*, rest in the house by night.   ' Between the

mother, with her fast-perishing lumber of superstition, folk-lore, dialect, and orally transmitted ballads, and the daughter with her trained National teachings, and Standard knowledge under an infinitely Revised Code, there was a gap of two hundred years as ordinarily understood. When they were together the Jacobean and the Victorian ages were juxtaposed.' ' Conjuror Fall was sometimes astonished that men could profess so little and believe so much at his house, when at church they professed so much and believed so little.' These Wessex stories abound in legends, myths, magical rites : such as those, with which the woodlanders amused the unprincipled prig Fitzpiers, so proud of his Shelley and his Schleiermacher : incidents, such as the divination by hemp seed on old Midsummer Eve, and South's horror of the great tree. A sense of old-world credulity pervades the books : we hear the voices of such haggard crones, as live for us in Horace, in Propertius, in Apuleius the magical : of witches from Thessaly or Lapland.

Apart from all speculation, about the natural tendencies of a rustic people, to keep something primitive and pagan in their religion, it is not hard to find historical reasons, for the permanence of such a tendency in England : we can consult in Bede the letter of Saint Gregory the Great to Saint Augustine, and read there, how the wise economy of the Church dealt with the pagan prepossessions of a convert people. But Protestantism, during the three centuries of its rule, has shewn no such wisdom in directing and in purifying, what the Master of Balliol calls, 'underground religion': that gloomier and more fearful strain of thought about things spiritual, which ancient Greece itself could never annul. When their reverent familiarity, with the things of faith, was gone, country folk, unmoved by the decent dulness of Protestantism, gave in the more to the pagan instinct : that instinct, which Catholicism had recognized, and partly turned into a purer sentiment. What remained, but that the simple folk should betake themselves to all manner of confused oracles, dubious rites, gross fancies ? That comely service and decorous liturgy ; so moving to the gracious spirits of Herbert and of Ken, so comfortable to the trained minds of Walton and of Johnson, so stately at Whitehall and at Oxford ; could it make much appeal to ruder spirits and to unlettered minds ? The country parson, the parson's clerk, the Sunday service, became official, legal, and conventional, in the eyes of rustics : but for stirring converse with unseen powers, for trembling emotion and awful fear, better the haunted places, the oracles of nature, the books of magic, the woodland solemnities and divinations, than the cold correctness of authorized religion. *Primus in orbe deos fecit timor* : we are told by Statius and Petronius : ' nous humanisons souvent la divinité,' writes Malebranche : the two tendencies, the habit of fear and the habit of literality, unchastened by higher habits of thought, produce just that rustic ' fetichism,' so strongly realized by Mr. Hardy. At the same time, it may be thought, that he too dwells more upon the letter of such habits, than upon the spirit ; he hardly

makes allowance for the struggling light, which finds
its blind way through that gross darkness covering
the people. Anthropologists know well, how honest
travellers, after long sojourn among savage races, will
report of them, atheism and unspirituality beyond
doubt : and how a closer investigation reveals their
jealous concealment of a wild theology. So too, it is
easy to fix our thoughts upon the peasant's outward
degradation of spiritual faith, without thinking of the
interior sentiment so rudely manifested. At the least,
I would apply to these Wessex ' pagans,' what Burke
said of the French peasants, and of the new light
poured upon them by the ' philosophers ' : ' I cannot
conceive, how a man's not believing in God can teach
him to cultivate the earth with the least of any additional skill or encouragement.' The quality of a
man's belief is hard to estimate : like the quality of a
man's pleasure, that famous problem, it is a matter of
very various degree : but you do not rob anything of
its value to its possessor, by treating it with a scientific
contempt, or with an artistic condescension.

The attitude of Mr. Hardy's country folk, towards
existing forms of worship, is that of customary adher-
ence to the ' old ancient ' ways, venerable by their
establishment for three centuries ; a religion of use
and wont ; not lightly to be renounced, not greatly
to be revered, but to be accepted naturally, as a fact
in the order of existing things. Joseph Poorgrass,
confessing to certain lapses from good conduct, was
unwilling to go too far : ' Your next world is your
next world, and not to be squandered off-hand.' So

serious a view roused his fellow tipplers at the Buck's
Head, that melancholy day : while Fanny Robin's
coffin lay in the cart without, under the dripping
boughs, in the chill air.

' " I believe you to be a chapel-member, Joseph.
That I do."

' " Oh, no, no !   I don't go so far as that."

' " For my part," said Coggan, " I 'm staunch
Church of England."

' " Ay, and faith so be I," said Mark Clark.

' " I won't say much for myself ; I don't wish to,"
Coggan continued, with that tendency to talk on
principles which is characteristic of the barley-corn.
" But I 've never changed a single doctrine : I 've
stuck like a plaster to the old faith I was born in.   Yes ;
there 's this to be said for the church, a man can belong
to the church and live in his cheerful old inn, and
never trouble or worry his mind about doctrines at
all.   But to be a meetinger, you must go to chapel in
all winds and weathers, and make yerself as frantic
as a skit.   Not but that chapel members be clever
chaps enough in their way.   They can lift up beautiful
prayers out of their own heads, all about their families
and shipwrecks in the newspaper."

' " They can—they can," said Mark Clark, with
corroborative feeling ; " but we Churchmen, you
see, must have it all printed aforehand, or, dang it all,
we should no more know what to say to a great person
like the Lord than babes unborn."

' " Chapel folk be more hand-and-glove with them
above than we," said Joseph, thoughtfully.

' " Yes," said Coggan.   " We know very well that
if anybody goes to heaven, they will.   They 've
worked hard for it, and they deserve to have it, such
as 'tis.   I 'm not such a fool as to pretend that we
who stick to the church have the same chance as they,
because we know we have not.   But I hate a fellow
who 'll change his old ancient doctrines for the sake
of getting to heaven.   I 'd as soon turn King's evidence for the few pounds you get." '

Of a piece with this religious constancy, preached
indeed by a theologian in his cups, but not the less
sincere for that, is the fatalism of the Wessex poor.
Throughout all Mr. Hardy's books, ' 'Twas to be,' is
the consolation, the justification, the meditation, of his
countrymen.   ' Fortune is a woman,' said Machiavel,
' and must be hectored to keep her down ': but Grand-
fer Cantle, or William Worm, or old Creedy, would but
find in that definition another reason for acquiescence,
submission, and resignation, with an almost humourous joy in the simplicity of life, thanks to the arrangement of fate.   ' Steeped in fancies and prefigurative
superstitions,' these people look upon life, less as a field
of battle, than as a place of ordeal : all are blindfolded :
but this man never sets foot upon the red shares, that
man never escapes them.   Hence the air, now of
peace, now of gloom, which hangs over the Wessex
stories : such tranquillity or such melancholy, as the
seasons of nature seem to feel.   The fields glow in
the sunlight : ' 'twas to be ' : the wind wails through
the bare branches : ' 'twas to be.'   **The Mayor of
Casterbridge, passionate and powerful, did not wrangle**

with his fate: 'his usual habit was not to consider whether destiny were hard upon him or not, the shape of his ideas in cases of affliction being simply a moody " I am to suffer, I perceive." ' The village tragedies owe half their tragedy to this impassive patience of men filled with strong passions : there is no wild anger against so natural a thing, as a predestination to sorrow and to loss. The rise and fall of families, upon which Mr. Hardy loves to meditate, strengthen the rural fatalist in his convictions : a vague sense of departed greatness, as a common thing, known from father to son, helps to make present afflictions bearable. Mr. Mozley, in his reminiscences of the Oxford movement, notes that many of his labouring parishioners in Devon had their coats of arms, their descent from noble houses : it is characteristic, as Tess pleaded, of all Wessex. These considerations explain that monumental, that almost mortuary, look of passionless calm in Mr. Hardy's books : an air of massive grandeur, which moulds their features, from long pondering upon the ways of time and of death. Sir Thomas Browne, with a far greater command of imagination, had no greater sense of human mutability, and of immitigable death, than has Mr. Hardy : in whom the place of Browne's ardent faith is taken by a volcanic spirit of protest and of pity, breaking out through the steady darkness.

' " Michael Henchard's Will.

" That Elizabeth-Jane Farfrae be not told of my death, or made to grief on account of me.

" & that I be not bury'd in consecrated ground.
" & that no sexton be asked to toll the bell.
" & that nobody is wished to see my dead body.
" & that no murners walk behind me at my funeral.
" & that no flours be planted on my grave.
" & that no man remember me.
" To this I put my name.

" MICHAEL HENCHARD."

' " What are we to do ? " said Donald, when he had handed the paper to her.

' She could not answer distinctly. " O Donald ! " she said at last, " what bitterness lies there ! But there 's no altering—so it must be." '

This naked misery and mere agony, sublimed to grandeur by endurance, seem commensurate with the great looks and ways of nature : like the sacred madness of Lear, this aching stoicism, in which all is petrified but one nerve of pain, escapes the charge of extravagance, through its affinity with the wild scene of its passion. It is a truth, of which Mr. Hardy often avails himself, that place and passion should be well matched : ' The new vale of Tempe may be a gaunt waste in Thule : human souls may find themselves in closer and closer harmony with external things wearing a sombreness distasteful to our race when it was young.' Ethelberta puts it in her melodramatic way : ' We must not be poor in London. Poverty in the country is a sadness, but poverty in town is a horror. There is something not without grandeur in the thought of starvation on an open mountain or in a wide wood, and your bones lying there to bleach in the pure sun and rain : but a back garret in a rookery and the other starvers in the room insisting on keeping the window shut—anything to deliver us from that ! ' It is to the harmony between themselves and their surroundings, that the country folk owe the singular impressiveness of their virtue and of their vice : they are not engulphed in vast crowds, distracted by the whirl of life : they retain a personality, clear and strong, which years and experience do but confirm. Brutal, ignorant, sottish, they are still full of character : kindly, wise, dignified, they are still full of distinction. Giles Winterborne and Gabriel Oak, by their exquisite congruity with their occupations and circumstances, force us to think of them, as masters in the art of life : as men who fulfil the duties, who possess the culture, demanded of them : men in their right minds and places, to a degree past attainment by men of the crowd. Here is a passage, which I read with just that feeling of respect, felt in reading of Cuvier or of Bentley.

' Gabriel proceeded towards his home. In approaching the door, his toe kicked something which felt and sounded soft, leathery, and distended, like a boxing-glove. It was a large toad humbly travelling across the path. Oak took it up, thinking it might be better to kill the creature to save it from pain ; but finding it uninjured, he placed it again amongst the grass. He knew what this direct message from the Great Mother meant. And soon came another.

' When he struck a light indoors there appeared

upon the table a thin glistening streak, as if a brush of varnish had been lightly dragged across it. Oak's eyes followed the serpentine streak to the other side, where it led up to a large brown garden-slug, which had come indoors to-night for reasons of its own. It was Nature's second way of hinting to him that he was to prepare for foul weather.

' Oak sat down meditating for nearly an hour. During this time two black spiders, of the kind common in thatched houses, promenaded the ceiling, ultimately dropping to the floor. This reminded him that if there was one class of manifestations on this matter that he thoroughly understood it was the instincts of sheep. He left the room, ran across two or three fields toward the flock, got upon a hedge, and looked over among them.

' They were crowded close together on the other side around some furze bushes, and the first peculiarity observable was that, on the sudden appearance of Oak's head over the fence, they did not stir or run away. They had now a terror of something greater than their terror of man. But this was not the most noteworthy feature : they were all grouped in such a way, that their tails, without a single exception, were toward that half of the horizon from which the storm threatened. There was an inner circle closely huddled, and outside these they radiated wider apart, the pattern formed by the flock as a whole not being unlike a vandyked lace collar, to which the clump of furze bushes stood in the position of a man's neck.

' This was enough to re-establish him in his original

L

opinion. He knew now that he was right, and that Troy was wrong. Every voice in nature was unanimous in bespeaking change. But two distinct translations attached to these dumb expressions. Apparently there was to be a thunderstorm, and afterwards a cold continuous rain. The creeping things seemed to know all about the latter rain, but little of the interpolated thunderstorm; whilst the sheep knew all about the thunderstorm and nothing of the latter rain.'

The passage fills me with a strange fear; so magical seems this warning of nature in the night: and with a strange shame; so little should I have understood it. The richness of the world in wonder is opened before us: and we come to comprehend, dimly and slowly, how the life of labouring men, away from the confused commerce of towns, is a life in which nature plays a direct part; with what influence upon soul and body, it is no light task to say. For crowds and multitudinous traffic, these men have the innumerable society of natural things, trees and winds and waters: they find companionship in creatures of the woodland and the field: their hopes, fears, experiences, sciences, their faith and love, sorrow and hate, are nourished by the Mighty Mother.

There are many features of the country folk in Mr. Hardy's books, upon which I have not touched: those village choirs, with their pleasant pride in a music, which, laugh over it, if you will, was a relic of artistic instincts, fast dying out among the rustics of to-day: scenes of rural feast and converse, drawn with delightful sympathy, and sometimes, as in that brief comedy of error, *The Three Strangers*, full of moving incident : all kinds of adventure, business, and stir, such as those, which go to the making of Mr. Hardy's Wessex ballad :

> ' There was skimmity-riding with rout, shout, and flare,
> In Weatherbury, Stokeham, and Windleton, ere
> They had proof of old Sweatley's decay ;
> The Mellstock and Yalbury folk stood in a stare
> (The tranter owned houses and garden ground there),
> But little did Sim or his Barbara care,
> For he took her to church the next day ' :

there is the happy pastoral of Dick Dewy and Fancy Day, deserving all praise for its simplicity, which is not forced, and for its reality, which is not unkind ; but Mr. Hardy's genius is very rich, and I make no attempt to illustrate its richness on all sides.

One point remains, which must not go without notice : Mr. Hardy's treatment of the Wessex dialect. An artistic interest in provincial dialect is older, than many men might think it to be : Shakespeare, of course, and Ben Jonson, have given us their impressions of the Irish, Welsh, and Scotch versions, of our English speech : Fielding and Smollett, with their Squire Westerns, their Lismahagos, their Morgans, their Seagrims, produced a rare Babel of tongues : but all this is incidental, and by way of casual diversion. Some instances there are, of an interest in provincial dialect more like that of Mr. Hardy ; an interest more scientific and serious : and of these, I know none more curious than ' An *Exmoor* Scolding,

in the Propriety and Decency of *Exmoor* Language,
between two sisters, *Wilmot Moreman and Thomasin
Moreman*, as they were spinning. Also an *Exmoor*
Courtship.' [1] These pieces, produced early in the
eighteenth century, though somewhat overdone, yet
have much in common with Mr. Hardy's manage-
ment of the Wessex speech : and they do not stand
alone. Our antiquarian ancestors did not bestow
all their horrified curiosity upon ' wild Irish ' and
' Highland savages ' : the barbarous and Gothic
peasantry of England, in the north and west countries,
had their share of attention.   Mr. Hardy has it always
in mind, that the Wessex dialect is the passport to
intimacy with the Wessex folk : not merely a means
of making his readers feel themselves carried into the
country.   He makes but a sparing use of local words ;
barton, *blue-vinnied*, and the like : he prefers, by
careful disposition of words, elaboration of sentences,
turns of phrase, and stresses of accent, to convey a
notion of that slow, emphatic speech, one of the
strongest spoken in England.   It abounds in peculiarities, which the erudite German may call ' diseases
of language ' : at least, they are ' dulcet diseases,' full
of charm and vigour.   A writer, less powerful than
Mr. Hardy, would have composed a terrible parody
of rustic language : a jargon neither to be repeated,
nor to be understood ; the resources of print would
have been ransacked for means of recording it ; there

---

[1] I have to thank my friend, Mr. Victor Plarr, Librarian of
King's College in the Strand, for calling my attention to these
and to other rare pieces.

would not have been three lines of common English put
into a rustic mouth. Mr. Hardy knows, that a novel
is not a phonograph, any more than it is a photograph :
and he contrives to reconcile the demands of truth
with those of art, in a way which brings Wessex before
our eyes, and the memory of its speech into our ears.
For accuracy, he is most noticeable : he tells us, how
ancient usages, *Ich* for *I*, *Ich woll* for *I will*, *er woll*
for *he will*, *er war* for *he was*, and the like, are ' still
used by old people in north west Dorset and Somerset ' :
and how ' Grammer Oliver's conversation in *The
Woodlanders*,' that story of the north west, is ' an
attempted reproduction.' He adds, that such forms
are dying rapidly, and only used by others than the
old, in moments of strong emotion : witness the
speech of Tess, with its sudden changes. I know not,
whether any part of England has been so glorified in
verse and prose of its own familiar speech, as Dorset
has been glorified by Barnes, the poet of Blackmore
Vale, and by Mr. Hardy, who has all Wessex to his
province.

' J'aimerais les paysans, si le paysan ne me dégoûtait,'
says the Abbé Roux, of those Limousin folk, whom
he depicts with so subtle a mingling of repulsion and
of love : I am not sure, that love for the best of Wessex,
or disgust for its worst, is the characteristic of Mr.
Hardy : so impassive is he, so reticent and restrained.
But of his fidelity I can see no question : if there be
fidelity in George Sand or in Turgeneff, in Count
Tolstoi or in M. Fabre, when they paint their rural
scenes, there is at least an equal fidelity in the Wessex

artist. Sitting in some humble, homely inn ; hung round, not with ballads, like Walton's ' honest alehouse,' nor with ' lavender in the windows,' but, like *The Three Tuns* in Sherborne, with bills of sale and agricultural notices ; ensconced in the old settle, black or white, and joining in talk with mine Hostess and her blue-coated gossips : many a time, I have almost dreamed myself into one of Mr. Hardy's books ; and awoken to marvel at the power of an art, so faithful without pedantry, so imaginative without exaggeration. Humane and high seriousness ; far reaching thoughts, and sympathies with the things of home : by these Mr. Hardy has made masterpieces, for which I cannot trust myself to thank him ; masterpieces of beauty, masterpieces of truth.

V

CHARACTERS OF MEN AND WOMEN

THE writer of this century, whom Mr. Hardy brings most often before my mind, is Wordsworth: that austere poet. Mr. Hardy's 'message,' his burden, is indeed not that of Wordsworth; it is no solemn exultation of mind, exaltation of soul, that fill us, while we read the Wessex stories: yet there is an ardent austerity about them, a grave joyousness now and then, which recall the temper and the mood of Wordsworth. The works of each bring before our minds the presence of a mind burning with passion, but strong to restrain it: a mind touched to its depths by the appeals of nature and of mankind, but disdainful of all light answers: a mind enamoured of meditation, but impatient of mere dreams. The style of both is massive in its simplicity, and moves to a solemn music; with sudden elevations of tone, which stir in us an indescribable pleasure: each style displays a rare mingling of richness and severity; that beauty of restrained art, which enchaunts us beyond all the charms of an art ever prodigal and gorgeous. Both writers love to deal with the spiritual magnificence of men in a humble station; with the unadorned majesty of natural lives; with things immemorial, the oldest signs and tokens of an ancient world ; with great passages of time, dissolutions, vanishings, and vicissitudes : both impress upon us the ' magnalities ' of the universe, alike throughout the whole unconceived eternity of things, and at each single point within it ; both are obedient to the vision of forms, laws, powers, ideas, awful and august, among which men walk, themselves mysterious and tragic. Both have so solicitous an impartiality and indifference in their dealings with the world, so perfect a loyalty, each to his sense of righteousness and truth, that their very virtues provoke us to some anger : we exclaim against this austerity, this iron mood, this unamiable serenity, this unbending dignity : and both go lumbering over low ground, when they relinquish their accustomed heights.   Both present men with a directness, a belief in the power of plain, strong figures, which sometimes creates an effect of awkwardness : the verse can be bald and barren, the prose can be wooden and stiff. A passionate prepossession by some few dominant thoughts must issue, either in works of singular and distinguished loftiness, or in works of a rigid and stark monotony : there is little room for flashing plays of thoughts and fancies, volatile, mercurial, rapid.   Like mailed men, these writers fall heavily, and lie grievously cumbered : in the manner of Sacrovir's iron troops, whose clumsy helplessness, Tacitus describes with so pleasant a zest.   Both writers are filled with the spirit of their country : when Wordsworth is uninspired, he has the mulish obstinacy of his dalesmen ; when Mr. Hardy is uninspired, he has the graceless perversity of his West Saxons : and when either indulges his genius in all its strength and beauty, he gives voice to the very earth under his feet. Yet these two writers are at variance, upon the fundamental principles and the crowning issues of life : the living writer has challenged the dead writer's faith.

The likeness between these two is worth a consideration here ; because the writer of established fame helps to explain certain qualities of the writer, whose very virtues, the ground of a future fame, are still in the making : Wordsworth, an idealist and a mystic assignable to no school, presents the formation and the exercise of character by certain methods ; which are also those of Mr. Hardy, a positivist upon many sides, but somewhat isolated, and sworn to no binding tenets. ' That the laws which nature has fixed for our lives are mighty and eternal, Wordsworth comprehended as fully as Goethe, but not that they were pitiless as iron. Wordsworth had not rooted in him the sense of Fate—of the inexorable sequences of things, of the terrible chain that so often binds an awful end to some slight and trivial beginning.' What Mr. Morley finds lacking in Wordsworth is plentiful in Mr. Hardy : who would subscribe to a saying in George Sand ; ' Il n'y a ni bien ni mal dans le vœu de la nature.' But both writers, by loyalty to their rival apprehensions of truth about things, apprehensions which they have treasured with a passionate attachment, come to resemble each other in virtue of that common tenacity : now they cure, now complement, each other ; they stand in antagonism, like the first sentence of Montesquieu and the first sentence of Rousseau ; they stand side by side, as all men in earnest must, whatever be their illusions about truth. Now it were hard to describe, without the pains of long circumlocution, the characteristics of the men and women in Wordsworth ; hard, apart from the fact that he is a lyrical and a meditative poet, not skilled in the direct narrative for its own sake : yet few characters live more in our memories, than those of Michael, of the Leech-gatherer, of Lucy, of the Highland girl. And it is Wordsworth's habitual openness to certain influences, his prepossession with ideas of a certain order, that make these characters at once so indelible from our memories, and so elusive of our descriptions. This is true of Mr. Hardy's characters also. As a teller of stories, a composer of situations and events, he is admirable ; it has already appeared, that he is independent of casual graces, a strict and stern master of design ; there is in him no baffling obscurity, nor blinding brilliance : yet, like Wordsworth, he has a vision of things so personal, from a point of view discovered by himself, that we do not at once recognize the familiar scenes of human passion. In the curious dialect of some modern critics, we might say, that his characters are subtly coloured, or chemically compounded, by the idiosyncrasies of his psychological analysis. To say so were an ugly affectation : but the saying would be true in substance. As in Wordsworth, the simplest things ; a gray stone, a gleam of light, a bed of flowers, a song of birds ; are so wrought into relation with human life, and human life so harmonized with them, that the world seems to suffer a transfiguration and a glory, which most eyes must be purged to see : so Mr. Hardy realizes the world of men and things in a severe harmony ; under the hard light of natural laws, whose alone is the supremacy ; with that pitying irony and chilled compassion, which play vainly in the shadow of those laws. The conclusions of the two men are far apart : but in both there is this concentration, this intensity, signs of a certain spiritual temperament, to be seen in a large class of strenuous minds. Lucretius, Pascal, Rousseau, Obermann, Hawthorne ; some mystical theologians of Germany and Spain ; certain devotees of passive despair, in philosophy and in poetry : many of these communicate fine truth, gold tried in the fire ; others yield only dust and ashes ; but, one and all, they are men of minds too intensely strained in one direction, to apprehend truth in its fulness and in its wholeness. Wordsworth was saved by that salt of common sense, which kept him human and wholesomely terrestrial, even at the height of his contemplations : he has more in common with the austerity and the strenuousness of Dante and of Milton, than with those of Lucretius and of Pascal : but he seldom fills us with a sense of that large and liberal wisdom, which seems to know no bounds. And in reading Mr. Hardy, whose books are never fanatical, we are forced now and then to pause, and to discount some phrase or tendency, by saying to ourselves : *The shield has another side.* That is to say, Mr. Hardy's prepossessions of a positivist sort are held with so firm a conviction, that all things, from farmyards to the stars, and all men whosoever, are touched by them : his novels are not written for a purpose, to prove the truth of something ; but with the prejudice, that it is a proven truth.   There are few English novels, controlled from end to end by a philosophic unity of ideas ; few, which do not show their writers playing fast and loose with their sovereign notions : but Mr. Hardy will not allow either his art or his philosophy, to lose anything by their conjunction ; rather, he would deny the possibility of any such loss.   He runs two risks : the risk of unpopularity among the unphilosophical and the inartistic : and the risk of dislike from lovers of another philosophy and of another art. For he does nothing to conciliate possible enemies : there are no concessions to a vulgar, or to a fastidious, taste : when once a character, or an event, or an issue of events, is conceived by him as true to the nature of things, he will present it with all the power of his art ; but he will not soften its asperity, nor herald it with deprecation, nor dismiss it with a palinode.   He is unlike that ancient Greek writer upon medicine, who in certain cases of *syncope* recommends, for the sufferer's support, an application of encouraging words and rose water.   It follows, that without some reasonable readiness to be patient under discomforts, an unsympathetic reader of Mr. Hardy will find constant provocation to ill humour : once let such a reader give way to a passion of controversial wrath, and the spell is broken, the book charms no more.   Were a few characters only, or a few events, brought under the great principle, so potent to displease, the reader might fasten upon the harmless remnants of the book, and find there his pleasure, in contempt of logic and of art : but the art of Mr. Hardy is a logical art, and is no more capricious than the facts of nature.

> ' Streams will not curb their pride
> The just man not to entomb,
> Nor lightnings go aside,
> To give his virtues room ' ;

nor will an honourable man be false to his vision of truth, for fear of offence : he may enjoy it in private, revealing nothing : but he may not misrepresent it. There are, then, two chief difficulties in the way of a criticism upon Mr. Hardy's characters : their relation to certain views of life ; and the method of their presentation, which follows upon an honest holding of those views. The first difficulty may be almost left for longer discussion, and with it, the character of Tess : let us rest content, for the present, with chiefly examining into some of Mr. Hardy's characters, as he presents them to us.

Throughout the preceding essays, I have laid stress upon the strength and the stability of character, which Mr. Hardy loves to present ; upon his souls of a somewhat pagan severity, grand in the endurance of dooms ; upon their simplicity, resoluteness, and power : yet I have also spoken of Mr. Hardy, as a novelist typical of modern literature in this, that he loves the complexity of things, the clash of principles and of motives, the encounter of subtile emotions. Both criticisms, as I dare think, are true ; and in these two characteristics, brought together, contrasted, made to illustrate each other, lies the power of Mr. Hardy's art. For he chooses to present the play of life, tragic and comic, first of all, in a definite tract or province of England ; in the Kingdom of Wessex : whither new influences penetrate but slowly. Secondly, he takes for his chief characters, men of powerful natures, men of the country, men of little acquired virtue in mind and soul : but men disciplined by the facts and by the necessities of life, as a primitive experience manifests them. Thirdly, he surrounds them with men of the same origin and class, but men of less strongly marked a power, of less finely touched a spirit : the rank and file of country labour. Fourthly, he brings his few men of that stronger and finer nature, his rustic heroes, into contact and into contrast with a few men, commonly their superiors in education, and sometimes in position, but their inferiors in strength and fineness of nature : men, whom more modern experiences have redeemed from being clowns, at the risk of becoming curs. Fifthly, he makes this contact and this contrast most effective, through the passion of love : to which end, he brings upon the scene women of various natures ; less plainly marked in character than the men ; for the most part, nearer to the flashy prigs and pretty fellows in outward sentiment, fashion, and culture ; but nearer to the stronger and finer men, in the depths of their souls. Sixthly, the narratives are conducted slowly at the first, and great pains are given to make clear the spirit of the country, with its works and ways : when that has been made clear, the play quickens into passion, the actors come into conflict, there is strong attraction and strong repulsion, 'spirits are finely touched' : then, there is a period of waiting, a breathing space, an ominous stillness and a pause ; till, at the last, with increased force and motion, the play goes forward to its 'fine issues' ; all the inherent necessities of things cause their effects, tragic or comic, triumphs of the right or of the wrong : and the end of all is told with a soft solemnity, a sense of pity striving against a sense of fate.

I do not say that any one novel presents those features, in precisely that way : it is but an attempt to construct a mechanical type, to which all Mr. Hardy's novels tend to conform. At the least, it is true of them all, that they present, either the resolution of a discord into a harmony, or the breaking of a harmony by a discord : always the contrast, and the various issue, according to the worth of the performers with that strange organ, the human mind. Tess was changing from peasant ignorance and convention, when she met Clare, changing from the conventional culture and belief of a higher station ; the woman struggling up from superstition, the man struggling free from prejudice : the two natures, breaking with the past, came together, she straining towards his level of thought, he stooping to her level of life : the result was a tragic discord. It might be interpreted in many ways. Perhaps the superstitious faith of the Durbeyfield household, and the Calvinist faith of the Clare household, were more nearly in accord with the essential verities of life, than the new aims and impulses of their

offspring : perhaps Tess and Clare carried right theories
into wrong practice : perhaps one alone did so : certainly, we have in this story a singular presentation
of the struggle between old and new, in various ranks
of life and ranges of thought ; of the contact of the
new in one rank and range with the new in another ;
of the curious reversion, in each case, of the new to the
old. Tess acts, on several occasions, from impulses
and in ways, which derive, so her maker hints, from
her knightly ancestors : Clare, at the crisis of her life
and of his own, falls back in cruel cowardice to the
conventional standards of that society, which he so
greatly scorns. Tess, again, having learned by ear
and heart Clare's arguments against Christian theology,
repeats them to her old betrayer, Alec D'Urberville,
then a fanatical convert to the Calvinism of Clare's
father : and she enables him thereby to become a
second time her betrayer. Finally, this tangled play
of new things upon old comes to its wretched end at
Stonehenge, the most ancient of religious monuments
in England, and at Winchester, the ancient capital of
England: religion, however stern, society, however cruel,
are vindicated in the presence of their august memorials.
The old, we are meant to feel, was wrong, and the new
was right : but the inhuman irony of fate turned all
to misunderstanding and to despair : the new devil
quoted the new scriptures in the ears of the new
believers ; and they went to the old destruction.

But the human comedy of Tess must be elsewhere
discussed in detail : now it merely serves to illustrate
a characteristic common to almost all Mr. Hardy's

books. Norris of Bemerton, 'the English Malebranche,' has this saying in his third *Contemplation* :
' 'Twas a Celebrated Problem among the Ancient
Mythologists, What was the *strongest* thing, what the
wisest, and what the *greatest* ? Concerning which
'twas this determin'd, that the *strongest* Thing was
Necessity, the *wisest* was *Time* ; and the *greatest* was the
Heart of Man.' That would seem to be the deter-
mination of Mr. Hardy also, at his best and deepest :
almost over conscious of the fatal strength, ever delighted with the growing wisdom, strongly moved by
the unsatisfied greatness, he sends out his characters
to that forlorn hope, life : forlorn, but not lost, and
promising at least the noblest of defeats. I remember
but few of Mr. Hardy's general sentiments, about the
meaning of the unconscious universe, or of conscious
mankind, with which I do not disagree : his tone of
thought about human progress, about the province
and the testimony of physical science, about the
sanctions of natural and social ethics, neither charms,
nor compels, me to acquiescence : but it is because I
am thus averse from the attitude of a disciple, that
I admire Mr. Hardy's art so confidently. Not even
unwelcome judgments upon those estranging matters,
the humane arts, can cool my zeal for this artist. He
writes of a house : ' It was Palladian, and, like all
architecture erected since the Gothic age, was a com-
pilation rather than a design.' *Saeva indignatio* were
a poor term, by which to describe my emotion upon
first reading that : yet my faith is unshaken. These
personal confessions are not impertinent, only because

M

they best help me to declare the power, the beauty, the fidelity, to his own visions of truth, which I reverence in this writer, as I reverence them in Lucretius. That wise impassiveness, which Mr. Hardy inculcates, seems in a measure to affect certain of his readers : for we come to read him at his best, this living writer about modern life, with that tranquil equability and cheerfulness, wherewith we read the twenty-eight Lucretian arguments against the soul's immortality ; and rejoice in the marvellous chaunt that follows, to the glory of deathless death.   There is but one living writer beside, who produces a like effect : that poet of vast, austere, and melancholy genius, M. Leconte de Lisle.

These conflicts, then, and antagonisms, between the forces of the world and the forces of the human soul, realized by Mr. Hardy with a sombre imagination, as though by some Hugo smitten suddenly unspiritual ; are of sufficient validity in the region of imaginative thought, to fill a story with the breath of life ; even for readers, who would give them another interpretation.   Such readers may indeed be forced, by some trenchant utterance of Mr. Hardy upon grave problems, to think themselves ' *sad* friends of Truth ' : but they are never impelled to cry out against any such distortions of thought and sentiment, as in these days so often pass for the last word of man upon the universe.   The hard sayings of this writer come from a commanding height of speculation.

His three classes, most worthy of consideration, for their displays of character, are the country heroes and lovers, Winterborne, Henchard, and their fellows : those examples of ' a poor Sixpenny Soul, a Subburb Sinner,' Fitzpiers and Clare, with the rest of that company : and the various women, Eustacia, Elfride, Grace, Elizabeth-Jane, and others of the sisterhood. To these may be added certain typical figures of different kinds : the youths, too delicate to be imperious, too gentle to be vicious, yet of a certain hardness ; Yeobright and Smith, Julian and Swithin, Somerset and Farfrae ; a whole chapter of ecclesiastics ; and other inhabitants of Wessex.

The first class shows the immitigable strength of Mr. Hardy at its best : a comparison of Winterborne and Henchard will serve our purpose. Winterborne was a plain countryman, skilled in woodland lore, honest and courteous and kind, but in no way a man of genius, in things worldly, or in things spiritual : his chief distinction was that simple refinement and habitual reverence, which in some country natures grow to a singular kind of grace. The woman, whom he loved with a great delicacy and awe in his passion ; a woman, trained to a certain height of taste and thought, above the old woodland level, but at some loss of its natural contentment ; fell in love with a man of origin, of education, and of interests, rarely met among the woodlands : she married him. Winterborne, upon whom other blows also fell, bore it with an unbroken dignity of sorrow, accepting his lot. Presently, Grace found her husband to be a man of unstable nature, loving her in a fitful way, yet careless of her : and vehemently drawn by the lures of another

woman, the great lady of the place, Felice Charmond,
known to him long since, abroad ; a woman of untempered and unregulated emotions. After much
misery, Grace and her husband parted : presently,
her father heard a wrong account of the new law of
divorce, imperfectly understood among so remote a
people : and he saw in it the one escape for Grace out
of her wretchedness, the one way to destroy the
reproach upon his house, and the means of making
amends to Winterborne. With the most gracious
care, lest he give any offence, Winterborne embraced
this hope : Grace, too, who had learned to know his
nature, wearied and distracted by her unhappiness,
accepted the prospect of deliverance and of peace.
But the mistake was discovered ; Grace was not
wronged enough : and the old troubles had to continue : at last, upon the return of her husband, Grace,
unequal to the endurance of her distress, resolved
upon flight to a friend at a distance. She was forced,
by circumstances, to ask the guidance of Winterborne
for a little way, to the market town, the first stage of
her evening flight : then came a storm of rain, pre-
venting her journey. In this distress, Winterborne
entreated her to remain, till morning, in his hut :
while he passed the night under some hurdles. But
his troubles and hard work, had already told upon
him : and that night's exposure ensured, as he had
foreseen, the overthrow of his strength. Grace, not
dreaming of his illness, agreed to his plausible arguments, that she should remain, where she was : until,
the fever prostrating him, he could no longer come to

speak with her. At last, the truth broke in upon her : and, going out to his wretched shelter, she found him unconscious. The rest need not be told : he died, a loyal sacrifice to the purity of her honour and of his love ; a reparation, partly, for his one act of ' treachery,' in having once suffered her to make him express his love, during her brief delusion into happiness ; when he had already learned, that it was a delusion.

In weak hands, such a character would have been weak also : the rustic lover, unsuccessful in his love, would have been either sullen or frantic : his hope of success at last, through the divorcing of his successful rival, would in itself have seemed nauseous or absurd ; and his behaviour in that hope, of necessity, undignified : even his death would have been but a blunderer's last chance of redeeming his blunders, by a self-sacrifice less resolute than dogged. There is none of this in Mr. Hardy's handling of the story : without idealizing the man ; without any dexterous enlistment of our sympathies, by hints of some finer strain in his nature, than the mere facts reveal ; without any shrinking from the homeliness and the rusticity of his life ; Mr. Hardy, through the strength of his belief in the truth and beauty of his conception, wins us without a struggle. Winterborne is not blameless, and therefore impossible to understand : nor is he perfect in mind and person, a tiresome model of the rustic proprieties : we can be amused by the arrangements of his household, and be shocked by his taste in hostelries : he is handed over to our scrutinies and to our mercies, a natural Wessex woodlander. Even when he lies dead before us ; and when the two women, who loved him, Grace, whom he never won, and Marty, whom he never loved, meet in his presence ; Mr. Hardy is not afraid to provoke our sense of humour : he knows, how much pity is at the springs of humour.

' To check her tears she turned, and seeing a book in the window-bench, took it up. " Look, Marty, this is a Psalter. He was not an outwardly religious man ; but he was pure and perfect in his heart. Shall we read a psalm over him ? "

' " Oh, yes, we will ; with all my heart ! "

' Grace opened the thin brown book, which poor Giles had kept at hand mainly for the convenience of whetting his penknife upon its leather covers. She began to read in that rich, devotional voice peculiar to women only on such occasions. When it was over Marty said, " I should like to pray for his soul."

' " So should I," said her companion. " But we must not."

' " Why ? Nobody would know." '

The conduct of the story is characteristic of its writer's fearlessness : the true lover might so easily have been rewarded, the unworthy husband put out of the way : the moral might have been pointed, how far better are simple happiness and contentment, than distracting passion and restlessness. As it is, the story has a bolder disentanglement : Grace and Winter-borne, her husband Fitzpiers and her rival Mrs. Charmond, teach each other lessons of bracing courage : husband and wife come together at last. We are not led to suppose, that Fitzpiers was radically changed by experience : but he was at least warned, reproved, and strengthened : and the love, which began to our dismay, ends in a possible happiness through purification. Grace and her husband go out to their new trial of life : and we are left with Marty South, standing by Winterborne's grave ; while the lines of an old, forgotten poet run in our minds :

> ' Since then, though more I cannot love,
>   Without thy injury :
>   As Saints that to an Altar move,
>   My thoughts shall be.'

The character of Michael Henchard, Mayor of Casterbridge, is in rich contrast with that of Giles Winterborne. Henchard was a hay-trusser : tramping, with his wife and child, along the road, he came to Weydon-Priors on fair-day. A turbulent man by nature, of a passionate habit, given to gusts of anger and discontent, he was a hard man to his weary wife. The wretchedness of their married life came to an end, for some twenty years, in a tent at the fair : drunk with ' laced ' furmity, Henchard sold his wife to a sailor for five guineas. She thought the transaction binding, for she was a woman of much simplicity, and went with the sailor and her child. Next morning, shamed and remorseful, Henchard made a solemn vow to touch no strong drink, during as many years, as he was old that day. Two years had yet to pass, at the opening of the next scene, before Henchard might touch strong drink with a clear conscience. A crowd was standing beside the chief hotel of Casterbridge, looking in at a dinner of the municipal magnates :

the worshipful Mr. Henchard was in the chair : among the crowd were three travellers, just come to the town. Two of them were Henchard's wife and child : the third was a Scotch youth, Donald Farfrae. The four actors were upon the stage together, all in an almost equal ignorance of their past, present, and future relationships, worthy of the Attic theatre. Henchard had worked his imperious way up to this height of prosperity, retrieving his self-respect, and concentrating his pride of will. The four actors mingled their fortunes : Henchard, under the guise of a new marriage, took back his wife, whose buyer, she said, was dead : she had found Henchard after a long search, telling Elizabeth-Jane, that he was a kinsman, but not the truth of the kinship. Farfrae became the Mayor's manager in his business of corn-dealer. The Mayor, then, had redeemed his past wrong, and was proud of his present prosperity : the rest of the story tells, how that past wrong had yet to bring its inevitable and grievous penalty of sorrows ; and how Henchard allied himself to his pursuing fate, through that stubborn pride and passion of his will, which had caused alike his old wrong doing, his repentance, and his prosperity. In the insanity of his jealous pride, he dismissed Farfrae, his most faithful servant and friend, to whose knowledge and skill he owed an increased prosperity : he would not have his man for his master : though the ' man ' was innocent of any such thought. Farfrae established himself in business, and against his own will, by the talents which had enriched Henchard, now drew away his prosperity :

and he crowned his unconscious offences by marrying
a lady, to whom Henchard, believing his sold wife to
be dead, had not only the right, but had been bound
by honour, to regard himself as pledged. After his
wife's actual death, Farfrae frustrated his wish to
fulfil that pledge. He felt little affection for his
daughter Elizabeth-Jane, while her mother lived :
but then, feeling his loneliness, he told her that not
the sailor, as she had believed, but he, was her father ;
giving her a kindly, falsified version of the old tragedy.
A warm love would have sprung up between them, to
the joy of both : and again Henchard became the
minister of his own downfall. Finding a paper left
by his wife, not to be opened till the girl's wedding
day, he disregarded the direction, and opened it : it
was his wife's confession, that Elizabeth-Jane was not
their child : that child died three months after the
fair : Elizabeth-Jane was the sailor's child. In mortification at the mockery of things, he treated her with
such harsh coldness, that she left him with his consent,
to live with a lady come to the town, whose acquaintance she had made : the lady was Lucetta, who was
to become Farfrae's wife. For though engaged to
Henchard, she fell in love with Farfrae : strengthened
in her consequent dislike to Henchard, by the publication of his early crime. The furmity seller, an old
woman fallen from that flourishing estate, was brought
before Henchard and the magistrates for drunken-
ness : and then, recognizing the actor in that scene
at her tent, she told the story : Henchard confirming
her. This scandal turned the scale against him in the

public judgment : and his affairs, rashly undertaken and roughly managed, since Farfrae's dismissal, ended in bankruptcy.   He hired two rooms of a cottage in a melancholy quarter : his landlord was a man, whom he had long ago cashiered or disappointed, to make room for Farfrae, then the bosom friend of his violent affections.   Farfrae bought his old house and place of business, treating Henchard with infinite tact and delicacy in offers of help : but Henchard, in a fit of half grim, half noble, humour at the vicissitudes of life, asked for a place among Farfrae's men.   The years of his vow were now ended : and drink brought him into a yet closer correspondence with his early fortunes, obliterating the signs of his advance in life, from his temper and from his will.   By an hundred ways, the reversal was completed.   Lucetta, his rival's wife, had written to him, during their former intimacy, letters of an effusive kind : these she begged him now to restore.   He gave them to his former victim and present landlord, to give to her : he first, in hatred of Henchard, reads them in a low haunt of poachers and loose women ; who learn that Farfrae, now Mayor, has a wife married to him in defiance of a previous engagement ; a chance for that uproarious form of public censure, the ' skimmity-ride.'   It was carried out : Lucetta, overcome with shame, fell into a violent disorder, and died with fearful suddenness.   Henchard, just before this, had nearly murdered Farfrae, in a seizure of wrath and madness : then, smitten with a horror of remorse, remembering all the past, had longed to make amends.   Upon the night of Lucetta's

shame, her husband was away : Henchard grasping
at his chance, hastened to meet him, with entreaties
to return at once : Farfrae, disbelieving his story, and
suspecting some scheme of violence, refused ; and
he returned to find his wife dying. Each step of these
miseries was Henchard's act, voluntary, or, against his
will, inevitable. Now one thing alone remained : the
love of Elizabeth-Jane, who still thought him to be her
father, and had sought him out, and tended him. All
his passionate affection went out towards this child of
the man, to whom he had sold her mother : nothing,
surely, could rob him of her love. Then came the last
blow : her real father was not dead ; but content to
let her mother think him lost at sea, because she had
heard in agony, that she still was Henchard's wife, and
not her buyer's by law and right ; and he now came
to find his daughter, knowing that her mother had returned to Henchard, and was now dead. Henchard
told him, that Elizabeth-Jane was dead too : hoping
against hope, that he would go away, believing it, not
rob him of that one solace, her companionship and
love. But, inevitably, the sailor came to find the truth :
and father and daughter met at last. Henchard had
schooled himself, with sore pains, to accept the fact,
that she was in love with Farfrae : who had loved her,
till Henchard, by his jealous action, threw him in the
way of Lucetta's fascination. But the return of her
father was more than he could bear, remaining among
the scenes of his long life : her contempt and dislike
would be intolerable. When, therefore, he learned that
she was about to meet a stranger, whom he knew to be

her father, the stranger having asked for an interview with her: he told her, that he would leave her to a happy married life, and leave Casterbridge, giving broken reasons for his resolve. He dressed again in rustic clothes, bought a new basket, ' cleaned up his old hay-knife and wimble,' and tramped out of the town, where he had been so eminent a citizen, the lowly figure, that entered it long ago. He first went to Weydon-Priors, the scene of his old disgrace : then, with bitterness at heart, wandered till he came into Egdon : and there he died, and was found dead by the married lovers, both of whom he had hated and loved so well.   I know few histories more poignant than this : none, which more perfectly fulfil the great demands of Aristotle upon the composers of dramatic plot, and the con-ceivers of dramatic character. There is no forced contrivance of artifices, by which to bring about so exact and relentless a retribution : for good and bad, Henchard is his own fate, and to himself ' both law and impulse ' : at the end of all, he cries aloud : ' My punishment is *not* greater than I can bear ! '   And there is no glamour about him, no halo of tragic greatness, as there were none about Winterborne. Henchard is no such splendid victim of his consuming passions, as are some northern men famous in romance : he is no Heathcliff, but a far more commonplace man. Yet his story moves almost as deep, if not nearly as fierce, a compassion : the man is so like a child in his sim-plicity, so like a hurt animal : he seems to feel the fatality of his own acts, and to make no complaint ; he has no vast self-pity. ' Misery taught him nothing

more than a defiant endurance of it ' : the fates were
so much more practised in the ways of life, than this
poor, passionate man, that we give him the pity, he
would not give himself : yet we own the justice of
his lifelong discipline. The book does but enforce
with fresh vigour, that ancient truth, by no one stated
more forcibly, than by the genial Neapolitan :

> *' Sumus hic tot Inferi, quot homines vivimus,*
> *Suusque quisque dirus est Erebus sibi.'*

These two men, Winterborne and Henchard, are
probably the best examples of Mr. Hardy's enduring
heroes : the rest seem allied in character to one or
other of them. John Loveday's carriage towards
Anne Garland has much of Winterborne's natural
courtesy, with something of a worldlier air, acquired
in his profession of arms. Farmer Boldwood, the
silent, keen man, driven desperate and maniacal with
passion for Bathsheba, has that intensity which we
could imagine in Henchard, had his fortune in love
been the same. In Diggory Venn the reddleman,
and in Gabriel Oak the shepherd, Mr. Hardy has
drawn portraits of the patient lover, with a more
decided insinuation of kindly humour into his work :
the reddleman's fantastic figure, as he lurks among
the Egdon hills and trenches, to surprise news of
import to his lost mistress Thomasin, has a touch of
the grotesque about it ; and Gabriel's devotion to
Bathsheba the farmer adorns a character, sturdy
indeed, but of less distinction, than we like to
admit.

The braggarts and roisterers compose a curious group : they are rustical with a twang of the town, ill conditioned and shifty fellows : or men of wider knowledge and of higher station, who show to disadvantage among the country folk : Wildeve, Sergeant Troy, Bob Loveday, Festus Derriman, Edward Springrove, Edred Fitzpiers, Angel Clare. Doubtless, it is not quite discriminating to class all these together : there are wide gradations of offensiveness between many of them. But a swagger of body, or a swagger of soul, is common to them all : a lack of good manners, in the bearing of mind or person. ' He that was only taught by himself,' says Ben Jonson, ' had a fool to his Master.' These men were so taught ; their masters were all foolish : for though one be a soldier, and one a sailor ; one a doctor of great science and good family, and one the enlightened son of that poor thing, a theologian ; one a small squire in the yeomanry, and one an engineer turned innkeeper : one and all follow their own wills and ways, not with a just pride, but with a jaunty petulance. Whether it be Festus, talking big about his gallantry and martial merits, to the placid cottagers of Overcombe ; or Angel, pluming himself upon his liberality of mind, in contrast with the timid orthodoxy of his brothers : it is to be surmised, that the valour and the freedom are but sorry stuff ; and the course of events in each case proves it is true. Against the insolent cowardice of Festus is set the quiet courage of John : against the vagueness of Clare is set the steadiness of Tess. Neither the man of blood, nor the man of thought, handsels well his valour or his freedom. All the men of this class have their excellent qualities, but qualities alloyed and damaged by an infusion of something impure : some spirit of selfishness, or of heartlessness, or of coxcombry, which obtains an exaggerated power in their compositions. There are no ' villains,' except Æneas Manston, and not wholly he, in Mr. Hardy's Wessex ; men of deliberate malice, vowed to the service of evil, and trustworthy in their service : we meet but irritable egoists rejoicing, neither in right nor in wrong, but in themselves. Some of them became laughingstocks of their own pretensions : Clare and Fitzpiers ; conscious, the one of finer aims and ideals, the other of wider knowledge and experience, than the people about them possessed ; made their acts a parody of their pretensions : Clare fell away from his high, theoretic rule of life, into just that petty, pharisaic disproportion, for which he blamed the world, and his own family ; Fitzpiers, who thought himself, whom his humble neighbours thought, worthier of Grace than one of themselves, knew nothing of her value, till his homely rival had died to serve her. Such men are schooled into distrust of self by mortification, shamed into modesty by mockery of their pride : the dimensions of their failure are a cruel comment upon the dimensions of their confidence : they are left thrilling and tingling from the scourge of an instructive irony. Most of the others in this set are less prigs, than scapegraces : not scapegraces, who take our hearts by storm, with their engaging follies ; but unamiable scapegraces, who drift and dangle into dishonour. Sergeant Troy indeed, whose character is illuminated by Mr. Hardy in ten most brilliant paragraphs, almost cajoles the reader into tolerance, as he cajoled women into admiration. ' He never passed the line which divides the spruce vices from the ugly ' : and thus, according to Burke's one sophism, his vices seem to lose ' half their evil.' But he is a flashy proficient in the elegances of vice. As he dazzled and enchaunted Bathsheba by his miracles of sword play, in that hollow among the ferns, so it was by the quick keenness and flashing assault of his manner and speech, that he won her heart, and what a contrast are those displays to the slow, laborious, faithful, ways of Gabriel ! A vulgar paladin, after all, the Sergeant : even when he and his wife meet over the coffin of Fanny Robin, the woman whom he had betrayed and abandoned, his agonies of contrite love for Fanny, and his deliber- ate insults to Bathsheba, are but sentiments, the most like sincerity possible, of a theatrical conscience. Bob Loveday, without the intellect of Troy, and with a sailor's professional temperament in place of a soldier's, is not unlike him : one can imagine both men, lace ruffles falling over their white hands, with an incom- municable air of elegance, insolence, and ease, the heroes of old comedy. They would have been at home there : the one hard and brilliant as a diamond, the other full of shallow sentiment and charm. These men bring into Mr. Hardy's most rural books a strain of wordliness, in the lighter sense of that condemna- tion, which the word implies. Wessex can furnish

its own great crime and sin : but its casual, careless
peccadilloes are uninteresting, unless some wider experience has touched them ; experience, however
contemptible and slight, some hint of superior education, some trace of the world's bustle and business ;
anything that flashes, or struts, or shifts, will serve
to pass across the scenes of a play, in which braggarts
and fops are wanted, as foils to more passionate and
steady natures.

Of the women, whose characters and fortunes are
pourtrayed by Mr. Hardy, most various opinions may
be held. Some have that winning audacity, the charm
of strength, which marks in diverse manners those
gentle ladies, Captain Keeldar, Sir Julius, and Count
von Rosen, the creations of other eminent hands ;
some are alternately ' cautelous ' and ' temerarious,'
old words of too exact a meaning to be lost : some
have a distant likeness to Miss Austen's great characters, a likeness that takes us by surprise : some
almost incur from Dr. Johnson the charge of flirta-
tion, since he defines a flirt to be ' a pert young hussey.'
I cannot think that any one of them is so powerfully
conceived and drawn, as are the best of Mr. Hardy's
men : but more cleverness, more adroitness and dex-
terity of wit, more research, have gone to their portraits.
An admiration of their versatility, in maintaining their
consistency, is the sentiment, which they provoke :
an amazed awe of the infinite ingenuities, which their
sincerity can devise for its protection. ' A very little
wit,' wrote Swift, ' is valued in a woman, as we are
pleased with a few words spoken plain by a parrot,'

N

That is too often the dangerous and ignorant view of woman's wit, entertained by Mr. Hardy's men, with distressing consequences.

Eustacia, Lucetta, Ethelberta, Bathsheba, Viviette, Felice, Elfride, and some of the noble dames, how admirable is the contrast between these and Anne, Faith, Grace, Elizabeth-Jane, Thomasin, Charlotte, Marty South ! Upon the one side, all shades and lights of passion, petulance, perversity : upon the other, of reticence, patience, and restraint. The violent or ambitious natures are more opulent and prodigal in their demeanour ; mood follows mood, they are always in a state of revolution against themselves : the quiet or constant natures are more refined and proud in their bearing ; they suffer, but in silence and with strength. Not one of them all is a copy of any other : but these are the general distinctions and divisions to be traced among them.

Eustacia is a masterpiece of pathetic satire. ' Queen of night,' she is described in the most gorgeous chapter, that Mr. Hardy has yet written : gorgeous, with a royal pomp and pride of magnificent phrases, but all perfectly restrained and measured. ' She had Pagan eyes, full of nocturnal mysteries ' : she was a dreamer of great dreams, and in love with the imageries of an heroic love : allied with the rich and solemn beauty of things, a votarist of supreme powers, majesties, and splendours, rather felt than conceived : her looks and ways, those of an antique divinity : *vera incessu patuit dea* : a lonely, passionate, and hungering spirit, in a marvellous form, among the wastes of Egdon : set apart for tragedy to come. Thus far, she is an imperial recluse, of a grandeur equal to that of Egdon itself : but Mr. Hardy did not create her, without indulging his sense of humour. She is drawn, a very rival of Rachel's great portrait in *Villette* : but she has not the tragic chances of the stage. In bitter contrast with her ideals, she has but the wretched wastes of Egdon, the stupid labourers, the maddening unworldliness of the wilderness : and she knew Budmouth in earlier days. Just as that respectable place was to her a modern Paris and an ancient Rome, so Damon Wildeve was a very prince of romance : a trivial fellow, of decent looks and a little education. Rejecting him for Clym Yeobright, she takes Clym for a born leader of men, who will go with her into all the brilliance of all the world : she finds him bent upon plain living and high thinking, and is in despair, desolate and famished, outside the whirl of pleasures, triumphs, joys. Her pitiful standards of greatness, pitiful ignorance of life, pitiful hunger of heart, not wholly vulgar nor absurd, yet in large measure both, make her a masterpiece : seldom has a woman's impatient craving for the fulness of life, and the freedom of action, been so set down in words ; one doubts, whether to call the portrait the most cruel of caricatures, or the most superb of likenesses. But without doubt, Eustacia was both lamentable and ridiculous : contrasted with Egdon, she could but suffer. Egdon ' reduced to insignificance by its seamed and antique features the wildest turmoil of a single man ' : and still more

the rushing rhetoric of this woman's vehement long-
ings, those

> ' Impériales fantaisies,
> Amour des somptuosités ;
> Voluptueuses frénésies,
> Rêves d'impossibilités ! '

Much, that is seemingly wayward in some of these
women, can be explained by Bathsheba's pleading
criticism : ' It is difficult for a woman to define her
feelings in language which is chiefly made by men to
express theirs ' : which recalls the quaint sagacity of
Clarissa in observing, that ' the men were the framers
of the matrimonial office.'   Mr. Hardy expresses well
that dissatisfaction with the refractory strictness of
language, which distresses a woman, when she would
speak, not the logic of thought, but the logic of emotion :
she has all manner of real convictions, hidden deep in
her consciousness, but only explicable by hints and
suggestions, which sound like the shifts of a pre-
varicator.   She feels, that ' the plain truth ' does but
give the lie to a great many obscure truths, hard of
definition, but profoundly true.   In some crisis, when
she must act ; at some question, to which she must
reply : she struggles against the necessity, shrinking
from the bluntness of a decision.   Thrice, Mr. Hardy
represents a woman, recoiling from her purpose in
this way.   Elfride made up her mind to tell Knight,
her engaged lover, that she was once engaged to Smith :
when the time came, she pretended that the matter of
her confession was merely her precise age, about which
she had led him into error.   Tess, in the same way,

could only bring herself to confess to Angel, that she was a D'Urberville : she could not confess the haunting secret of her history. Lady Constantine, having sent for Mr. Torkingham the parson, to disclose certain confidences about her husband and herself, sent him away in ignorance, and chose Swithin the young astronomer for her confidant. In the case of Elfride and of Tess, there appears a justification for the cowardice and the deception, in the conduct of Knight and of Clare, when the truth at last appeared : both men heard that they had been forestalled, with an unreasoning jealousy and anger ; that temper, which has so often roused the laughter and the scorn of Mr. Meredith. A strange impression is left upon the reader by these characters, half crafty and half agonized ; the sense, that they are snared and tangled in a net ; birds, so trapped, cower down, very still, with bright, wild eyes, then flutter desperately : just so, these various troubled women have their times of quiet resignation to harsh facts, succeeded by breathless battle. Much that at first offends us, as a representation of women, almost insulting, proves on reflection to be a tribute to their honesty : they are bewildered and distracted, where men would see no difficulty and require no casuistry, from their incapacity to see all sides of the case. Elfride had three engagements and one marriage ; Bathsheba had three engagements and two marriages : and there were circumstances in either instance, which demand a somewhat delicate justification. To those who would seriously censure Elfride or Bathsheba, I would say in Miss Austen's words :

' Your reasoning is very good, but it is founded on ignorance of human nature.' Equally free from reproach is the momentary falseness of Fancy Day, in accepting Mr. Maybold ; carried away, despite her love for Dick, by the sudden chance of ' stepping into history,' or at least, of entering an higher rank of life : just as Margery Tucker's romantic friendship with the Baron amply excused her perverseness. Indiscretion, the defect of that good quality, a quick wit, is often imputable to these various characters : the child Elfride, and the great lady, Viviette, are not wholly blameless ; the innocence of Elfride, and the experience of Viviette, should have hindered, even whilst they caused, the rashness of the first, and the intoxication of the second. Sometimes Mr. Hardy illustrates that different feeling about the relative value of things, entertained by an emotional woman, and by a man, whose intellect has grown faster than his emotion. Swithin, the young astronomer, with the beauty of Nero, the heart of a child, and the ardour of Copernicus, talked to Viviette about the stars, in a rapture of intellectual enthusiasm : Lady Constantine merely said, ' Say some more of it to me ' : no words could express more heartily her sentimental pleasure in watching the boy's eloquent, beautiful face, in hearing his inspired voice. ' Say some more of it to me ' : the hopeless inadequacy of the phrase to the occasion is inimitable.

It is a relief to turn from these to less disquieting characters : to women who, like Anne Garland, could reconcile ' dignity with sweetness ' : of whom it could

be said ; ' beneath all that was charming and simple
in this young woman there lurked a real firmness, un-
perceived at first, as the speck of colour lurks unper-
ceived in the heart of the palest parsley flower.'
Perhaps none of these strong and quiet women is more
gently attractive, than Faith Julian ; whom one does
not immediately learn to esteem at her true value : it
requires the wearying agility of Ethelberta's ambition,
to set off the restful charm of Faith. It was true of
Ethelberta, that ' the oscillations of her mind might
arise as naturally from the perfection of its balance,
like those of a logan-stone, as from inherent lightness ' :
but such perfections are doubtful blessings. Faith,
Elizabeth-Jane, Anne, and a few more, are more stable
natures, not rocking in a perpetual indecision : nor
yet, by the alternative perfection, motionless from
inability to choose one of two bundles of hay ; like
Buridan's famous ass, which so greatly puzzled Bayle.
They do not fill a book with their flighty humours,
nor show us the perplexity of their minds, and the
troubles of their souls, upon every page : *bene latent*,
they are well cloistered in the seclusion of their own
thoughts. A very haunting scene is that in the British
Museum, where Faith, intent upon her sense of a
wonderful reality, face to face with the sculptures of
Nineveh, visionary kings and cities of Scripture,
eternized in that barbaric art, listens to her brother's
story of his rejection by Ethelberta, without hearing a
word of it : her mind enthralled by the sudden spell
of a great antiquity. Henchard too knew the spell of
an unworldly art, transporting him to the land, ' that

is very far off,' even farther than old Assyria : ' with Henchard music was of regal power. The merest trumpet or organ tone was enough to move him and high harmonies transubstantiated him.' Elizabeth-Jane found a strength and stay in the Roman traditions of Casterbridge : and to Marty South the woods were full of sad, wise voices. These women, at least, ' have some roses from Pieria.' There is no trace of uncomely sternness or defiance, coldness or firmness, in these women : but they are not weak : harassed by the bewilderment of love, they do not fall into danger or indignity. A certain manliness in such perfect women gives them a curious grace of courage : and they shape their sorrows into finer forms, than do men. Mr. Hardy's art in his presentations of women, whatever be their natures, might well draw to him readers, whom Wessex does not win by itself : for his fertility of imagination is greatest, when the fortunes of a woman's soul are his study. He knows the wealth of meaning in a woman's acts : meaning, not to be come at by any brutal impatience of meditation, by the laziness of hasty epigram. In three novels, two of old fame, one of recent success, *Villette, The Marble Faun,* and *The New Antigone,* there is an identical scene : a woman, in the first two cases not a Catholic, in the third not a Christian, suddenly mastered by the appeal of the confessional, to disburden her conscience there. The three scenes are outwardly identical : inwardly, there is no single feature common to them. It is so with all the acts and circumstances of life : there is no repetition : and Mr. Hardy has brought home to us that variety, by his diverse treatment of passion in characters and under conditions, outwardly often uniform. That singular group of Noble Dames, disinterred from the decaying traditions of Wessex, furnished him with an humourous means of illustrating the diversity of women's character, in strange and trying ways : the book is a gothic work of the quainter sort ; an indulgence of truth in whimsical evidences. It is true, that he has now and again allowed himself satire, to which the ill-disposed may impute an element of contempt : but the contempt, if it be there, is a contempt of men. ' An evill spirit, your beautie haunts Me still,' sang Drayton to his *Idea* :

> ' Thus am I, till provok'd to every Evill,
>   By this good wicked Spirit, sweet Angell Devill.'

It were a mistake, to attribute malice to Drayton's muse, in that simple confession of his own embarrassed and unequal love.

There is an attractive set of youths, as characteristic of Mr. Hardy's books, as Marius, Sebastian, Gaston, are characteristic in the works of Mr. Pater : these are the youths, who with a simplicity native to the soil, a literal humility, combine an energy, often artistic, which has raised them to another level. Somerset, Owen Graye, and Smith, are architects : Christopher Julian is a musician : Swithin St. Cleeve is an astronomer : Yeobright is an idealist upon ways of life and thought : Farfrae is an artist in commerce, with a moving gift of sentiment and song. They have a charming persuasiveness in their eager, brilliant, ways

and looks ; or in their dreamy persistence, a gentle
serenity of purpose, which effects much, and seems to
effect nothing.   Julian had ' an under feeling ' always
in him, ' that at the most propitious moment the distance to the possibility of sorrow is so short, that a
man's spirits must not rise higher than mere cheerfulness out of bare respect to his insight.'   A thoroughly
Greek piece of natural wisdom : and a later sentiment
of the young musician in love is Greek also.   ' His
habit of dreaming instead of doing led him up to a
curious discovery.   It is no new thing for a man to
fathom profundities by indulging humours : the active,
the rapid, the people of splendid momentum, have
been surprised to behold what results attend the lives
of those, whose usual plan for discharging their active
labours has been to postpone them indefinitely.   Certainly, the immediate result in the present case was,
to all but himself, small and invisible : but it was of
the nature of highest things.'   It was, that his lost
mistress might become to him a ' Creature of Contemplation,' and thus ' almost a living soul ' : a lover's
perverse theory of ideas, Platonic twice over.   As a
rule, it is the function of these youths, active or con-
templative, to be drawn by virtue of their temperaments, and by the same virtue to draw others, into
love : commonly with the result, that they prove to
have, and to have been, attracted wrongly.   Their
peculiar blessing of a genius, apparent in and through
their youthfulness, misleads their mistresses into
thinking them all beautiful and all young, ignoring the
necessary hard grounds of all effective genius : while

the youths find a natural charm in the condescension of a woman's love, without the prosaic foresight of considering its kind. Yeobright and Eustacia, Swithin and Viviette, are cases in point : perhaps also, Farfrae and Lucetta, Ethelberta and Julian. At the least, a delightful vivacity, or a delicate pensiveness, pervades some of Mr. Hardy's books, thanks to this band of youths.

Such, then, are a few of Mr. Hardy's chief characters: and what a multitude of others throng his Wessex ! He has dispossessed it of the living, to people it with the creatures of his art : rather, the two peoples have become one. The very memories of literature in Dorset fail to impress us, when our minds are full of Mr. Hardy's pageant. In the north-east, we forget that Voltaire walked ' on Dorset Downs ' with Young, under the auspices of Dodington, Thomson's patron, Browning's victim : we forget how Gibbon, during his military career, tasted ' the dissipations of Blandford,' that birthplace of ' Virgil ' Pitt and of ' Lucretius ' Creech : in the south-west, we forget that Wordsworth wrote his dreadful tragedy at Racedown, first meeting Coleridge there : that Mill in his laborious childhood visited Bentham at Ford Abbey : that Wyatt died, and Raleigh lived, at Sherborne. On Portland, it is not the drowning of Wordsworth's brother, when his ship went down off the Bill, but Anne Garland's sorrow, that we remember. Upon the Dorset coast, Keats wrote his last great sonnet : it was the last English earth under his feet : but Mr. Hardy's storm off Swanage, is more in our minds. If we think of

George III., at sight of that equestrian monarch cut in chalk by Osmington, or along the shores of Weymouth, it is less history than Mr. Hardy's fiction, that guides our thoughts about the kindly king. Lyme Regis, indeed, is sacred to Anne Elliot, in the eyes of Miss Austen's lovers ; and, ' seven miles from Dorchester,' lived Evelina and the Reverend Mr. Villars, at ' dear Berry-Hill ' ; at Stour, Fielding displayed the disastrous luxury of his married life ; Eustace Inglesant was killed at Minterne Inn : but the whole of Dorset belongs to Mr. Hardy.

The characters, which have at once least power and least originality, are those of sundry gentlemen, who have no great parts to play : even Knight, who is of vital importance in the story of Elfride ; Neigh, who helps much to intensify the comedy of Ethelberta ; Power, the domineering uncle of Paula the heiress ; Lady Constantine's brother, who provides her with a husband in the Bishop of Melchester ; the Baron Von Xanten, mysterious and dyspeptic ; are not characters, that arrest us very greatly. Knight, in particular, contrives to disappoint us : he is so dryly real, that he ought to be more interesting. Like the others, whom I have mentioned, and many beside, ' He was at the brightest period of masculine growth, for his intellect and his emotions were clearly separated : he had passed the time during which the influence of youth indiscriminately mingles them in the character of impulse, and he had not yet arrived at the stage wherein they become united again, in the character of prejudice, by the influence of a wife and family.'

It may be to that very clear separation between the
intellect and the emotions, that the lack of interest
is due : that process is more than a separation, it
is a divorce.

Mr. Hardy's divines must not be left without a word
of gratitude : they are of many kinds, and all excellent. There is old Mr. Clare, most loveable of stern
Calvinists : the Baptist minister, whom young Somerset
confronted upon Pædobaptism, for the support of
the backsliding Paula : the Bishop of Melchester, so
cruelly fooled in his marriage : Mr. Swancourt, a
genial aristocrat with the gout, beneficed at the ends
of the earth : others, whose acquaintance we make
best through the criticisms of their flocks. Fitz-
gerald, in angry letters about Dorsetshire to Carlyle
and to Mr. Tennyson, describes the two main kinds
of country parson, with whom Mr. Hardy deals. The
one has a touch of Parson Trulliber, and a touch of
Parson Adams : ' quaint and humourous,' Fitz-
gerald calls such an one, ' quiet and saturnine ' :
' a poor Rector in one of the most out-of-the-way
villages in England—has five children—fats and kills
his pig—smokes his pipe—loves his home and cares
not ever to be seen out of it.' But he also found
Dorset much given over to the ' Pugicides,' as the
rustics termed the energetic clergy, so loathed by the
late Rector of Lincoln. The villagers of Mellstock
held strong views upon clerical duty.

' " Ah, Mr. Grinham was the man ! " said
Bowman. " Why he never troubled us wi' a visit
from year's end to year's end. You might go any-

where, do anything : you 'd be sure never to see him ! " '

But Mr. Grinham's successor was not, in Addison's phrase, a ' reverend vegetable ' : he disestablished the stringed instruments, and provoked this perfect utterance from the schoolmistress : ' Vicars look so miserable and awkward, when one's house is in a muddle ; walking about and making quaint impossible suggestions in academic phrases, till your flesh creeps and you wish them dead.' The rural clergy in these Wessex novels provide admirable mirth, and quite good-humoured.

It is a rare praise, to say of a book that it is passionate, without a necessity to add, that it lapses into rhetoric and rant : it is largely true of Mr. Hardy's books. There are few passages, in which the passion swells into big words : but many, in which it uses the heightened tones of nature, words powerful and moving, in all the keys of emotion, yet utterly free from bombast. Mr. Hardy has written some scenes, created some characters, of a passion almost unbearable for poignancy : but with little more ' fine language,' than we find in Thucydides' Sicilian Expedition, or in Caesar's Siege of Alesia. There are some popular novelists just now, romantic, passionate, grandiose, who can scarcely be read, without recalling Dryden's happy wit. He writes of diseased authors : ' Another, who had a great *Genius* for *Tragedy*, following the Fury of his natural *Temper*, made every Man and Woman too, in his Play, stark raging mad : there was not a sober Person to be had for Love or Money :

All was tempestuous and blustering : Heaven and Earth were coming together at every Word ; a mere Hurricane from the beginning to the end ; and every Actor seem'd to be hastening on the Day of Judgement.'

Mr. Hardy's control over his art is a good example, for our day of tempestuous writing : an example of sanity, of beauty, and of strength.

VI

SINCERITY IN ART

' IT requires a talented omission of your real thoughts
to make a novel popular, for one thing.' Knight in-
dulged his rather acrid temper in that sarcasm : and
Elfride consoled him with more sarcasm unawares.
' Is that really necessary ? Well, I am sure you could
learn to do that with practice.'

It is often asserted, that practice has made most English novelists perfect in this art of omission, and that
popularity has rewarded hypocrisy: there are shrill pro-
phets among us, who denounce our average novel, as
our national vice. Whenever lamentations and denun-
ciations rend the air, come they from Tory or from
Radical, the poor listener would do well, to recall the
wisdom of Savile the Trimmer : ' What do angry men
ail, to rail so against moderation ? Does it not look
as if they were going to some very scurvy extreme,
that is too strong to be digested by the more considering part of mankind ? ' It is none too easy a task, to
determine the just proportions, which right reason
would assign to the contending elements in artistic
work : the senses and the imagination, the claims of
constraining morality and the claims of creative desire,
are in persistent warfare. ' In the present day,' said
Cardinal Newman, ' mistiness is the mother of

wisdom ' : it is tempting to cut the knot, by declaring that art and morals have nothing in common : or that one must give way to the other. These theories might be rational in Utopia, and lucid in a Land of the Fourth Dimension : they are inexpressibly meaningless, here and now. Not even music, that art so independent of matter, is disconnected from morality : the great Greek critics of art and morals would have been astounded at that notion. So long as art proceeds from, and appeals to, men of a whole and harmonious nature, art must express that wholeness and that harmony : an artist is forbidden, by the facts of his natural structure, to dissociate his ethics from his aesthetics : as well might he try to live by bread alone, without exercising reason, or by reason alone, not eating bread. Certainly, he can mutilate his mind : not indeed, as yet, by a physical mortification or excision of his conscience ; but by a culture of morbid tendencies in thought and will ; of which the end is to find

> ' his moral powers gone idiot,
> And his intellect sane, to watch them.'

Not a few writers of our time are engaged in those watches of the night : not a few are fascinated by another variety of contemplation ; they ' shut their eyes, and look into their stomachs, and call it introspection.' Further, there is no little cant upon all sides : writers of the poorest stuff, which is not literature at all, talk boldly of their high, artistic mission : they cry out, with Lady Wishfort in the play ; ' If you think the least scruple of carnality was an ingredient ! '

o

These suspicious and suspected persons, could we believe them, are all for the dignity of sacred art : just as the loudest clamourers against many public burdens are those, who do not bear them. Now, as in Swift's age, ' some men, under the notion of kneading out prejudice, eradicate virtue, honesty, and religion ' ; and now, as in Swift's age, ' when a true genius appears in the world, you may know him by this sign, that the dunces are in confederacy against him.' Extremes are just now in fashion and in favour, with this unfortunate result : that catholicity of taste is set down, as the sign of lukewarmness and of half-heartedness : he must be indifferent to the great issues at stake, the great principles involved, who can see ' much to be said on both sides.' It is very tiresome : ' life with substantial ills enough is cursed,' as the tragic Smollett observes, without this additional pest of artistic parties : may we not be allowed to like Dr. Ibsen, and to dislike M. Verlaine ; or to like M. Verlaine, and to dislike Dr. Ibsen ; or to like or dislike them both ; without being held guilty of a mortal sin ? We are so violent in these days ; and, to our irreparable loss, there is no Arnold left to charm us into serenity : there are four noisy schools, who deafen us with their controversies. There are those, who preach the principle of art for art's sake : those, who preach the principle, that art is bound to preach the dogmas of Christianity : those, who preach the principle, that art is bound to preach the dogmas of almost everything else : and those, who preach the principle, that art has no principles at all. Like most heresies, these doctrines contain, each a distorted fragment of truth : and, like orthodoxy, art survives all its abuses. ' What Art can be more pernicious,' asks Sir Henry Wotton, ' than even *Religion* itself, if itself be converted into an Instrument of Art ?   Therefore, *Ab abuti ad non uti negatur consequentia.*'

Mr. Hardy has written an essay upon *Candour in English Fiction*, expressing his sense of the difficulties, under which the novelist lies : difficulties, due to the trammelling of his thought, by the puritan shackles of his readers ; difficulties, created by ' the censorship of prudery.' The essay, it hardly need be said, is admirably dignified and grave : there is nothing in it of the fanatic's excitement. But it states a few reasons, why so large a proportion of English novels compose ' a literature of quackery ' : a literature false to truth, afraid of truth. ' The crash of broken commandments,' writes Mr. Hardy, with equal force and fineness, ' is as necessary an accompaniment to the catastrophe of a tragedy as the noise of drum and cymbals to a triumphal march.' English readers, the vast majority of them, coercing, and coerced by, the commercial producers and distributors of books, will not endure that music of the nether sphere : they are all for a lulling, soothing, comfortable strain. Upon this, two remarks may be made. First, the writer cannot with justice complain, if the public taste be against his works : he can only regret it. By the act of publication, the writer gives over his work to the public judgment : he has no rights over that judgment. He can think it a foolish judgment, a stupid

and a dull judgment : he may strive to bring the
judges to a better mind, to purge their blind eyes, and
to enlighten their dark minds : he may find solace in
the thought of time, the final arbiter and judge of
appeal. But he has no right to command applause
and the verdict of success : he trades in a fine art,
and offers his best to the public : the public is under
no obligation to like it. Secondly, it is not criminal to
enjoy poor art, provided that the enjoyer do not enjoy
it for artistic reasons : let us consider the example of
Darwin. In early life, he loved great poetry, painting,
and music : immersed in scientific studies, he lost
those tastes, and loathed the great arts : the ' dulness '
of Shakespeare ' nauseated ' him. But, on the other
hand, ' novels, which are works of imagination, though
not of a very high order, have been for years a wonderful relief and pleasure to me, and I often bless all
novelists. A wonderful number have been read aloud
to me, and I like all if moderately good, and if they
do not end unhappily—against which a law ought to
be passed.' I do not say, that novelists with a high
respect for their art will return the blessing of Darwin :
but need they beat the breast, and be indignant ?
Here was a man, whose life was devoted, in the face of
vehement antagonism, to the discovery of great facts
about physical science ; a man incapable of loving
falsehood, or of concealing truth : his devotion to
science caused an atrophy of his aesthetic tastes : yet
some refreshment he must have, in the midst of his
labours ; and he found it in stories, that took him
away from the fierce storms of human life, from the

vision of conflict and of pain in the physical order ;
pleasant, charming, trifling inventions, all about happy
people and fortunate events. Had the writers of
these stories prefaced them by saying, that they contained a ripe philosophy of life, the mature fruits of
wise consideration, Darwin would not have been deceived : but his favourite novelists made no such pretensions. They pourtrayed life in bright colours :
they wrote fictions, not facts : their aim was to give
simple pleasure, by charming men into a paradise for
a little while : they looked at the world, and chose out
certain cheerful incidents of life, rejecting certain
others : and so doing, they soothed and rested one
of the noblest men, that have yet enriched our knowledge. From pretty tales of happy marriages, Darwin
turned with fresh zest and vigour to an unflinching
pursuit of hard, inexorable, and momentous facts.
The majority of men and women turn from their work
and occupation, in the same spirit, to the enjoyment
of novels : they have no taste for art, they have no
interest in its difficulties, nor in its triumphs : they
want to be amused, and they find amusement in plausible stories about pleasant things. ' Why do you
write such melancholy things ? Life is melancholy
enough without that,' is their reproach to the serious
writer : a reproach, which shows two things. The
cheery, trivial stories do not mislead them, they wish
to be caressed and charmed into an illusion of happiness : and they know nothing about the joy of an
artist in making beauty out of all things, glad or sad.
And they have great allies : Dr. Johnson said to Mrs.

Sheridan : ' I know not, Madam, that you have a
right, upon moral principles, to make your readers
suffer so much ' : and Arnold has immortalized that
saying of Joubert about the soul's cry, ' You hurt me ! '
Even Mr. Hardy has protested against ' the gratuit-
ous infliction ' of miseries.   Doubtless, there are limits
to the right of a smiling author to prophesy smooth
things : when Bentley presents Milton with two new
concluding lines for *Paradise Lost*,

> ' Then hand in hand with social steps their way
> Through Eden took, with heavenly comfort cheered,'

we do well to be exceeding angry : the principle of
' happy endings ' has gone too far.   But I must be
allowed to think it an hard task, to discern infallibly
all transgressions of common sense, let alone, of art,
in these matters.   To take a famous instance : the
sounding letter of Sulpicius to Cicero, upon the death
of Cicero's daughter.   ' On my return from Asia, as I
sailed towards Megara from Ægina, I fell to surveying the prospect.   Behind me lay Ægina, before me
Megara, to right of me Piraeus, to left of me Corinth :
fallen from their high estate, all fallen !   And in this
our day, what men of shining fame are perished !
How is the empire of the Romans minished !   How
are the provinces convulsed and shaken !   And now :
*in unius mulierculae animula si iactura facta est, tanto
opere commoveris ? '*   The futile elegance of those
sentiments, set to sonorous phrases, after a sentimental journey !   Your child is dead : I am so sorry !
But Ninus and Assaracus are dead too : think of that,

and be comforted! Yet I can hardly doubt, considering much indubitable evidence about Stoic endurance and Epicurean calm, that Cicero received comfort from such rhetoric : his experience of the world, and of his own heart, did not wholly give the lie to its consolations.

For these reasons, then, I think that there is some exaggeration in the complaints, even of Mr. Hardy : and the best proof of it is his own work. In that, there is no courting of the popular tastes, no mutilation of thought or of invention, no pandering to prejudice or to preference of any kind. His last book shows his courage and conscientiousness : he need have no concern for the artistic demerits of lesser men, who do not claim to be great artists. But, before proceeding to an examination of Tess, we may well consider one point in Mr. Hardy's general view of things, which may have been some hindrance to his popularity : that is, his love for ' the note of revolt.'

In a public letter about the recognition of literary merit by the State, Mr. Hardy writes : ' The highest flights of the pen are often, indeed mostly, the excursions and revelations of souls unreconciled to life ; while the natural tendency of a government would be to encourage acquiescence in life as it is.' In his sombre Egdon novel, he asks : ' Was Yeobright's mind well proportioned? No. A well-proportioned mind is one which shows no particular bias ; one of which we may safely say that it will never cause its owner to be confined as a madman, tortured as a heretic, or crucified as a blasphemer. Also, on the

other hand, that it will never cause its owner to be
applauded as a prophet, revered as a priest, or exalted
as a king.   Its usual blessings are happiness and mediocrity.   It produces the poetry of Rogers, the paint-
ings of West, the state-craft of North, the spiritual
guidance of Sumner ; enabling its possessors to find
their way to wealth, to wind up well, to step with
dignity off the stage, to die comfortably in their beds,
and to get the decent monument which, in many cases,
they deserve.   It never would have allowed Yeobright
to do such a ridiculous thing as to throw up his business to benefit his fellow-creatures.'   Throughout
Mr. Hardy's books, this spirit burns with a passionate
flame : his anger grows sometimes to a white heat :
under the grandeur of his eloquence, Roman and
massive, leaps, hardly to be controlled, this fervour
of scorn and wrath.   Shelley was not more grandly
angered against Lord Eldon, than is Mr. Hardy
against the powers and the influences, of an unjust
society, and of a false religion.   Accepting, for the
moment, the righteousness of such anger, I yet cannot
assent to this attitude : it is possible to have right
motives for revolt, yet to revolt wrongly.   How, and
when, and where, must be considered in all things,
according to the eternal common sense of Aristotle :
or the remedies may prove worse than the diseases.
Here is the sober counsel of one who, like his own
Heine, was a Knight in the War of Liberation : ' Dissolvents of the old European systems of dominant
ideas and facts we must all be, all of us who have any
power of working ; what we have to study is that we

may not be acrid dissolvents of it.' Those ' old
European ' systems, in religion at the least, I regard
as eternal and ideal, neither old nor European : but
how wise, with all the wisdom of a child of this generation, is the courtesy of Arnold's counsel ! For again,
' the perfection of culture is not rebellion, but peace ' :
rebellion is but a lamentable, necessary means to
an end, at best. The great literature has always
expressed the sanity, the measure, the harmony, of
the world : we may confront Mr. Hardy's irony about
the well-proportioned mind, with the history of great
revolutionaries. Contemplate Socrates in prison, and
Dante in exile : contrast them with Shelley and with
Byron. There is nothing more pathetic, and nothing
more triumphant, than the figure of Socrates, drawn
by his disciple in the *Crito* : Socrates is urged to
fly from prison, and to take refuge in Thessaly : the
laws have condemned an innocent man : why should
he respect them, and not rather save a life, full of light
and strength to many ? But Socrates hears the voice
of the Laws murmuring in his ears : ' Will you fly
to Thessaly, the land of disorder ? Will you break
our commands, because men have used us wrongly ?
Will you return evil for evil ? Will you go to death and
to the lower world, to be received by our brothers,
the Laws of that world, as an enemy ? But, going in
innocence, you go a sufferer of wrong, and not a doer
of it.' Dante also : the fruit of his exile was no strain
of revolt alone : he denounced injustice and wrong,
he had no fear of wickedness in high places : but his
solemn meditations, his ' contemplation everywhere

of the sun and stars,' issued in the most perfect poem
of an universal harmony : modern taste seems to
prefer Ovid's *Tristia*. Socrates, or Plato speaking for
him, and Dante, who certainly speaks for himself, had
minds well balanced, with a ' particular bias ' towards
the solution of life's doubts and difficulties, not by
captious, querulous, lamentations, but by a generous
and patient exposition of the best truth known to
them. A revolt, which finds no better expression
than weeping and wailing, or than flouts and sneers,
is not a little contemptible. There are personal convictions of sorrow and of wrong, which are not ignoble
to entertain, but very ignoble to make public : many
sufferers should ' die, and make no sign ' : many
should ' learn in suffering,' that silence may sometimes teach more, than any song. Most modern
preachers of revolt in literature resemble some among
those men, turned into beasts, noble and ignoble, upon
the Island of Circe :

> ' *Hinc exaudiri gemitus, iraeque leonum*
> *Vincla recusantum, et sera sub nocte rudentum ;*
> *Saetigerique sues, atque in praesepibus ursi*
> *Saevire, ac formae magnorum ululare luporum.*'

But the lions are few : the swine, and bears, and
wolves, are many. Mr. Hardy has an austere habit
of style, which but seldom changes into flippancy :
human life is too sacred a thing in his eyes, to be
lightly treated : but at times the passion, that informs
his work, seems to break out in fitful phrases, which
impede his story without the justification of being
solid arguments. The novels, which ' vindicate the

ways of God to man,' are indeed wearisome : but
fully as wearisome are those, which vindicate the ways
of man to God : and it is because *Tess of the D'Urbervilles* contains so much insinuated argument of this
kind, to the detriment of its art, that I cannot rank it
so high, as certain other of Mr. Hardy's books. Its
spirit is nothing new, for all Mr. Hardy's books proceed from the same range of thought : but none of
them show quite this irritability of casual comment :
this refusal to let the facts of the story convey their
own moral, without the help of epigrammatic hints.
At times, they read like quaint, modern imitations
of those marginal glosses, which adorn the *Pilgrim's
Progress* and the *Ancient Mariner* : ' Here Tess illus-
trateth the falling out betwixt Nature and Society,' or,
' In this place did Angel mock at Giant Calvinist, for
that he taught an untenable redemptive theolatry.'

There can be no need to repeat the story of Tess :
her guiltless seduction ; her love for Clare ; his rejection of her, within a few hours of their marriage,
upon learning her early fate ; her piteous fidelity to
him, among hard scenes, in his absence ; his tardy
return, repentant of his desertion, to find her won
back by the arts of her seducer, who played upon her
love for her outcast family ; the meeting of husband
and wife at the house of her bondage and of her shame ;
her murder of her seducer, in a revulsion of agony
and love ; her wandering fortunes with her husband,
ending in her capture at Stonehenge, and her execu-
tion at Winchester. The story goes with a surge and
sweep, a magnificence of movement ; a cloud of vast

forces, labouring at the fates of one poor girl, over-shadows every page : Hugo, and, to dare a greater illustration, Æschylus, so wrought out their mighty tragedies. But in this vital point, the illustrations fail : *Les Misérables* and the *Oresteia* carry conviction, not in the telling merely of their tragedies, but in the presentation of their moral imports : *Tess of the D'Urbervilles* does not. ' A Pure Woman faithfully Presented,' writes Mr. Hardy upon his title page : the second and fourth words would be the better for some definition. Let us set down, for consideration, some passages from the book.

The Durbeyfield household is described, with these comments. ' All these young souls were passengers in the Durbeyfield ship—entirely dependent on the judgment of the two Durbeyfield adults for their plea-sures, their necessities, their health, even their exist-ence. If the heads of the Durbeyfield household chose to sail into difficulty, disaster, starvation, disease, degradation, death, thither were these half-dozen little captives under hatches compelled to sail with them—six helpless little creatures, who had never been asked if they wished for life on any terms, much less if they wished for it on such hard conditions as were involved in being of the shiftless house of Durbey-field. Some people would like to know whence the poet whose philosophy is in these days deemed as profound and trustworthy as his verse is pure and breezy, gets his authority for speaking of " Nature's holy plan." '

Twice Mr. Hardy suggests, that some act of Tess

was an hereditary impulse : once, that her suffering was in retribution for her ancestors' sins. Upon the latter theory he comments : ' But though to visit the sins of the fathers upon the children may be a morality good enough for divinities, it is scorned by average human nature ; and it therefore does not mend the matter.'

When at home after her first great sorrow, Tess only walked out after dark. ' It is then that the plight of being alive becomes attenuated to its least possible dimensions. She had no fear of the shadows ; her sole idea seemed to be to shun mankind—or rather that cold accretion called the world, which, so terrible in the mass, is so unformidable, even pitiable, in its units. . . .

' At times her whimsical fancy would intensify natural processes around her till they seemed a part of her own story. Rather they became a part of it ; for the world is only a psychological phenomenon, and what they seemed they were. The midnight airs and gusts, moaning amongst the tightly-wrapped buds and bark of the winter twigs, were formulæ of bitter reproach. A wet day was the expression of irremediable grief at her weakness in the mind of some vague ethical being whom she could not class definitely as the God of her childhood, and could not comprehend as any other.

' But this encompassment of her own characterization, based on shreds of convention, peopled by phantoms and voices antipathetic to her, was a sorry and mistaken creation of Tess's fancy, a cloud of moral hobgoblins by which she was terrified without reason.   It was they that were out of harmony with the actual world, not she.   Walking among the sleeping birds in the hedges, watching the skipping rabbits on a moonlit warren, or standing under a pheasant-laden bough, she looked upon herself as a figure of Guilt intruding into the haunts of Innocence.   But all the while she was making a distinction when there was no difference.   Feeling herself in antagonism she was quite in accord.   She had been made to break a necessary social law, but no law known to the environment in which she fancied herself an anomaly.'

Her baby is born : ' Alone in a desert island would she have been wretched at what had happened to her ? Not greatly.   If she could have been but just created, to discover herself as a spouseless mother, with no experience of life except as the parent of a nameless child, would the position have caused her to despair ? No, she would have taken it calmly, and found pleasure therein.   Most of the misery had been generated by her conventional aspect, and not by her innate sensations.'

Her baby dies : ' So passed away Sorrow the Un-desired—that intrusive creature, that bastard gift of shameless Nature who respects not the civil law ' ; . . .

Some time has passed : ' Almost at a leap Tess thus changed from simple girl to complex woman. Symbols of reflectiveness passed into her face, and a note of tragedy at times into her voice.   Her eyes grew larger and more eloquent.   She became what would have been called a fine creature ; her aspect was fair and

arresting ; her soul that of a woman whom the turbulent experiences of the last year or two had quite
failed to demoralize. But for the world's opinion
those experiences would have been simply a liberal
education. . . . Was once lost always lost really
true of chastity ? she would ask herself. She might
prove it false if she could veil bygones. The recuperative power which pervaded organic nature was
surely not denied to maidenhood alone.'

At the dairy farm, the three milkmaids were in love
with Angel Clare. ' The air of the sleeping-chamber
seemed to palpitate with the hopeless passion of the
girls. They writhed feverishly under the oppressive-
ness of an emotion thrust on them by cruel Nature's
law—an emotion which they had neither expected
nor desired. . . . The full recognition of the futility
of their infatuation, from a social point of view ; its
purposeless beginning ; its self-bounded outlook ;
its lack of everything to justify its existence in the eye
of civilization (while lacking nothing in the eye of
Nature) ; the one fact that it did exist, ecstasizing them
to a killing joy ; all this imparted to them a resignation, a dignity, which a practical and sordid expecta-
tion of winning him as a husband would have destroyed.

Clare considered his position towards Tess. ' Despite his heterodoxy Clare was a man with a conscience. Tess was no insignificant creature to toy
with and dismiss ; but a woman living her precious
life—a life which, to herself who endured or enjoyed
it, possessed as great a dimension as the life of the
mightiest to himself. Upon her sensations the whole

world depended to Tess; through her existence all her fellow-creatures existed, to her. The universe itself only came into being for Tess on the particular day in the particular year in which she was born.

'This consciousness upon which he had intruded was the single opportunity of existence ever vouchsafed to Tess by an unsympathetic First Cause—her all; her every and only chance.'

After some time passed at the dairy farm, Clare felt the spirit of his home foreign and uncongenial. 'Latterly he had seen only Life, felt only the great passionate pulse of existence, unwarped, uncontorted, untrammelled by those creeds which futilely attempt to check what wisdom would be content to palliate.'

Tess at last consented to marry Clare, and kissed him passionately in earnest of her love: 'She had consented. She might as well have agreed at first. The "appetite for joy" which pervades all creation, that tremendous force which sways humanity to its purpose, as the tide sways the helpless reed, was not to be controlled by vague lucubrations over the social rubric.'

On her hard way to work, after Clare's desertion, Tess passed a night in a wood, disturbed by strange noises: in the dawn, she found that they were the sound of wounded pheasants, falling from their perches: she put them out of their pain. '" Poor darlings—to suppose myself the most miserable thing on earth in the presence of such misery as this!" she exclaimed, her tears running down as she killed the birds tenderly. " And I have not a twinge of bodily pain about me!

I am not mangled and I am not bleeding, and I have two hands to feed and clothe me." She was ashamed of herself for her gloom of the night, based on nothing more tangible than a sense of condemnation under an arbitrary law of society which had no foundation in Nature.'

Tess was hanged for killing her seducer : ' " Justice " was done, and the President of the Immortals (in Æschylean phrase) had ended his sport with Tess.'

To these passages, we may add three or four from the earlier writings, of the same character, but there more rarely found. Henchard reflected, as he visited the scene of his old disgrace, upon the strange issues of his act : ' It was an odd sequence that out of all this wronging of social law came that flower of Nature, Elizabeth. Part of his wish to wash his hands of life arose from his perceptions of its contrarious inconsistencies—of Nature's jaunty readiness to support bad social principles.' Had Eustacia been made a goddess, the world would have felt no change in its government : ' There would have been the same inequality of lot, the same heaping up of favours here, of contumely there, the same generosity before justice, the same perpetual dilemmas, the same captious alternation of caresses and blows as we endure now.' Again, ' In Clym Yeobright's face could be dimly seen the typical countenance of the place. Should there be a classic period to art hereafter, its Phidias may produce such faces. The view of life as a thing to be put up with, replacing that zest for existence which was so intense in early civilizations, must ultimately enter so thor-

P

oughly into the constitution of the advanced races
that its facial expression will become accepted as a
new artistic departure. People already feel that a
man who lives without disturbing a curve of feature,
or setting a mark of mental concern anywhere upon
himself, is too far removed from modern perceptive-
ness to be a modern type. Physically beautiful men—
the glory of the race when it was young—are almost
an anachronism now ; and we may wonder whether,
at some time or other, physically beautiful women may
not be an anachronism likewise.

' The truth seems to be that a long line of disillusive
centuries has permanently displaced the Hellenic idea
of life, or whatever it may be called. What the Greeks
only suspected we know well ; what their Æschylus
imagined our nursery children feel. That old-fashioned
revelling in the general situation grows less and less
possible as we uncover the defects of natural law, and
see the quandary that man is in by their operation.'
Yeobright did not share his mother's views of social
advancement. ' He had no desires of that sort. He
had reached the stage in a young man's life when the
grimness of the general human situation becomes clear ;
and the realization of this causes ambition to halt
awhile. In France it is not uncustomary to commit
suicide at this stage ; in England we do much better,
or much worse, as the case may be.' Wildeve also
had his perversities : ' To be yearning for the difficult,
to be weary of what offered ; to care for the remote,
to dislike the near : it was Wildeve's nature always.
This is the true mark of the man of sentiment. Though

Wildeve's fevered feeling had not been elaborated to real poetical compass, it was of the standard sort. He might have been called the Rousseau of Egdon.' Swithin, the young astronomer, recovered from his sickness, through his strong desire to study the appearance of a new comet: 'his example affords another instance of that reflex rule of the vassal soul over the sovereign body, which, operating so wonderfully in elastic natures, and more or less in all, originally gave rise to the legend that supremacy lay on the other side.' Once more, Mr. Hardy's essay speaks of an original treatment required for the presentation of that high tragedy, which modern taste now relishes, as it was relished in the days of Pericles and of Elizabeth ; but a tragedy, differing in its dramatic motives from those old tragedies : it is a treatment, ' which seeks to show Nature's unconsciousness not of essential laws, but of those laws framed merely as social expedients by humanity, without a basis in the heart of things ' ; not that there must be any ' prurient treatment of the relation of the sexes, or . . . any view of vice calculated to undermine the essential principles of social order ' ; nor should literature ' for a moment exhibit lax views of that purity of life upon which the wellbeing of society depends.' Finally, writing upon the Dorset labourers, Mr. Hardy observes : ' It is among such communities as these that happiness will find her last refuge on earth, since it is among them that a perfect insight into the conditions of existence will be longest postponed.'

I have read *Tess*, some eight or ten times : at first,

with that ravishment and enthusiasm, which great art, art great in spite of imperfection, must always cause. Still the grandeur of the book, its human tragedy, holds and masters me : ' how largely it is all planned ! ' as Goethe said of Marlowe's *Faustus*. But gradually, difficulties, unfelt under the first spell of enchantment, begin to appear : it were unjust to Mr. Hardy to ignore them. Doubtless, there is something prosaic in scrutinizing, with unmoved tranquillity, the argument of so piteous a story : why not accept its simple beauty and its simple pity, the moving passion of it ; without curiously considering those places, where the writer's personal convictions have expressed themselves in irony and in anger ? That is impossible : because *Tess* is more than the history of a woman's life and death ; it is also an indictment of ' Justice,' human and divine, as the *Oresteia* is its vindication. Either the story should bear its own burden of spiritual sorrow, each calamity and woe crushing out of us all hope, by its own resistless weight : or the bitter sentences of comment should be lucid and cogent. But had Mr. Hardy denied himself all commentary, and left the story to carry its own moral into our hearts ; I doubt, whether we should all have received quite the same moral : to prevent any such ' perverse ' resistance to his intended moral, Mr. Hardy has not denied himself the luxury, or perhaps the superfluity, of comments at once inartistic and obscure. The sincerity of the book is indubitable : but the passion of revolt has led the writer to renounce his impassive temper ; and to encounter

grave difficulties, in that departure from his wonted
attitude towards art.

In art, nothing is more difficult than to turn theories
of ethics, or of metaphysics, into living motives : than
the expression of them through the treatment of human
characters and of human actions : the genius of Browning could not always overcome that difficulty. For a
false step here is irrecoverable : a false thought may
vitiate the whole book. It is not so with the treatment of facts, for their own sake, as great things to see
or hear : a mistake is deplorable, but not fatal. Hugo
may give us impossible science, grotesque history,
confused learning : but it is not that, which can condemn him, just as it is not absurdities of detail, which
can condemn Euripides : it is bad logic, bad infer-
ence, misrepresentation of a mind. Various artists
have various ways : Lucretius, whose argument is
much that of Mr. Hardy, has no hesitation in stating
his plain reasons in unadorned language, one by one,
orderly and simply : that done, the spirit of poetry
leaps from its restraint, and chaunts the dirge of worlds
and men. Shakespeare goes delicately, suffusing all
his work with the spirit of his thought. But it is useless to attempt a combination of methods : when the
reader is following the fortunes of Tess, he hates to
fall into some track of thought, which leads him to
the debateable land, where he must listen to Aristotle
and Rousseau, Aquinas and Hegel, Hobbes and Mill,
Sir Henry Maine and Mr. Herbert Spencer. It is a
question of manner : things, intolerable in one manner,
are delightful in another. If I wish to study certain

aspects of English melancholy, at various times, I can
turn to Burton's *Anatomy*, to Cheyne's *English Malady*,
to Thomson's *City of Dreadful Night* : if French
melancholy be my study, there are Pascal, Rousseau,
Baudelaire, ready at hand : all these tell their tale
with greater or with less felicity : their spirit and
their form, are well consorted.   But Mr. Hardy is not
content to frame his indictment, by the stern narration of sad facts : he inserts fragments of that reasoning, which has brought him to his dark conclusion.
They are too many, too bitter, too passionate, to be
but an overflow, as it were, from his narration : they
are too sparse, too ironical, too declamatory, to be
quite intelligible.   After enjoying their grimness, I
want definitions of *nature*, *law*, *society*, and *justice* :
the want is coarse, doubtless, and unimaginative ; but
I cannot suppress it.   It is the fashion of to-day to
mock at those scholastic disputations, which en-
livened the scholars of old time : logical quibblings,
we say, useless and trivial, a vain logomachy !   But
we greatly need something of their discipline now :
for there will presently remain few words of philosophic
language, unburdened with several meanings in several
mouths.   To one man the phrase, *physical realism*,
suggests a question in the metaphysics : to another,
a question in the arts.   Many misty persons, who
exercise ' the right of the individual to general hazi-
ness,' would feel most unhappy, confronted with the
great Doctors, the Subtile, the Irrefragable, the
Special, the Admirable, the Solid, and the Profound.
Without doubt, Mr Hardy is a man of his mind, with

careful conclusions upon perplexing points : but his thought is something elusive, in such passages, as I have quoted.

Nature's plan is not ' holy,' as Wordsworth taught, because children come unconsulted into a world, where endless miseries may await them. Nature has no respect for the civil law, and none for the conventions of society about sexual commerce. Nature's law is cruel : exciting sensations, which cannot be gratified ; and desires, which civilization cannot justify. Tess felt herself condemned by an ' arbitrary ' social law, with no foundation in Nature : yet the law, which she was made to break, was a ' necessary ' social law. She rebuked herself for her self-pity, because she was suffering no physical pain, in a world full of animal pains : and she was wrong in feeling a consciousness of guilt, among the scenes and creatures of the woods, because, like any other animal, she had but fulfilled a physical function of nature. Not her ' innate sensations,' but the conventions of society, caused most of her misery at the thought of her unmarried motherhood : upon a desert island, she would have taken pleasure in it : but for public opinion, her seduction and her motherhood would have been but ' a liberal education.' After all, organic nature is full of recuperative power : does not that power extend to lost maidenhood ? After all, men and women are helpless before that ' appetite for joy,' which rules all creation, and is far too strong to be controlled by disquisitions about social rites and customs : its full force cannot be checked by creeds, but only paltered with and winked at by wisdom : it leads, at worst, in Lovelace's phrase, to 'a transitory evil, an evil which a mere church-form makes none.' And the world is only a psychological phenomenon : and the First Cause is unsympathetic : nay, is fiendish, because the children suffer for the fathers ; and sportive, because the fate of Tess was a prolonged caricature of justice, ending in the supreme jest of her violent death.

I know not, who can lie under a stronger necessity to realize the sorrow of the world, than a Catholic : but he lies under no obligation to abnegate his reason : and I cannot, with all the will in the world, to understand Mr. Hardy's indictment, understand one word of it. Making all allowance for mere sentiment, and all deductions for mere passion, I can see in it but a tangle of inconsistencies. What is this ' Nature,' of which or of whom, Mr. Hardy speaks ? Is it a *Natura naturata*, or a *Natura naturans* ? Is it a conscious Power ? or a convenient name for the whole mass of physical facts ? The Doge of Genoa might well propound his difficulties :

> ' My thoughts are fixed in contemplation,
> Why this huge earth, this monstrous animal,
> That eats her children, should not have ears and eyes.
> Philosophy maintains that Nature 's wise,
> And forms no useless or unperfect thing.
> Did Nature make the earth, or the earth Nature ?
> For earthly dirt makes all things, makes the man,
> Moulds me up honour, and like a cunning Dutchman,
> Paints me a puppet even with seeming breath,
> And gives a sot appearance of a soul :
> Go to, go to : thou liest, Philosophy.

Nature forms things unperfect, useless, vain.
Why made she not the earth with eyes and ears ?
That she might see desert, and hear men's plaints :
That when a soul is splitted, sunk with grief,
He might fall thus, upon the breast of earth ;
And in her ear halloo his misery :
Exclaiming thus, O thou all-bearing earth,
Which men do gape for, till thou cram'st their mouths,
And chok'st their throats with dust : oh chaune thy breast,
And let me sink into thee. Look, who knocks ;
Andrugio calls. But oh, she 's deaf and blind :
A wretch but lean relief on earth can find.'

Let us take Nature to be no more than a personifica-
tion of physical facts : neither moral nor immoral :
' power is in nature,' says Emerson, ' the essential
measure of right ' ; that is a calm statement, prefer-
able to Mr. Hardy's ' cruelty ' : and M. Renan may
give us a graceful statement of nature's productive
desire, in place of Mr. Hardy's ' tremendous force.'
' Si la nature était méchante, elle serait laide. . . .
La nature a du goût : seulement elle ne va pas à la
morale ; elle ne va pas au delà de l'amour.' All this
is but the doctrine of modern science about the physical
conditions of life : conflict and survival, both caused
by strong forces of impulse. But Mr. Hardy juggles
with ' Nature ' : now she is cruel, which is a reproach
to divine justice ; now she is kindly, whereas society
is harsh. ' To remove and cast off a heap of rubbish
that has been gathering upon the soul from our very
infancy requires great courage and great strength of
faculties. Our philosophers, therefore, do well deserve
the name of *esprits forts, men of strong heads, free-
thinkers*, and such like appellations, betokening great

force and liberty of mind. It is very possible the heroic labours of these men may be represented (for what is not capable of misrepresentation ?) as a piratical plundering, and stripping the mind of its wealth and ornaments, when it is in truth divesting it only of its prejudices, and reducing it to its untainted original state of nature. Oh nature ! the genuine beauty of pure nature ! ' Thus Alciphron, in the manner of Mr. Squeers upon the same theme : and thus Euphranor, in answer. ' You seem very much taken with the beauty of nature. Be pleased to tell me, Alciphron, what those things are which you esteem *natural*, or by what mark I may know them.' Whereat Alciphron falls into the prettiest confusion possible. And Mr. Hardy's praise of nature is in the very dialect of the eighteenth century : the suggestion, that on a desert island, away from censorious eyes, Tess would have felt innocent and unashamed, is worthy of Rousseau. Nature alone has essential laws : society has but expedient laws ; ' arbitrary,' in the sense that they are *only* expedient ; ' necessary,' in the sense that they *are* expedient. Such seems to be Mr. Hardy's position. Now, the misfortune of Tess, her seduction, was in conformity with Nature, as a simple, physical occurrence : it was out of conformity with Society, because it broke a social law, necessary, if arbitrary : but a state of Nature precedes a state of Society, and has therefore deeper, wider, larger laws : Society, then, was but prejudiced in favour of its own well-being, when it condemned Tess : therefore Society was unjust, preferring its necessary laws of expediency to the

great fundamental laws of Nature. Tess, from ful-
filling against her will her natural function, was driven
on by iron forces, till at last she committed murder :
she could not help herself : why was she hanged,
unless to amuse God ?   True, she was at first haunted
by a sense of guilt : but conscience is a conventional
thing, the utilitarian product of racial experience : it
merely meant, that her misfortune, though nothing
in the sight of Nature, belonged to a class of acts pre-
judicial to Society : true, she yielded at the last to her
old seducer ; but that was in despair, and to help her
family ; she was but *vulning* herself, as heralds say of
the pelican in her piety ; and, once more, since the
rabbits and the pheasants would have seen no harm
in it, why should she, merely an animal, higher in the
scale of physical development ?

It is perplexing : some one, some thing, must be
to blame. It cannot be Nature, because you cannot
blame an abstraction : it cannot be Society, unless you
would have it commit suicide : it must be God.

> ' Like flies to wanton boys, are we to the gods :
> They kill us for their sport.' [1]

There is almost a delicious irony in the thought : no
need for reverence remains : if this be true, no *gami-
nerie* can be too bitter an insult to the God of Israel
and of the Christians. One can but stand up in
righteous wrath, and repeat the severe rebukes of
Mill, against so monstrous a divinity. It might be
thought, even so, that dignity counselled silence and

---

[1] This chapter was written before, and has not been altered
since, the publication of Mr. Hardy's new preface to *Tess*.

endurance : *Gloria in terra Homini*, beyond question :
but perhaps it were only respectful to add, with
Lucretius, *et in caelo pax deis nullius voluntatis* : to
assume, that the gods are at rest in an impassive peace ;
and to revile some blind Will, or superior Fate, instead.
But that were to forego much occasion of rhetoric :
' *Victrix causa deis placuit, sed victa Catoni* ' : ' morality
good enough for divinities, but scorned by average
human nature ' : ' " Justice " was done, and the President of the Immortals (in Æschylean phrase) had
ended his sport with Tess.'

It is characteristic of Mr. Hardy to quote the *Prometheus* : that one play of Æschylus, which may be
thought to show a malevolence of God to man.

> ' Do you not see, dear friend, that thus
>   You leave Saint Paul for Æschylus ? '

asks Browning : but Mr. Hardy has left even Æschylus,
for ' nursery children ' ; the babes and sucklings of
our disillusioned day, to whom ' the grimness of the
general situation ' is revealed, and out of whose mouths
is pessimism perfected. But I am content with
Æschylus.

> ' *O prima infelix fingenti terra Prometheo !*
>   *Ille parum cauti pectoris egit opus :*
>   *Corpora disponens mentem non vidit in arte.*
>   *Recta animi primum debuit esse via.*'

If Propertius were right in so criticising the labours of
Prometheus, Zeus were also right in refusing to bless
them : but it is no true criticism. Nor have we a
right to infer the faith of Æschylus, from but one part
of a mutilated trilogy : as well might we reason about

the faith of Dante, with sole reference to the *Inferno*.
In the *Oresteia*, those three poems beyond all human
praise, Æschylus has declared the grounds of his faith
in a just ordering of the world. I believe, speaking
in reverence and under correction, that a simple, full,
literal exposition of Æschylus' moral system would be
found to correspond, without any forcing of phrases,
with the catholic doctrine of sin, punishment, free-
will, and fate. That no man is compelled to sin ; that
sin is the act of a bad will ; that punishment is the
correlative of sin ; that suffering is discipline ; that
no inherited tendency to sin is too strong for a good
will ; that with God is no caprice nor tyranny : all this
is the faith of millions to-day. There is no literature
more melancholy, from end to end, than the Greek ;
but it is often with a gracious wistfulness : and there
is no literature more full of faith in a divine justice.
With Plato in his *Gorgias*, the great spirits of men
have constantly upheld the teaching, that to do evil is
worse than to suffer it : and that to go unpunished is
an injustice to the evil-doer. *Nulla poena, quanta
poena !* As Herbert said, the ' divine regiment,' the
government of God, is ' clad in simpleness and sad
events ' : and elsewhere he wrote a word of spiritual
cunning :

> ' life's poore span
> Make not an ell, by trifling in thy woe.'

It is Mr. Hardy's apparent denial of anything like
conscience in men, that makes his impressive argument so sterile : granted, that there is no sign of

conscious morality in the world, apart from man ; and
it is a vast concession ; yet, to place man upon the
level of other animals is to ignore the whole weight of
evidence from the history of mankind in general, and
of single men in particular ; and also to ignore difficulties connected with the nature of the mind, which
no man of commanding science has even professed to
explain.   When Amiel asked M. Renan, what he made
of sin ? M. Renan, with a sweet unreasonableness,
replied : ' Je crois bien qu'en effet je le supprime.'
That is practically Mr. Hardy's answer : and his view
of conscience is scarce more convincing, than that of
Swedenborg's men of medicine : who defined it to
be ' an uneasy pain, which seizes both the head and
the *parenchyma* of the heart, and thence the *epigastric*
and *hypogastric* regions beneath.'   The unhappy sentiments of Tess are attributed to a vague sense of social
misdemeanour, to a wandering drift of superstitious
ideas, to a childish misconception of her experience,
that ' liberal education ' : not to any deep cry from
the heart and soul, bearing true witness to the wrong,
that she had suffered.   It is a pity, that she was
ignorant of Hume's doctrine upon the nature of
chastity : it might have established her in a rational
content, and in ' a cool self-love.'   As it was, she did
but illustrate, in her darkling conscience, a great
sentence of Leo XIII. : *Ita magnam in animis coelesti
doctrina carentibus vim habuit natura rerum, memoria
originum, conscientia generis humani !*
   Mr. Hardy would not for a moment have literature,
restored to its freedom, ' exhibit lax views of that

purity of life upon which the well-being of society
depends ' ; but he pleads that, ' the position of man
and woman in nature, and the position of belief in the
minds of man and woman—things which everybody
is thinking but nobody is saying—might be taken up
and treated frankly.' But there is little advantage to
be gained, by showing the unsocial position of man
and woman, as nature regards them, to an age of social
thought and practice : it is like Diderot's exposition
of naked beatitude in the Pacific Isles. ' Men cannot
enjoy,' wrote Burke, ' the rights of an uncivil and of a
civil state together ' : looking back upon vast ages of
the world's history, Burke was but using the voice of
common sense, when he declared ; ' I have in my
contemplation the civil social man, and no other.'
No more than in his day, have we ' subtilized ourselves
into savages ' : like the Englishmen of his day, ' we
know that *we* have made no discoveries ; and we think
that no discoveries are to be made, in morality ' ; we,
too, as members of ' eternal society,' are loth ' to
separate and tear asunder the bands of our subordinate
community, and to dissolve it into an unsocial, uncivil, unconnected chaos of elementary principles.'
And the present age also has discovered, that ' men of
letters, fond of distinguishing themselves, are rarely
averse to innovation.' Mr. Hardy's writings are, in
the main, far too austere of tone, to expose him to
the least suspicion of a desire, to loosen the social ties
of life : yet I cannot conceive, what may be his design
in elaborately descanting upon the fact, that man and
woman in ' nature ' are not the same, as man and

woman in ' society.' Lucretius knew that : but he
drew thence the lesson, that with family life, and the
cessation from wild promiscuity of living, came the
first signs of social concord : no longer *Homo homini
lupus*, but *Homo res sacra homini*. Life ' according to
nature ' means many things : Aristotle at least saw in
the phrase nothing inconsistent with another phrase,
that ' man is by nature a social animal ' : just as Burke
declared him to be ' a religious animal.' It was reserved for a distinguished philosopher of our times, to
dictate the following delightful counsels : ' It is important,' writes Hartmann, ' to make the life of beasts
better known to our youth ; as the truest source of
pure nature, wherein youth may learn to understand
its true being, in its simplest form ; wherein to rest
and refresh itself, after the artificiality and deformity
of our social state.' Plato, on the other hand, somewhat mistrusted ' the wild beast in the soul,' already
there, and not rashly to be encouraged : and Dr.
Johnson's comment upon the German's advice would
probably surpass his sensible wrath against Rousseau.
There is a tendency in *Tess* to treat women, with a
curious lack of dignity : we hear of ' the charm which
is acquired by woman when she becomes part and
parcel of outdoor nature ' : and Angel Clare, at the
dairy farm in Var Vale, experienced an ' aesthetic,
sensuous, pagan pleasure in natural life and lush
womanhood ' : the latter phrase expressing, not a
simple buoyancy of spirits, enhanced by unsophisti-
cated life in the open air, among rural scenes and
duties, but a positive absence of any higher qualities.

The hunger to be rid of social hypocrisies has led to a mere materialism, in which neither material earth, nor material mankind, preserve their charm. This seeming declension from the hardly won, firm ground of social concord ; this lust after ruinous and abandoned ways ; compel a melancholy anger. To what end has the human race discovered, through ages of strife and struggle, the better way : if, provoked by its imperfections, men are to fall back into the old confusions ? But the sanctions of Christian marriage, the ethics of Christian civility, are something stern, you say, and austere : They are : do you expect much softness and much ease in an honourable life ? Boethius was wiser :

> ‘ *O felix hominum genus,*
> *Si vestros animos amor,*
> *Quo coelum regitur, regat !* ’

It may be presumptuous to require in a novel the rigour of a treatise : but Mr. Hardy himself has led us to require it of his novels. They are nothing, unless they be the outcome of his own most honest thought. It is little hindrance to us, if we miss the force of some rhetorical term in Seneca : but we are wholly thrown out of the way, if we miss the force of some logical term in Aristotle. Mr. Hardy has accustomed us to look for the same closely knit fabric of thought and word : but in this book, great as it yet is, there are many places, where *Tace ! dictum est Aristoteli* by Mr. Hardy ; in another sense to that, in which Abelard sang. Is it, that he is carrying out the polite doctrine : ‘ Nous devons la vertu à l’Éternel : mais nous avons

Q

droit d'y joindre, comme reprise personnelle, l'ironie ' ?
In that case, one is tempted to reply, with Valentine :
' Lass unsern Herrn Gott aus dem Spass': only
the most spiritual, or the most undisciplined, of
humourists, Plato or Heine, can be trusted with such
jesting.

It is hard, to feel bitterly against even so bitter a
book : it is harder to say anything, that can for an
instant move other minds, to share my view of it :
against the grandeur of such a book, criticism unadorned has the poorest of chances. Indeed, the
book and the age are in many ways good friends : for
both are full of humanitarian sentiment, often most
true and fine ; and both incline towards the same
philosophy.   The late Mr. Cotter Morison, in a book
of strenuous rhetoric, began a sentence with the words :
' But a deeper philosophy, or, rather, biology ' : the
popular voice speaks in that astounding substitution.
We have long since forgotten Hume's irony : ' All this
is metaphysics, you cry : That is enough : there needs
nothing more to give a strong presumption of falsity.'
And in matters of practical ethics, Mr. Hardy is no
solitary champion : Molière is grown obsolete ; his
Madelon is a woman of advanced thought, his Gorgibus
is antiquated. ' *Madelon.* " Ah, mon père ! ce que
vous dites là est du dernier bourgeois. Cela me fait
honte de vous ouïr parler de la sorte ; et vous devriez
un peu vous faire apprendre le bel air des choses."
Gorgibus. " Je n'ai que faire ni d'air ni de chanson.
Je te dis que le mariage est une chose sacrée, et que
c'est faire en honnêtes gens que de débuter par là."

'*Madelon.* " Mon Dieu ! que si tout le monde vous ressemblait un roman serait bientôt fini ! " '

Mansel, thirty years ago, speaking of a novel called *Recommended to Mercy*, observed : ' The moral that would be drawn up by the author may be conjectured from the title of the book ; that which will be drawn by many of its readers may be summed up in the comfortable doctrine of Hans Carvel's wife,—

' That if weak women went astray,
Their stars were more in fault than they.'

In truth, we much doubt the wisdom of the morality of drawing fictitious portraits of noble-minded and interesting sinners, by way of teaching us to feel for the sinner while we condemn the sin.'

Prior's lines have not lost all their point yet : though we do not speak of astrology, but of heredity. Astrology is indeed discredited : but is heredity proved ? Doubtless, from the days of Ezekiel and of Æschylus, men's minds have been occupied by the thought of transmitted tendencies and of vicarious sufferings : but only in our day has the creed of ' determinism ' taken body and form : and that, with a somewhat premature decision. Considering the great conflicts of opinion upon the matter of heredity, among leading men of science, we can only assume the truth of it, in any one form, at some risk of reputation to come. But Mr. Hardy keeps ever in our view the inherited impulses of Tess : by hints and fanciful suggestions, he turns our minds towards the knightly D'Urbervilles, men of violence and of blood, lawless, passionate, rude. Whether she throw her glove in Alec's face, or stab

him with a knife, we are led to look upon her, as an
inheritor of ancestral passions : society demands her
punishment, in reparation and in self-defence : but,
since she was at the mercy of her inherited nature, she
claims our pity and our pardon.   Certainly, no one
can read her story, and be unmoved :

> ' Io son fatta da Dio, sua mercè, tale,
>   Che la vostra miseria non mi tange,
>   Nè fiamma d'esto incendio non m'assale.'

So she seems to say, all through her troubled life : and
to take for epitaph :

> ' Weep only o'er my dust, and say, Here lies
>   To Love and Fate an equal sacrifice.'

Not indeed, ' so made by the compassion of God '
as to pass unscathed among the flames of this world :
but so made by the indifference of Nature, as to be
forced among them, to suffer them, yet to be at heart,
innocent and pure.

But, winning and appealing as she seems, there
remains in the background that haunting and disen-
chaunting thought, that upon the determinist principle,
she could not help herself : she fulfilled a mechanical
destiny.   There is nothing tragic in that, except by
an illusion : like any other machine, she ' did her
work,' and that is all.   Those, who held the automatic
theory of the lower animals, were yet compelled to
speak of them in the common, illogical language, as
capable of cognition : just so, Tess is pitiable, because
we retain the illusion of freedom.   Tragedy, said
Chaucer, versifying the old view of it,

'Tragedie is to sayn a certain storie,
As olde bookes maken us memorie,
Of him that stood in gret prosperitee,
And is yfallen out of high degree,
In to miserie, and endeth wretchedly.'

The tragedy of Tess does indeed rouse in us ' pity
and fear ' : it does indeed purge us of ' pity and fear ' :
but with what a parody of Aristotle !   For, as Butler
has it, ' Things are what they are, and the consequences of them will be what they will be ; why, then,
should we desire to be deceived ? '   Upon Mr. Hardy's
principles, there was no real struggle of the will with
adverse circumstance, no conflict of emotions, nor
battle of passions : all was fated and determined : the
apparent energies of will, regrets of soul, in Tess, were
but as the muscular movements of a dead body :
' Simulars ' of freedom and of life.   Our pity and our
fear are not purified merely : they are destroyed, and
no room is left for them : in Cudworth's phrase, we
have but ' Belluine Liberty and Brutish Force.'   It
may be urged, that in the very illusion lies the tragedy :
' All this passion, sorrow, and death, inevitable and
sure, to come upon one poor girl, whose struggles were
ordained by the same force, that ordained their vanity !
Is there no tragedy in that ? '   I can find none : I
can find in it nothing, but a reason for keeping unbroken silence.   Least of all, do I find in it an excuse
for setting up a scarecrow God, upon whom to vent our
spleen.   *Quid superbis, terra et cinis ?* asked *Ecclesiasticus* of man : but if dust and ashes be all, there is no
question more of pride : we had best read Hawthorne's

allegory, and say nothing.   It is in the conflicts of will
with will, and of force with force, that Tragedy finds
a voice :   men battling with the winds and waves, or
with the passions and desires ;   men played upon by
the powers of nature, or by the powers of mind ;   men
struggling with the powers known to science, or with
the powers known to conscience :   an eternal warfare,
and no illusion of battles in the clouds :   a theatre,
not of puppets, but of men.   If our will be no more
than a powerless yearning, life is a farce, much too
tedious to amuse.

It is not cheerful acquiescence in life, an oblivious
and partial view of it, that have marked the great vin-
dicators of human will, and therefore, of human
tragedy.   ' When I see the blindness and the misery
of man ;   when I survey the whole dumb universe,
and man without light, left to himself, and lost, as it
were, in this corner of the universe ;   not knowing who
has placed him here, what he has come to do, what
will become of him when he dies, and incapable of any
knowledge whatever ;   I fall into terror, like that of a
man who, having been carried in his sleep to an island
desert and terrible, should awake, ignorant of his
whereabouts, and with no means of escape ;   and
thereupon I wonder, how those in so miserable a state
do not fall into despair.'   That is Pascal :   this is
Newman.   ' Starting then with the being of a God,
. . . I look out of myself into the world of men, and
there I see a sight which fills me with unspeakable
distress.   The world seems simply to give the lie to
that great truth, of which my whole being is so full ;

and the effect upon me is, in consequence, as a matter
of necessity, as confusing as if it denied that I am in
existence myself. If I looked into a mirror, and did
not see my face, I should have the sort of feeling which
actually comes upon me, when I look into this busy
living world, and see no reflexion of its creator. This
is, to me, one of those great difficulties of this absolute
primary truth, to which I referred just now. Were it
not for this voice, speaking so clearly in my conscience
and my heart, I should be an atheist, or a pantheist,
or a polytheist, when I looked into the world. I am
speaking for myself only ; and I am far from denying
the real force of the arguments in proof of a God,
drawn from the general facts of human society
and the course of history, but these do not warm me
or enlighten me ; they do not take away the winter of
my desolation, or make the buds unfold and the leaves
grow within me, and my moral being rejoice. The
sight of the world is nothing else than the prophet's
scroll, full of " lamentations, and mourning, and woe." '
Then follows a period embracing, in sad and unsparing
detail, the sorrows of the world : with a somewhat
large experience of such sorrowful literature, I still
know nothing that approaches this confession of Newman, in its piercing apprehension of the world's innumerable sadness. It was no blindness to the facts
of life, that made it impossible, for Pascal and for
Newman, to draw such conclusions from the world, as
logic is forced to draw from *Tess*, upon a scrutiny of
each word and sentence. But without changing a
single incident of the story, it is possible to reject Mr,

Hardy's moral : read it apart from his commentary, and it loses nothing of its strength : rather, it gains much.   Tess is no longer presented to us, as pre-destined to her fate : she once more takes the tragic place.   Beginning in ' great prosperitee,' as a girl of generous thought and sentiment, rich in beauty, rich in the natural joys of life, she is brought into collision with the harshness of life : she may have inherited impulses, vehement abettors of her temptations : circumstances may be against her always : the conflict will be an agony between the world and the will.   Like Marty South, she might have been austerely strong, with a bitter maceration of her desires : like Teresa of the Carmelites, she might have learned to long for suffering or for death, *aut pati aut mori*, as a more joyous denial of joy, than any ' appetite for joy ' : with Miss Rossetti, she might have said, ' Bitterness that may turn to sweetness is better than sweetness that must turn to bitterness.'   Since she was so ' Hellenic,' she might have realized with the Greeks, that happi-ness is lower than beatitude, and prosperity than blessedness.   She did none of those things : the world was very strong ; her conscience was blinded and bewildered ; she did some things nobly, and some despairingly : but there is nothing, not even in studies of criminal anthropology or of morbid pathology, to suggest that she was wholly an irresponsible victim of her own temperament, and of adverse circumstances. *Oportet te transire per ignem et aquam, antequam veneris in refrigerium* : like Maggie Tulliver, Tess might have gone to Thomas à Kempis : one of the very few writers, whom experience does not prove untrue. She went through fire and water, and made no true use of them : she is pitiable, but not admirable.

Mr. Hardy's last book, then, contains much that may be disliked, much that may seem untrue, and much that may seem inartistic : but it is among the books of most ardent sincerity, that I have yet read. There is nothing in it capable of producing even a ' labefactation of principles ' : or, at the least, nothing directed to that end. Mr. Hardy's art is not of the sort described by Bishop Blougram :

> ' Our interest 's on the dangerous side of things.
> The honest thief, the tender murderer,
> The superstitious atheist, demirep
> That loves and saves her soul in new French books—
> We watch while these in equilibrium keep
> The giddy line midway : one step aside,
> They 're classed and done with.'

Tess is ' good, but not religious-good,' as a rustic casuist of Wessex puts it. Much hostile criticism comes of the eternal separation between man and man : that isolation, alone with his thoughts, in which each man lives, and which no intimacy can abolish. For, as Newman said in one of his Dublin lectures upon literature, all literature and style are personal, the expression of a personality : with the greatest pains, no reader can perfectly pass into the writer's mind : nor can the writer draw him in thither. And so, if I see in this or that passage of Mr. Hardy, what he has called ' an odd mixture of scientific earnestness and melancholy distrust of all things human,' my own temperament may disqualify me for a criticism of that mixture.   I will but say, that in the new battle between the philosophy of faith, and a philosophy of the senses, Mr. Hardy seems to take the vehement part of a Luther, Calvin,Knox,rather than the serene part of an Erasmus, Colet, More.   Yet he belongs to a nobler company of artists, than they who are simply clamouring for some new thing, and his works witness to his sincerity : *nemo enim illic vitia ridet, nec corrumpere et corrumpi saeculum vocatur.*   He has never condoned corruption, as *saeculum*, the spirit of the age : or, as the silly dialect of the day has it, as *fin de siècle.*   It is hard, indeed, to sympathize with much of his sentiment upon man's position in nature : as Carlyle said of the material world, ' mere circlings of force there, of iron negation, of universal death and merciless indifference': but its meditative grandeur is unquestionable.   Here are two passages, in which two aspects of it are seen : both prompted by the stars and night, to which, with their mistress or handmaid, Astronomy, he appears to have a devotion.   ' The sky was clear—remarkably clear—and the twinkling of all the stars seemed to be but throbs of one body timed by a common pulse. The North Star was directly in the wind's eye, and since evening the Bear had swung himself round it outwardly to the east, till he was now at a right angle with the meridian.   A difference of colour in the stars—oftener read of than seen in England—was really perceptible there.   The kindly brilliancy of Sirius pierced the eye with a steely glitter, the star called Capella was yellow, Aldebaran and Betelgueux shone with a fiery red.

' To persons standing alone on a hill during a clear
midnight such as this, the roll of the world eastward
is almost a palpable movement. The sensation may
be caused by the panoramic glide of the stars past
earthly objects, which is perceptible in a few minutes
of stillness, or by the better outlook upon space that
a hill affords, or by the wind, or by the solitude ; but
whatever be its origin, the impression of riding along
is vivid and abiding. The poetry of motion is a phrase
much in use, and to enjoy the epic form of that gratifi-
cation it is necessary to stand on a hill at a small hour
of the night, and, having first expanded with a sense of
difference from the mass of civilized mankind, who
are horizontal and disregardful of all such proceedings
at this time, long and quietly watch your stately progress through the stars. After such a nocturnal re-
connoitre among those astral clusters, aloft from the
customary haunts of thought and vision, some men
may feel raised to a capability for eternity at once.'

There is the beauty of night and stars, as our poor
eyes can see them, and our poor poetical imaginations
dream of them : but Astronomy is tragic : and Swithin
displayed with pride its tragedy to Viviette. He would
not let her call the actual universe ' grand.'

' The imaginary picture of the sky as the concavity
of a dome whose base extends from horizon to horizon
of our earth is grand, simply grand, and I wish I had
never got beyond looking at it in that way. But the
actual sky is a horror.' He dilated upon the monstrous
Immensities. ' There is a size at which dignity
begins ; further on there is a size at which grandeur

begins ; further on, there is a size at which solemnity begins ; further on, a size at which awfulness begins ; further on, a size at which ghastliness begins. That size faintly approaches the size of the stellar universe. So am I not right in saying that those minds who exert their imaginative powers to bury themselves in the depth of that universe merely strain their faculties to gain a new horror ? ' Then he dwells upon the ' weirdness ' and ' pitifulness ' of the decay of stars. ' Imagine them all extinguished, and your mind feeling its way through a heaven of total darkness, occasionally striking the black, invisible cinders of those stars. . . . If you are cheerful, and wish to remain so, leave the study of astronomy alone. Of all the sciences, it alone deserves the character of the terrible.' This is the truth of all that beauty, in which our deceived senses take unalloyed delight. And what becomes of Addison's hymn ? From such contemplations, Mr. Hardy turns away to earth :

> ' Your chilly stars I can forego,
> This warm, kind earth is all I know ' :

or perhaps,

> ' Not till the fire is dying in the grate,
> Look we for any kinship with the stars.'

And yet, from that ' heaven of total darkness ' there falls an horror upon earth also, chilling its warmth and kindness : and our dying fires do but remind us of the ' eternal ' fires, that also waste and die. It is in passages like these, that we feel the gloomy power of Mr. Hardy : such contemplations, and the pictures of human life drawn by such a contemplator, must be dignified, grand, solemn, if not awful and ghastly. The stars may look charming, and wonderful, and sublime, and so may human life : but look far and well into both, and you will be stricken with horror.

Both conclusions deal but with one side of the matter : Sir Isaac Newton is able to face the heavens, knowing their reality, and to say : *Elegantissima haecce solis, planetarum, et cometarum compages non nisi consilio et dominio entis intelligentis oriri potuit.* And Berkeley is no whit behind Mr. Hardy in grasping the doctrine of the heavens : ' Astronomy is peculiarly adapted to remedy a little and narrow spirit. . . . These ideas wonderfully dilate and expand the mind. There is something in the immensity of this distance that shocks and overwhelms the imagination ; it is too big for the grasp of a human intellect : estates, provinces, and kingdoms, vanish at its presence.' Lucretius also deplored, how the contemplation of *Nox et noctis signa severa* may bring enlightened minds back to the superstitions of religion : whilst the infinite spaces did but terrify Pascal.

When Oliver Madox Brown lay upon his death-bed, the first chapters of *Far from the Madding Crowd* were read to him : the story was appearing in the *Cornhill Magazine*, which had just refused a story of his own : ' No wonder,' the boy exclaimed, ' they did not want *my* writing ! ' Time has shown, that there is little writing by modern men, which is more wanted, more acceptable, than the writing of Mr. Hardy. Think what we may of his implicit philosophy, of its rationality and truth, we can hardly refuse our praise to a writer of so much power.   Like Crabbe's ideal poet :

> ' He loves the Mind, in all its modes, to trace,
> And all the Manners of the changing Race ;
> Silent he walks the Road of Life along,
> And views the aims of its tumultuous throng :
> He finds what shapes the Proteus-Passions take,
> And what strange waste of Life and Joy they make ' ;

and that, because

> ' 'Tis good to know, 'tis pleasant to impart,
> These turns and movements of the human Heart.'

Good to know, and pleasant to impart : no phrases of a more perfect precision could be found.   There is nothing so dreadful and so dark, that art cannot take pleasure in moulding it into fine form, nor the mind be bettered by the knowledge thus won.   In Mr. Hardy's fifteen books, there is a wealth of fine form, enclosing a wealth of good knowledge.

' If thou hast in thee any Country-Quicksilver,' come and watch the lives of country ' souls ' : find tragedy and comedy in poor men trudging to their work, along the lanes of Wessex : understand, in spite of Sappho, how even ' a peasant girl,' with no acquired courtliness, can ' charm the heart.'   The country folk of Mr. Hardy, with their Wessex homes and labours, are the material of his great achievements : of these he is a master, and his work in this kind will surely stand the test of time.   It is the work of long thought about familiar things : the two conditions of the best writing. There is much, that may grow dim with time, though to us it have a living brilliance : it is not within our

province to discuss that. But we have the right, looking back over the history of literature, and assaying
by that test the books of Mr. Hardy, to pronounce,
that if posterity care nothing for him, posterity will
have come to care nothing for many a name, which
generations of men have venerated. Not even in art,
is it ' in mortals to command success ' : but there is no
sphere of human action, in which they, who deserve
success, more commonly achieve it. Much, again, of
Mr. Hardy's work is an austere descant upon ' the
dust and ashes of things, the cruelty of lust, and the
fragility of love ' : unwelcome truths ; and not all the
truths, there are. But they are very old and very
grave truths : and Mr. Hardy presents them with a
consciousness of their greatness. By the severity of
thought and of style, which he rarely deserts, he takes
his place among those writers, who from the early
ages of literature have expressed in art a reasonable
sadness. That deep solemnity of the earth in its
woods, and fields, and lonely places, has passed into
his work : and when he takes it in hand, to deal with
the passions of men, that spirit directs and guides him.
I do not find his books quite free of all offence, of anything that can hurt and distress ; but I never find them
merely painful : their occasional offences are light
enough, and unessential ; the pain, they sometimes
give, is often salutary, even for those who still hold,
with Æschylus, to the truth of that ancient doctrine,
which makes the sorrow of the world, a discipline :
*The Gods are upon their holy thrones : the grace of the
Gods constraineth us.*

W. Strang. 09.

THE POETRY OF THOMAS HARDY

BY

J. E. BARTON

The published poetical works of Mr. Hardy have appeared in the order that follows :

Wessex Poems	1898
Poems of the Past and the Present . . .	1901
The Dynasts (Three Parts) . . .	1903-1908
Time's Laughing-Stocks	1909
Satires of Circumstance	1914
Moments of Vision	1917
Collected Poems (including, with slight revisions, all previous works except *The Dynasts*) .	1919
Late Lyrics and Earlier	1922

THE POETRY OF THOMAS HARDY

I

IN 1894, when Lionel Johnson's admirable chapters were first printed, Mr. Hardy had already disclosed his maturer powers as a novelist, but his genius as a poet was not yet revealed. This accident of chronology misled many readers, including some good critics ; and even to-day, when the published poems have attained impressiveness if only by their total bulk, it is a common mistake to approach them with the preconception that they are in some way subsidiary, or at best an aftermath, to the novels.

We can see, now, that the transition from fiction to verse had nothing abrupt. The continuous devotion to verse, which has marked Mr. Hardy's later years, is only the resumption of a primal, fitfully courted, and never quite neglected, love. If we had the poems alone, one reader here or there might conjecture : These are the poems of a novelist. If we had the novels alone, nobody could read them without declaring : These are essentially the novels of a poet. The poetic spirit inhabits almost every page of Mr. Hardy's prose. And the novels and the poems are so inseparable and complementary in their effect on the mind, that it would be idle to analyse their unity of power, in the hope of discovering where the novelist ends and the poet begins.

In both forms of art, Mr. Hardy has laid himself open to those imputations of ' pessimism,' with which we are tediously familiar, and to which indeed he has made some personal retort in the remarkable *Apology* prefixed to *Late Lyrics and Earlier*. But poetry has this advantage over fiction, that its challenge is more direct, and therefore more disconcerting. Stupid readers may enjoy a tale, in their way, without noting its moral or philosophic import. When they approach a poet, their first conscious aim is to extract what they call his ' ideas,' and to praise or reject him according as those ideas agree or disagree with their own. In dealing with Mr. Hardy's poems, this course is fatal ; or to put it more truly, this course is always fatal, but Mr. Hardy's poems illustrate the fatality in a peculiar degree. His view of the world is not conventional nor cheerful. Good souls, who vaguely imagine that poetry exists to confirm their own parochial complacency or bright orthodoxy, are shocked ; so shocked that in secret, probably, they wonder why so dangerous a writer enjoys so high a reputation. If they had enough intelligence to see how undermining he really is, they would write letters of protest to *The Times*.

These people have never learned, and never will learn, that when you *extract* a poet's ideas, they cease to be his. They cease to be poetic. You have committed the absurdity of trying to separate the matter from the form in a work of art. Instead of considering the lilies of the field how they grow, you are examining specimens in what botanists call a herbarium. Everybody knows the sort of volumes that apply the herbarium method to the judgment of poetry, and can guess their devastating titles : *Tennyson as a Teacher, Sheaves from Shelley*. No doubt some kinds of verse invite and deserve the herbarium method, but that is only because they are bad kinds : verse that is not poetry at all, because the ideas it embodies are not subtle and implicit, but crude and undissolved. Nobody will ever compile a book called *Hope from Hardy*. But let us get one point clear : the people who find no pleasure in Mr. Hardy's poetry, because it is ' pessimistic,' are deluded in thinking they enjoy Browning's poetry because it abounds in optimism. They miss the actual poetry in both poets alike.

The unconventional outlook of Mr. Hardy as a poet only makes him a test case of the general proposition, that poetry is not to be judged as an answer to a request for some map or chart, brought up to date, of human destiny with its problems and uncertainties. ' Their doctrines are but tentative, and are advanced with little eye to a systematized philosophy warranted to lift " the burthen of the mystery " of this unintelligible world. The chief thing hoped for them is that they and their utterances may have dramatic plausibility enough to procure for them, in the words of Coleridge, " that willing suspension of disbelief for the moment which constitutes poetic faith." ' This attitude, which Mr. Hardy deliberately assigns to his supernatural Intelligences in *The Dynasts*, may symbolize not unfairly his own attitude, as the poet-spectator of man's relation to the universe. Poetry should always be tentative, more or less ; for the prime concern of a poet is to be true to his own temperament. Even the ethical value of poetry, in the long run, depends not at all on its incorporation of stock moralities, but on the power and sincerity with which it achieves that temperamental order of truth. The undogmatic sort of truth, which poetry supplies, can only be apprehended as it is created : by means of imagination and emotion. The artist can only be judged through the medium of his art. Truth in poetry is by no means the same thing as truth in science, or in theology. Poetically, the book of Ecclesiastes ranks high among the books of the Bible ; it ranks exceedingly low as a provider of what were once described, in a Puritan tract, as ' hooks and eyes for believers' breeches.'

A prosaic and literal mind, if it were also logical, would go on to ask why Mr. Hardy should continue till extreme old age, writing poetry which on the face of it amounts to a gospel of suicide. Why, indeed ? And how comes it that these suicidal pages are packed with so strange and convincing a passion of life ? The answer is, that what a *poet* thinks, in his poetry, is not to be found at all within the sphere of the *thinker*, so-called. The poet's belief is the artist's sort of belief : a passionate apprehension of life for its own sake, which creates eternity out of a moment of time, and thus rises to a plane on which art becomes, not perhaps identical with religion, but certainly parallel to it.

The poetry of so profound a poet as Mr. Hardy is not an accomplishment, nor an adjunct, but the one central thing in him. As a reader, your function is to let him absorb you, for the time being, into the vortex of that central experience. When we speak of the beauty of such poems, we do not mean agreeableness in the easy sense, nor comfortable delineations of the world : ' beauty ' is simply a name we give to the thrill of vital contact between the poet's spirit and ours. This, at any rate, is the modern, and what I may define as the *intrinsic*, conception of poetic beauty ; and whether you accept it or no, it has the advantage of covering all the cases, whereas other æsthetic theories of poetry cover some cases only.

No writer has excelled Mr. Hardy in the power of convincing us that he writes from experience. We feel that poetry is for him a mode of being, rather than a trick of utterance. The surface of his verse, as we shall see, is obstinate, knotty, and close-grained. It presents those ' signs of discovery, of effort and contention towards a due end,' which Pater regarded as the ' special charm ' in a certain order of style. The ' charm of ease ' is not to be looked for. But all truly destined readers of Mr. Hardy are induced in time, with whatever reluctance, to lay aside their prepossessions of opinion or taste, and to emulate the poet's own faculty of absorption.

An ordered review of Mr. Hardy's poetic volumes, from *Wessex Poems* to *Late Lyrics*, is beyond the scope of this essay. In any case such treatment would be inappropriate. Poets who begin to publish quite early, and unload their batches of new verse methodically at intervals through life, may lend themselves to the chronological diagnosis which modern critics affect. But Mr. Hardy's work is not readily dateable in that fashion. His early verse has not appeared at all, except in so far as it has passed the scrutiny of his riper judgment. New volumes have contained old poems. And even if we arranged all the lyric pieces—where other evidence of date is lacking—in the order of their publication, the result is likely to baffle those readers who plume themselves on tracing a main line of development. The twenty-odd years, it is true, have seen a continuous growth of variety and poetic content. As a metrist, Mr. Hardy's boldness of invention has increased with age. But on the whole his lyric work is surprisingly homogeneous in its inspiration. There are no points or stages at which he seems to break conspicuously new ground, whether of substance or of treatment. On the other hand, he escapes the fate of so many poets, whose mature technique not quite disguises their loss of vernal vigour : reminding us of first-class oarsmen, who keep their form to the end of a race, though a close spectator knows they are pumped out. To sustain their poetry, over many years, is reserved for the austerer poets. Poets of a luscious gift may learn restraint when they have lost their magic. Their best wisdom is to die young. Poets like Milton, or

Wordsworth, or Mr. Hardy, owe their poetic longevity to a restraint which is inherent, not acquired. They have missed certain moments of ecstasy, but find their compensation in a gain of staying power. Emotion and reflection are balanced. Their poetic imagination is consistent and durable, because it drapes always a vertebrate anatomy of thought.

Essentially true to its author in conception, material, and texture, *The Dynasts* is nevertheless regarded, by most admirers, as a *tour de force*, exotic to the main body of Mr. Hardy's poetry. In a sense, it stands midway between his poetry and his fiction. The Napoleonic menace, disturbing the orbit of quiet lives and pastoral scenes, provides a recurrent theme or echo in several of the novels and tales. To raise this favoured subject to the epic plane, where terrestrial throes may be surveyed with poetic philosophy, and qualified by the commentary or intervention of universal intelligences, was a characteristic ambition. The creation of ' an epic-drama ' so novel in form, on a scale so imposing, and fortified by close historical research, might be expected to interrupt or divert that continuity, which has just been remarked, in Mr. Hardy's lyric expression. But the innate sense of design, observed by Lionel Johnson in the Wessex novels, enabled Mr. Hardy to resume the lyric form in its true proportions, in spite of long preoccupation with a vast panoramic scheme. The truth is that from the beginning, both in prose and verse, Mr. Hardy has always added a cosmic sweep of imagination to his close grip of the immediate and visible. Were he less human, his turn for immensities and abstractions—however personified—might have lured him into regions of arid vagueness, where art withers. In *The Dynasts* he gave free rein to his synoptic and metaphysical genius; but this development, fortunately, has only tinged the later poetry, without overweighting it.

Indirectly, the writing of *The Dynasts* could not fail to affect his subsequent style, by enlarging his verbal resources. Its versatility of diction is prodigious. In this enormous composition, he presses into service all conceivable turns of speech. Uncouth or musical, colloquial or grandiose, drab or romantic—all come alike to him, and are hammered to his purposes.

We are sometimes told that Mr. Hardy is deficient in spontaneous lyric art. This is true enough, if it implies that the twentieth century is not the Elizabethan age; or that careless raptures are hardly to be demanded from a poet of reserves and of second thoughts. But many poems could be quoted, which have caught a modern melancholy in lines of crystal concentration. *Regret not Me*, for example, has the true lyric purity, with a cumulative appeal that partial quotation must impair:

> ' Now soon will come
> The apple, pear, and plum,
> And hinds will sing, and autumn insects hum.

> ' Again you will fare
> To cider-makings rare,
> And junketings ; but I shall not be there.

'Yet gaily sing,
   Until the pewter ring,
Those songs we sang when we went gipsying.

   'And lightly dance
   Some triple-timed romance
In coupled figures, and forget mischance ;

   'And mourn not me
   Beneath the yellowing tree ;
For I shall mind not, slumbering peacefully.'

Another instance is *The Farm-Woman's Winter*,
with its characteristic third line :

'If seasons all were summers,
      And leaves would never fall,
   And hopping casement-comers
      Were foodless not at all,
   And fragile folk might be here
      That white winds bid depart ;
   Then one I used to see here
      Would warm my wasted heart ! '

A lyric quality, not less clear if more diffused, may
be found in numberless verses of a narrative or reflec-
tive intention, such as *Night in the Old Home*, or
The Clock Winder, with its pensive monotone :

'. . . Up, up from the ground
   Around and around
   In the turret stair
   He clambers, to where
   The wheelwork is,
   With its tick, click, whizz,
   Reposefully measuring
   Each day to its end
   That mortal men spend
   In sorrowing and pleasuring.
   Nightly thus does he climb
   To the trackway of Time.' . . .

No poet is more sensible of the burden of modernity. Introspection, he knows, must check the purely instinctive gush of song. The 'mindless outpourings' of childhood, in the 'drowsy calm' of *Afternoon Service at Mellstock*, are recalled without the sentimentalizings to which an inferior poet might yield ; but

> '. . . I am not aware
> That I have gained by subtle thought on things
> Since we stood psalming there.'

Mr. Hardy's poetry admits the latter-day disease of self-consciousness, but his inborn hatred of cant or moral rhetoric gives to all his utterances the stamp of something fundamental. Many of them have the acid flavour we should expect from one who declares himself always the 'tart foe of smugness.' His view of social conventions, as an artist, sums up and alchemizes the scientific thought of his epoch. He avoids, I need not say, that shallow Bohemianism of thought which has long become a counter-convention among poetasters ; but the standard morals of society are always viewed, in his poetry as in his fiction, from the outside. He holds up no banner of rebellion against them. He can see that on the whole they are a good safe thing for little people ; but he regards them as the modern naturalist might regard the inherited habits of the bower-bird, or the agitations of an ant-hill. Mr. Hardy is a democratic poet, in so far as his poetic psychology disregards class distinctions ; but like all great poets without exception, he is an individualist. His deep instinct of pity is

directed to the individual ; and when with a telling
word he flouts some crude social dogma, he seems
to be saying : These rules are well enough for those
who have not been trapped and hurt within their
meshes, but I am thinking of this victim who *is* hurt
and trapped ! He perceives also that what may be
good collective morality is not necessarily conducive
to the highest life of the rare people who are capable
of great emotions. The delicate satire of *The Conformers* puts well his sense of the contrast. ‘ Stolen
trysts ’ are now to be replaced by lawful cohabita-
tion ‘ in a villa chastely grey ’ ; so that

> ‘ When down to dust we glide
> Men will not say askance,
> As now : “ How all the country side
> Rings with their mad romance ! ”
> But as they graveward glance
> Remark : “ In them we lose
> A worthy pair, who helped advance
> Sound parish views.” ’

It would be misleading to call Mr. Hardy a revolutionary. He is a revolutionary artist—by no means
the same thing. *An Invitation to the United States*
is rejected courteously but definitely. Even if that
new world tells the truth in claiming to be free from
the ‘ long drip of human tears,’ he shrinks

> ‘ to seek a modern coast
> Whose riper times have yet to be.’

As artist, he prefers an old world, whose accumulated tragedies he can count as part of his own experience. He is not one of those modernists who

dispense with the past. All survivals of perished man, all root paganisms of thought and custom, intrigue him. No other poet comes near Mr. Hardy, in his power of linking human life with its own remoter vestiges, or with the age-long earth whose outshapings, here and there, disclose them. His prose has nothing more wonderful, in its way, than the short piece entitled *A Tryst at an Ancient Earth-work*. All readers are familiar with his appetite for prehistoric and Roman traces on Wessex soil. In the poetry, it appears not only by way of particular subjects or titles—*The Roman Road*, *The Roman Gravemound*, *By the Barrows*, *By the Runic Stone*— but repeatedly, as an intensifying accessory to living drama. Ghosts of the past are habitual dwellers in Mr. Hardy's poems. He is so susceptible to history that no eventful region or site can exist for him, without its own impalpable and ' filmy ' emanations. A late poem of weirdly Biblical fancy, *Jezreel*, conjectures that even ' war-men at this end of time,' in such a place, may be aware of ' strange things and spectral.'

II

Over his own countryside, as we see it in the poems, Mr. Hardy has so established his intellectual dominion that for us it will always hereafter wear the unmistakable lineaments of his mind. This is the true task of the artist. In youth, we admire art because it reminds us of nature. In our riper development, we admire nature in so far as it reminds us of art. The world of the novels and marvellous short stories reappears, with enchanting new vividness, in the poems. To glance into their contents pages at random—*The Dead Quire, Seen by the Waits, A Trampwoman's Tragedy, The Dance at the Phoenix*—is to renew our imaginative experience of a rural world, once for all visualized by great art, and therefore more real than anything mere knowledge could create. Church choirs and country dances, shadows of the graveyard yew, rustic quaintnesses and heart-aches, the spreading heath whose colour is lost in a sense of undulation and elemental space—such things are touched again with that romantic hand, so stubbornly individual yet so intensely local, and gain in poignant power, if that were possible, from the poetic brevity with which their significance is distilled.

The pregnancy of Mr. Hardy's titles must often have been noted. They communicate not only local, but moral and dramatic atmosphere: *The Temporary*

*the All, The Death of Regret, Beyond the Last Lamp,
The End of the Episode, Rain on a Grave, On the
Departure Platform, The Blinded Bird, He fears his
Good Fortune, The Vampirine Fair, Middle-Age Enthusiasms.* How precisely a title-phrase can reflect
the half-tones of a poem itself, one verse from the
last-named piece may show :

> ' We joyed to see strange sheens
> Leap from quaint leaves in shade :
> A secret light of greens
> They 'd for their pleasure made.
> We said—" We 'll set such sorts as these ! "
> We knew with night the wish would cease.'

Some people would describe as ' morbid ' the power
to endue quite innocent aspects of nature (as they
seem to us) with some sinister motive. No doubt
there is always something abnormal in the kind of
imagination which can *drench* external things with a
subjective and personal essence. Coleridge had that
kind of imagination ; and so, in a lesser degree, had
Edgar Allan Poe. Call it morbid if you will ; but
whether you admire this capacity in Mr. Hardy or
not, you will hardly deny that it is native to his mind.
He stands *In a Wood*, and is aware of the fight for
existence among the envious trees :

> ' Touches from ash, O wych,
>   Sting you like scorn !
> You too, brave hollies, twitch
>   Sidelong from thorn.
> Even the rank poplars bear
> Lothly a rival's air,
> Cankering in black despair
>   If overborne.'

This obliqueness of view, this looking askance even at the life of trees, is no studied perversity. It really is Mr. Hardy's temperamental standpoint: and what is more, it presents just that side of reality from which most of us avert our gaze, comfortably unaware of our own disingenuousness. Nature's indifference to man's moods or creeds, time's havoc, God's automatism, the chilling of fancy by realization—these aspects of life elicit some of the finest of the poems. But to say this, of course, is not to describe the poems themselves. What raises them to poetry is their direct and clear emotion—the more felt, by reason of its restrained expression.

If a single poem were to be chosen as a sort of manifesto—a statement of what (if we were not talking of poetry) might be called the ' position ' of Mr. Hardy's mind—I fancy it would be *The Sign-Seeker*. In this masterpiece of poetic statement he speaks for man, as the intellectual heir of the ages, from whom the vision of faith has been withheld :

'. . . There are who, rapt to heights of trance-like trust,
These tokens claim to feel and see,
Read radiant hints of times to be—
Of heart to heart returning after dust to dust.

' Such scope is granted not to lives like mine . . .
I have lain in dead men's beds, have walked
The tombs of those with whom I had talked,
Called many a gone and goodly one to shape a sign,

' And panted for response. But none replies ;
No warnings loom, nor whisperings
To open out my limitings,
And Nescience mutely muses : When a man falls he lies.'

S

In *Shut out that Moon*, the same mood becomes more lyrically personal :

> ' Close up the casement, draw the blind,
>   Shut out that stealing moon,
> She wears too much the guise she wore
>   Before our lutes were strewn
> With years-deep dust, and names we read
>   On a white stone were hewn.

> ' . . . Within the common lamp-lit room
>   Prison my eyes and thought ;
> Let dingy details crudely loom,
>   Mechanic speech be wrought :
> Too fragrant was Life's early bloom,
>   Too tart the fruit it brought ! '

In a similar vein, even those who are prepared to refute *Yell'ham-Wood's Story* must regard it as a masterly miniature of style :

> ' Coomb-Firtrees say that Life is a moan,
>   And Clyffe-hill Clump says " Yea ! "
> But Yell'ham says a thing of its own :
>   It 's not " Gray, gray
>   Is Life alway ! "
>   That Yell'ham says,
> Nor that Life is for ends unknown.

> ' It says that Life would signify
>   A thwarted purposing :
> That we come to live, and are called to die.
>   Yes, that 's the thing,
>   In fall, in spring,
>   That Yell'ham says :—
> " Life offers—to deny ! " '

Just praise has been accorded to Mr. Hardy's gift of ' under-statement.' This self-control, which always adds solidity to speech of any kind, is never absent from his best work. How reticent, and therefore how moving, the last verse of his memorial poem, *Before Marching and After* !

' When the heath wore the robe of late summer,
   And the fuchsia-bells, hot in the sun,
   Hung red by the door, a quick comer
   Brought tidings that marching was done
   For him who had joined in that game over-seas
   Where Death stood to win, though his name was to borrow
   A brightness therefrom not to fade on the morrow.'

The thrill of grief is raised to monumental beauty, so that we feel there is something *final* about it. Several poems of the series dated 1912-13 have this character. The poem called *Lament*, realistic in detail, is supremely felt, most dignified, and strikes not a note of stressed or false pathos.

Of his love poems, few are more affecting than *In Death Divided*, with its second stanza closing in a miraculous last line :

   ' No shade of pinnacle or tree or tower,
       While earth endures,
     Will fall on my mound and within the hour
       Steal on to yours ;
     One robin never haunt our two green covertures.'

The author of such verse is no thin-lipped sage, built only for what he defines as ' crooked thoughts on life in the sere.' He has blood, affection, sex, with all those sensuous perceptions and convivial responses that are necessary to the artist, though they may be unnecessary to the philosopher. His alleged pessimism is not at all inhuman. When he has *A*

Merrymaking in Question, he wants his fiddle, his dance, and his ' mead, cider, and rum.' The head-stones that mock him, and the gargoyles that ' mouth the tune ' instead, are not the fantasy of a mental dyspeptic. They are the disillusion of a nature endowed for joy, but acquainted with tragic springs. He has found, as Shakespeare found, that enjoyment and suffering are twin capacities of the soul, and that only suffering teaches the poet to plumb reality.

Ironies of circumstance, as we might expect, abound in the poems not less than in the novels. It does not surprise us that *The Two Rosalinds*—the actress charmer of long ago, and the hag hawking theatre programmes—turn out to be the same person. Coincidences and contradictions of the ironic type attract Mr. Hardy even in trivial instances. *Architectural Masks*, for example, are houses inhabited by the wrong people : vulgarians in a Tudor manor house, taste and refinement in a hideous villa.

Irony of some kind is always visible in Mr. Hardy's poetic humour, with its tang of rustic dryness. No doubt he enjoys his own ferocity, in slighter pieces that avoid the universal intention of serious poetry. Lionel Johnson goes far, in interpreting this special mood of Mr. Hardy's as ' an uncanny sort of pleased and sly malevolence.' In a sentimental age, cynical veracity has its uses. Some of the rhymes called *Satires of Circumstance*, that conclude the volume so named—thumbnail episodes unsparing in their realism —were not penned, I imagine, without a caustic chuckle. The man *In the Cemetery* points to the mothers squabbling over the identity of their respective infants' graves : the truth being that

> ' all their children were laid therein
> At different times, like sprats in a tin.
> And then the main drain had to cross,
> And we moved the lot some nights ago,
> And packed them away in the general foss
> With hundreds more. But their folks don't know,
> And as well cry over a new-laid drain
> As anything else, to ease your pain ! '

Refreshingly horrid, too, is the anecdote of *The Curate's Kindness.* Bound for the workhouse along with his wife, a poor old man consoles himself by the thought that husbands and wives, in that well-ordered establishment, will occupy different wings. Suddenly arrives a young parson, flushed with the joy of philanthropic meddling, and tells the party that ' the harsh regulation is altered ' : so that wife and husband may now harry each other till death. The pathos of the ballad turns mainly on the fact that our old man is already in the workhouse vehicle, and has lost the chance of drowning himself. This piece may be commended to reciters at village concerts, by way of antidote to G. R. Sims or Ella Wheeler Wilcox.

Other good grim jests are the lines beginning ' *Ah, are you digging on my grave ?* ' with its admirable climax, and the stanzas about *The Levelled Churchyard*, where corpses and epitaphs are reduced to embarrassing confusion by what is known in the jargon of architects as a ' thorough ' restoration.

The final petition might well be incorporated in our
Litany :

> ' From restorations of Thy fane,
>   From smoothings of Thy sward,
> From zealous churchmen's pick and plane,
>   Deliver us, good Lord ! '

Written many years ago, but once more up to date
in its application, is the frolic on a single rhyme,
The Respectable Burgher on the Higher Criticism.
The burgher, having heard what reverend dignitaries
have to say about their own creeds, is impelled to
the decision :

> ' Since thus they hint, nor turn a hair,
>   All church-going will I forswear,
>   And sit on Sundays in my chair,
>   And read that moderate man, Voltaire.'

This sardonic temper of mind, expressed in its
various range from lofty despair to biting wit, is
the side of Mr. Hardy best known to his casual readers.
But the central Hardy, the Hardy with a message
(for those whose appetite for ' messages ' must be
appeased), is the poet who assigns eternal value to
great moments of experience, as Keats saw eternal
beauty in the arrested idyll on a Greek vase. When
Keats proclaims that a thing of beauty is a joy for
ever, he means literally what he says. He does not
mean only that agreeable things linger agreeably in
the memory even when they are faded. He means
that beauty, in the artist's sense, is something not
corruptible by time. No modern poet has vindicated
this standpoint more keenly than Mr. Hardy. The

lover in that fascinating soliloquy, *To Meet or Otherwise*, decides that he will ' sally and see the girl of his dreams,' despite the chastening reflection that life is short.

> ' By briefest meeting something sure is won :
>> It will have been :
> Nor God nor Demon can undo the done,
>> Unsight the seen,
> Make muted music be as unbegun,
>> Though things terrene
> Groan in their bondage till oblivion supervene.'

The substance of this thought lies deeper than *carpe diem*. Mr. Hardy neither cries with Browning, ' Leave " now " for dogs and apes,' nor advises with Herrick, ' Gather ye rosebuds while ye may.' He says what is more exactly true, for the modern mind, than either. He says to us : Seize *quality* from this world of material standards, and in so far as you are doing that, you may defy time, fate, orthodoxy, and all the furies !

In *The Minute before Meeting* he gives another turn to the same idea :

> ' I would detain
> The few clock-beats that part us ; rein back Time,
> And live in close expectance never closed,
> In change for far expectance closed at last ;
> So harshly has expectance been imposed
> On my long need while these slow blank months passed.'

Those last four lines startle us with a sense of familiarity. They are lines which Shakespeare forgot to write in one of his Sonnets. Here the supreme moment is consciously weighed : to encounter supreme moments unwittingly—as the poet realizes in *Best Times*—is tragic.

This pivotal theme of Mr. Hardy's poetry has found no simpler rendering than his memorable lyric, *Great Things*; a poem most typical of the principle that ideas in poetry should not be abstract, but implicit in sensuous and concrete images. He looks back on symbolic hours of life's high-water mark : cider at the wayside hostelry, the nightlong dance, the secret love-meeting : and concludes with a true poet's defiance :

> ' Will these be always great things,
>   Great things to me ?
> Let it befall that one will call
>   " Soul, I have need of thee ! "
> What then ? Joy-jaunts, impassioned flings,
>   Love and its ecstasy,
> Will always have been great things,
>   Great things to me.'

To the moralist, who might ask by what criterion these great things are measured, Mr. Hardy would probably return the intrinsic poet's answer, that life is its own valuer. His qualitative sense of life is suggested with extraordinary power in a poem of the 1913 series, *At Castle Boterel*; a poem condensing so much of his atmosphere, passion and cadence that it may almost seem to epitomize him.

Vitality is never explicable, but it is significant that Mr. Hardy's continuous vitality as a poet is both nourished and revealed by his abiding freshness of observation. Wordsworth at the age of seventy-five could note, as for the first time, the beauty of the mountain-daisy's ' star-shaped shadow, thrown on the smooth surface of a naked stone.' Mr. Hardy, still more advanced in years, is similarly impressionable. He has kept himself imaginatively young, not only by obeying Wordsworth's precept of keeping the eye on the object, but by living close to his object all the time. Like an old tree, the older he gets, the further he pushes his roots into his own soil. Too often the young modern poet, emboldened by slight fame, is drawn to a metropolis, lives in a coterie, lectures round the planet, and wins his way simultaneously to public limelight and poetic perdition. To poetry, at any rate, metropolitanism and cosmopolitanism are fatal. When the League of Nations gets into full swing, it may give us many things. Poetry will not be one of them. Mr. Hardy has brooded over Wessex until its very soul exhales under his nostrils. He has watched the passage of the generations, the flowing away of life, time's incrustations or hollowings, as they only can be watched in some quiet provincial region. Intimacy with tangible things has been his sheet-anchor. With the Gospel, he seems to praise those people whose singleness of mind impels them to fix their thought and emotion, steadily, on one simple object at a time : like the labouring man *In the British Museum*, who gazes at the base of an Athenian column, and cannot get over the fact that the stone he sees ' once echoed the voice of Paul.' Mr. Hardy, by this silent and intense watching, from youth to patriarchal old age, has attained a form of second sight. Milton showed

judgment, when he associated ' something like prophetic strain ' with a knowledge of ' every star ' and
of ' every herb that sips the dew.'

The basis of poetic observation is art, not science.
Tennyson may remind us, legitimately and vividly
in the context, that ' ash-buds in the front of March '
are black : but editors are misguided when they
define this piece of observation as poetic. Poetic
observation is not to be confused with amateur botany.
Few people, it is true, work up the energy to scruti-
nize ash-buds ; but the mere knowledge that ash-
buds have a black period is well within the compass
of any person whom we might describe (malevo-
lently) as well-informed. Poetic observation consists in seeing what all men have seen, but seeing it
with a difference : seeing it with love, noting it emo-
tionally. *The Five Students* is a short poem that
covers the human seasons. On a bright spring
morning,

> ' The sparrow dips in his wheel-rut bath.'

In autumn,

> ' The leaf drops : earthworms draw it in
> At night-time noiselessly.'

You and I have seen the things a hundred times. The
poet sees them with a rich fervour, and so rescues
them from transience. In this poetic sense, Mr.
Hardy is devoted to the ' innocent creatures,' as he
calls them, that creep, flutter, or fly. He likes to
think of himself as dying

> ' during some nocturnal blackness, mothy and warm,
> When the hedgehog travels furtively over the lawn.'

He invests with tender romance the 'hopping case-ment-comers,' the 'one robin' that will never haunt love's divided graves, and the 'little ball of feather and bone' which, while it lived, was Shelley's sky-lark.

III

Isolated study of a great poet's technique—as if
points of style were only attributes or accidents—
leads to error. It may not be quite so fallacious as
the consideration of ideas, apart from form ; but it
is only permissible to critics who recognize how pro-
visional, at best, such analysis must be. Let us then
forget, for the moment, that Mr. Hardy is a poet,
and regard his poems solely as exercises in descriptive writing. From this standpoint, no competent
reader can fail to be astounded, time after time, by
their manipulative skill, their virtuosity of exact
phrase. *Old Furniture* recalls past owners :

> ' I see the hands of the generations
>   That owned each shiny familiar thing
>   In play on its knobs and indentations,
>   And with its ancient fashioning
>   Still dallying :
>
> ' Hands behind hands, growing paler and paler,
>   As in a mirror a candle-flame
>   Shows images of itself, each frailer
>   As it recedes, though the eye may frame
>   Its shape the same.
>
> ' On the clock's dull dial a foggy finger,
>   Moving to set the minutes right
>   With tentative touches that lift and linger
>   In the wont of a moth on a summer night,
>   Creeps to my sight.'

In *The Convergence of the Twain* a sunken liner is imagined :

' Steel chambers, late the pyres
Of her salamandrine fires,
Cold currents thrid, and turn to rhythmic tidal lyres.

' Over the mirrors meant
To glass the opulent
The sea-worm crawls—grotesque, slimed, dumb, indifferent.

' Jewels in joy designed
To ravish the sensuous mind
Lie lightless, all their sparkles bleared and black and blind.

' Dim moon-eyed fishes near
Gaze at the gilded gear
And query : " What does this vaingloriousness down here ? "

Or take this passage from *The Pedigree* :

' The uncurtained panes of my window-square let in the watery
light
Of the moon in its old age :
And green-rheumed clouds were hurrying past where mute
and cold it globed
Like a drifting dolphin's eye seen through a lapping wave.'

In simile and metaphor, Mr. Hardy's modern range of imagery is always supported by a classic avoidance of the obscure. The paradox of Swinburne's *Poems and Ballads*, in a mid-Victorian society, appeals to him

' as though a garland of red roses
Had fallen about the head of some smug nun.'

Shakespeare too was no doubt an exotic in his day :

' So, like a strange bright bird we sometimes find
To mingle with the barn-door brood awhile,
Then vanish from their homely domicile—
Into man's poesy, we wot not whence,
    Flew thy strange mind,
Lodged there a radiant guest, and sped for ever thence.'

At no period has Mr. Hardy accepted any academic standard of poetic diction. Since *The Dynasts*, he has moved with complete assurance as a cosmopolitan among words. The later nineteenth century saw a phase of incalculable change in the English language. Modern thought and discovery had brought in a deluge of new names for things new or old. In words, as in society, a fusion of classes was at work. Nothing can abolish the distinction between words of emotional value, available for poetry, and words too hard and specific for the poet's use. But this broad distinction, so essential in theory, is highly elusive in practice. The emotional value of a word is fluid, not static. Words answer to things ; and novelties of language embody fresh experience, or readjusted vision, of life itself. Modern poets, in a world of changing susceptibilities, must feel their way to new verbal valuations. Stevenson declared the word ' hatter ' to be impossible for emotional verse. Mr. Hardy's poetic lexicon, to say the least, is more elastic. A word like ' waggonette ' has no terrors for him, even in a poem of profound feeling. He does not shun the unusual word. He stalks it, and if it will serve his turn, he takes it captive, sometimes with brutal lack of ceremony. He is a tyrant, who yokes his strange and intractable verbal forms into teams of startling new beauty.

Addiction to clanging Latinisms may disconcert the mealy-mouthed, but will seem natural to those who discern the Roman affinities of Mr. Hardy's mind. Laboriously but triumphantly evolved, his style presents an original synthesis of classically-derived and strong native elements, precisely suited to his packed and sinewy habit of thought. For twentieth-century poetry, an expanded vocabulary is inevitable. On what lines such expansion may proceed, no writer has indicated more suggestively. At an age when genius itself might well have stereotyped its coinage of speech, Mr. Hardy is still audaciously eclectic. Conventional taste, which makes a wry face at the unfamiliar, can find in his verse innumerable words and phrases that will stick in its gullet. Readers brought up in a smooth tradition, and coming as novices to Mr. Hardy, will admire such a lyric as *In Death Divided*, but tell us they do not like the word ' covertures ' in the line already quoted. For those who can breathe the air of his style, the pleasure offered by that special word is exquisite. The disagreement may be less a matter of taste than of acclimatization. His warmest votaries would admit that sometimes Mr. Hardy lapses into mannerism, and gives us eccentric or heavy words without the inspiration to carry them off. But sooner or later we discover that most of his verbal irregularities are not capricious, nor extraneous to the style itself. They indicate, rather, a supersaturation of the subject-matter by an intensely personal quality of thought.

With all his reserve, Mr. Hardy can utter phrases violent in their impact, or savagely condensed. The disillusioned bridegroom threw himself

> ' Over the slimy harbour wall.
>   They searched, and at the deepest place
>   Found him, with crabs upon his face.'

When life's show is over, *Exeunt Omnes*, and the poet's world looks like a deserted fair-ground :

> ' There is an air of blankness
>   In the street and the littered spaces ;
> Thoroughfare, steeple, bridge and highway
>   Wizen themselves to lankness ;
>   Kennels dribble dankness.'

The art of the novelist often comes out, in the mastery with which a few lines of verse transfix the core of a human situation. Two little stanzas, *The Moon looks in*, imprison a microcosm of tragedy :

> ' I have risen again
>   And awhile survey
>   By my chilly ray
>   Through your window-pane
>   Your upturned face,
>   As you think, " Ah—she
>   Now dreams of me
>   In her distant place ! "

> ' I pierce her blind
>   In her far-off home :
>   She fixes a comb,
>   And says in her mind,
>   " I start in an hour ;
>   Whom shall I meet ?
>   Won't the men be sweet
>   And the women sour ! " '

In the plots of Mr. Hardy's novels and short stories, dramatic use of some fantastic incident or device is frequent. *The Moth-Signal* is one of many instances that occur in his verse. A wife sits with her husband in the lamp-lit room : her lover, waiting outside in the darkness, summons her by inserting a moth through the door-crack, and she sees the ' pale-winged token ' burnt in the flame.

Close followers of Mr. Hardy's poetic style will see how clearly it retains the stamp of his architectural training. By natural bias, as well as by upbringing and association, he is architecturally-minded. He has the instincts of a draughtsman. His own account of the drawings that accompany his *Wessex Poems* is modest in the extreme, but some of them are quite remarkable. Their unity with the spirit of the poems is not less striking than their firm and delicate design. To look at these slight vignettes and tail-pieces—now preserved, with the manuscript, in Birmingham Art Gallery—is to see at once that Mr. Hardy's originality, like the totally different genius of William Blake, might have found parallel expression in the literary and graphic arts. Not only outline and proportion, that mean so much in architecture, engage him : he loves noble works of the architect and mason for their personal character, their durability, their moral truth in identifying beauty with purpose, and ornament with structure. He writes a poem in memorial of one whom he calls, eulogistically, *A Man* : a workman who preferred loss of employment to the paid task of

T

demolishing a fine old house. A poem in the latest
volume portrays *The Old Workman* who finds satisfaction in the true laying of certain blocks, though
their weight has crippled him incurably. As a piece
of art criticism embodied in narrative verse, and set
off by a most ingenious bit of circumstantial fiction,
The Abbey Mason is unique in literature. It relates
the origin of ' perpendicular ' design at Gloucester,
in the brilliant fourteenth - century solution of a
structural problem. Those who know Gloucester
choir, where Gothic genius drapes the cavernous
Romanesque elevation, and achieves consummate
unity from floor to glorious vault, are entranced
by Mr. Hardy's tribute to this famous church : not
least if, like the present writer, they grew up within
its shadow.

The architectural instinct is in keeping with the
strange fact that throughout Mr. Hardy's work—
poetry and prose alike—form invariably predominates
over colour. He visits Chartres cathedral, but of
its early glass—the colour-miracle of the Western
world—he sees, or says, nothing. The feature he
observes, and mentions with relish on several occasions, is the scaly arrangement of the roof-tiles on
the south spire. For edges and profiles he has a
curious affection : he sees the moon with

' the curve hewn off her cheek as by an adze.'

Take up his very last book, and you will find that
all his happiest figures are plastic in their suggestion
—concerned with shape or surface. A beldame is

' time-trenched on cheek and brow.' Care is ' cup-
eyed.' The sea is ' foam-fingered.' Ghosts in an
old house are ' thin elbowers.' Old violins are of
' glossy gluey make.' Like Crabbe, whom he otherwise resembles in astringent savour, Mr. Hardy
virtually eliminates colour from landscape.

> ' Above the slender sheaf
> The slimy mallow waves her silky leaf ;
> O'er the young shoot the charlock throws a shade,
> And clasping tares cling round the sickly blade ;
> With mingled tints the rocky coasts abound,
> And a sad splendour vainly shines around.'

Every word of this characteristic Crabbe passage
might be Mr. Hardy's. He would not tell us, any
more than Crabbe tells, what the ' mingled tints '
are. The East Anglian poet finds a pale landscape
ready to his mood. Mr. Hardy, with force more
original and compelling, persuades the green counties
of Wessex to utter repressed passion by means of
configuration. Man's work, in tumulus or mono-
lith, becomes one with nature's. The earth, as Mr.
Hardy sees it, is capable of emotional heavings,
like the sea. His eye dwells intently upon concaves,
protuberances, horizons : clouds of fantastic simili-
tude, like that which Hamlet saw : ' the wind-warped
upland thorn,' the silhouette of a gibbet on the dark
hill.

How piquant and modern a mixture—this un-
rivalled *flair* for form, allied to a temperament in-
timately romantic, and moved continually by the
clear sounds of stringed instruments ! The plain-

tive music of strings, plaintive in its gaiety, repeats itself interminably, as a kind of diaper pattern, in the background of Mr. Hardy's poems. In that unforgettable poem *Jubilate*, the tavern stranger recounts his midnight glimpse of the dead, making music with their ' dulcimers, hautboys, shawms, violoncellos, and a three-stringed double bass,' and minueting, under the snow of the churchyard, through which he saw them ' as it were through a crystal roof.'

The influence of old English music, with its free continuous rhythm—Shakespeare's ' stretchéd metre of an antique song '—has had something to do (we may suspect) with Mr. Hardy's novel and progressive exploits in metrical form. Where copious quotation is impracticable, a few lines may indicate the flexible sort of rhythm he has developed :

' Plunging and labouring on in a tide of visions,
    Dolorous and drear,
  Forward I pushed my way as amid waste waters
    Stretching around,
  Through whose eddies there glimmered the customed landscape
    Yonder and near,

' Blotted to feeble mist.   And the coomb and the upland
    Coppice-crowned,
  Ancient chalk-pit, milestone, rills in the grass-flat
    Stroked by the light,
  Seemed but a ghost-like gauze, and no substantial
    Meadow or mound.'

These verses open the *Satires of Circumstance* volume, dated 1914, and throughout his succeeding verse

Mr. Hardy's experimentalism in metre has shown no pause, but perennial zest. His late unceasing exploration of rhythmic subtleties is analogous to later developments in Milton's verse, culminating in the choruses of *Samson Agonistes*.

In general, Mr. Hardy's poetry does not readily lend itself to æsthetic criticism. His welding of style and substance defies the pedant or the mere connoisseur. Quite lately he has reminded his critics ' of Coleridge's proof that a versification of any length neither can be, nor ought to be, all poetry.' Like the great mediaeval builders whose work he admires, he reaches beauty indirectly, by seeking first the appropriate and unhackneyed statement of his own sincere thought, fancy, mood, or vision. There is something Gothic in his energy, which can vitalize a weighty material and transform it into a growing thing, full of sap and thrust. The cant phrase about his poetry is to say that it is rough-hewn. So it is, by comparison with sand-papered or pomaded verse : but incidentally it achieves a thousand thrills and fascinations of surface, let alone the total impression of power. Subdued to Mr. Hardy's strong consistency, we soon detect a strain of flabbiness in some quite reputable poets of the orthodox and consoling order. From facts, as he sees them, Mr. Hardy never flinches, and his poetic interpretations of life are often stern and cruel. If he were called upon to justify his art in a moral sense, he might reply by quoting the words of Jeremy Taylor in a sermon about charnel-houses and human dissolution : ' It is necessary to present these bundles of cypress.'

In the matter of popularity, his poetry falls between two stools. It will never make headway with the domestic circle, nor be quoted at tea-meetings. On the other hand, it makes no appeal to the propagandist type of intellectual, so numerous to-day, whose feverish activities for ' social welfare ' usually include some patronage of serious-minded song. Mr. Hardy may take satisfaction in the knowledge that his poetry is written for those readers, and those only, who love poetry because they cannot resist it. The vulgar conception of poetry, as of all art, is to think of it as a nice thing, just because it is not a necessary one. People for whom poetry is indispensable, who fasten upon it with famished eagerness, will waste little time in arguing with Mr. Hardy about his ' views,' when once they are subjugated to his poetic spell. They may not share his sombre outlook on life, nor any of his personal judgments and opinions about it. What they will share with him is a form of life itself, in the poetic experience he communicates—that mysterious transfusion of vitality, effected by art, which exhilarates and raises the imagination ; just as, in the religious sphere, the soul is raised by contact with genuine sanctity.

If the poetry of Thomas Hardy can mean little or nothing for those who assess poetry by non-poetic standards, this is just as well. It is the intrinsic lover of poetry, and none other, who controls in the long run what is humorously known as 'the verdict of posterity.' That verdict, indeed, is now on the way : for the crowd and its journalists already treat Mr. Hardy with the distant veneration willingly accorded to poets reputed great, but suspected to be unpalatable. To do the crowd justice, it has never pretended to care for poetry, and avoids the unconscious hypocrisy of suborning the poet to ends of cheap edification.

Among the growing number of Mr. Hardy's readers there are not a few who do care for poetry, but whose contact with his poems has been so intermittent that they still waver between hesitation and acquiescence, and have never passed from acquiescence to delight. They glimpse his power by flashes, but have not pierced what seem to them his unyielding idiosyncrasies of expression. They do not realize that most of those obstacles are the actual medium of a penetrating, consistent, and enveloping sense of beauty. Beauty under a new form, and belonging to that permanent order of beauty which only the artist can create, has a way of long eluding us : but if we persevere, its subtle contagion may fill the mind quite suddenly. In poetry, even more conspicuously than in prose, the work of Thomas Hardy typifies the principle laid down by Wordsworth : 'Every author, so far as he is great and at the same time original, has had the task of creating the taste by which he is to be enjoyed.'

THOMAS HARDY
A BIBLIOGRAPHY OF FIRST EDITIONS
[1865—1922]
BY
JOHN LANE

A BIBLIOGRAPHY OF FIRST EDITIONS
OF THOMAS HARDY

How I BUILT MYSELF A HOUSE. Article in *Chambers's Journal*, Saturday, March 18, 1865, pp. 161-164 (unsigned).

Reprinted in Vol. lxv., No. 389, May 15, 1922 (pp. 497-551) of *The Review of Reviews*.

DESPERATE REMEDIES. | A NOVEL. | ' Though a course of adventures which are only connected with each other by | having happened to the same individual is what most fre-quently occurs in | nature, yet the province of the romance-writer being artificial, there is more | required from him than a mere compliance with the simplicity of reality.' | SIR W. SCOTT | IN Three Volumes. | London : | Tinsley Brothers, 18, Catherine St., Strand. | 1871. | [*The Right of Translation is Reserved.*] Post 8vo. Vol. I., pp. vi+304 ; Vol. II., pp. v+291 ; Vol. III., pp. vi+274.

The original MS. was destroyed.

UNDER THE | GREENWOOD TREE | A | RURAL PAINTING OF THE DUTCH SCHOOL. | By the | Author of ' Desperate Remedies.' | In Two Volumes | London : | Tinsley Bro-thers, 18 Catherine St., Strand. | 1872. | [*All Rights reserved.*] Post 8vo. Vol. I., pp. 215 ; Vol. II., pp. 216.

The original MS. is in the possession of Mrs. Hardy, and Mr. John Lane owns the receipt for the copyright of this book, duly signed by Mr. Hardy on July 21, 1872.

A PAIR OF BLUE EYES. | A Novel. | By Thomas Hardy, | Author of | 'Under the Greenwood Tree,' 'Desperate Remedies,' etc. |

> 'A violet in the youth of primy nature,
> Forward, not permanent, sweet, not lasting,
> The perfume and suppliance of a minute ;
> No more.' |

In Three Volumes. | London : | Tinsley Brothers, 8 Catherine St., Strand. | 1873. | [*The right of translation and reproduction is reserved.*] Post 8vo. Vol. I., pp. 303 ; Vol. II., pp. 311 ; Vol. III., pp. 262.

Tinsley's Magazine, vols. xi. and xii., Sept. 1872 to July 1873, A Pair of Blue Eyes, by the Author of 'Under the Greenwood Tree,' 'Desperate Remedies,' etc. With 11 Illustrations.

This story was offered to Tinsley under the title of 'A Winning Tongue had He,' but this was altered before publication.

The original MS. of four of the instalments (those for September and October 1872, and January and July 1873) are in the possession of Mr. John Lane who would be interested to hear of the existence of the remainder.

FAR FROM THE MADDING CROWD. | By Thomas Hardy, | Author of | 'A Pair of Blue Eyes,' 'Under the Greenwood Tree,' etc. | With Twelve Illustrations. | In Two Volumes. | London : | Smith, Elder & Co., 15, Waterloo Place. | 1874. | (*All rights reserved.*) Demy 8vo. Vol. I., pp. iv+333, with 6 full-page Illustrations by Helen Paterson ; Vol. II., pp. iv+342, with 6 full-page Illustrations by Helen Paterson.

Cornhill Magazine, vols. xxix. and xxx., Jan. to Dec. 1874, FAR FROM THE MADDING CROWD. (Unsigned.) 12 Illustrations by H. Paterson (Mrs. Wm. Allingham).

The original MS. is in the possession of Mr. A. E. Newton of Philadelphia.

THE HAND OF ETHELBERTA | A COMEDY IN CHAPTERS | By | THOMAS HARDY | Author of ' Far from the Madding Crowd,' etc. | Vitæ post-scenia celant—*Lucretius* | With Eleven Illustrations | In Two Volumes | London | Smith, Elder, & Co., 15 Waterloo Place | 1876 | [*All rights reserved*] Demy 8vo. Vol. I., pp. viii+322, with six full-page Illustrations by George du Maurier ; Vol. II., pp. viii+318, with five full-page Illustrations by George du Maurier.

Cornhill Magazine, vols. xxxii. and xxxiii., July 1875 to May 1876, THE HAND OF ETHELBERTA. 12 Illustrations by George du Maurier.

THE | RETURN OF THE NATIVE | By | THOMAS HARDY | Author of | ' Far from the Madding Crowd,' ' A Pair of Blue Eyes,' etc. |

> ' To sorrow
> I bade good morrow,
> And thought to leave her far away behind ;
> But cheerly, cheerly,
> She loves me dearly ;
> She is so constant to me, and so kind.
> I would deceive her,
> And so leave her,
> But ah ! she is so constant and so kind.' |

In Three Volumes | London | Smith, Elder, & Co., 15 Waterloo Place | 1878 | [*All rights reserved*] Post 8vo. Vol. I., pp. vi+303 ; Vol. II., pp. vi+297 ; Vol. III., pp. vi+320.

Belgravia, vols. xxxiv., xxxv., xxxvi., xxxvii., Jan. to Dec. 1878, THE RETURN OF THE NATIVE, by THOMAS HARDY. 12 Illustrations by Arthur Hopkins.

The original MS. is in the possession of Mr. Clement Shorter.

New Quarterly Magazine, vol. x. (Chatto & Windus), April to October 1878, pp. 315-378, AN INDISCRETION IN THE LIFE OF AN HEIRESS, by THOMAS HARDY. Part I., pp. 315-347; Part II., 347-378.

(Not reprinted.)

From ' The Athenæum,' Nov. 30, 1878.

'DIALECT IN NOVELS.

' A somewhat vexed question is re-opened in your criticism of my story, "The return of the Native"; namely, the representation in writing of the speech of the peasantry, when that writing is intended to show mainly the character of the speakers, and only to give a general idea of their linguistic peculiarities.

' An author may be said to fairly convey the spirit of intelligent peasant talk if he retains the idiom, compass, and characteristic expressions, although he may not encumber the page with obsolete pronunciations of the purely English words, and with mispronunciations of those derived from Latin and Greek. In the printing of standard speech, hardly any phonetic principle at all is observed ; and if a writer attempts to exhibit on paper the precise accents of a rustic speaker, he disturbs the proper balance of a true representation by unduly insisting upon the grotesque element; thus directing attention to a point of inferior interest and diverting it from the speaker's meaning, which is by far the chief concern where the aim is to depict the men and their natures rather than their dialect forms.   THOMAS HARDY.'

(Not elsewhere reprinted.)

New Quarterly Magazine, vol. ii. (new series), pp. 469-473. Unsigned REVIEW of 'Poems of Rural Life, in the Dorset Dialect,' by Wm. Barnes, amongst the 'Selected Books' of the quarter (Oct. 1879).

(Not reprinted.)

THE TRUMPET-MAJOR | A TALE | By | THOMAS HARDY | In Three Volumes | London | Smith, Elder & Co., 15 Waterloo Place | 1880 | [*All rights reserved*] Post 8vo. Vol. I., pp. vi+295; Vol. II., pp. vi+276; Vol. III., pp. vi+259.

Good Words, Jan. to Dec. 1880, THE TRUMPET-MAJOR, by THOMAS HARDY. 32 Illustrations by John Collier.

The original MS. is in the possession of H.M. King George V. (Windsor Castle Library).

A LAODICEAN; | OR, | THE CASTLE OF THE DE STANCYS. | A STORY OF TO-DAY. | By | THOMAS HARDY, | Author of | 'Far from the Madding Crowd,' 'A Pair of Blue Eyes,' etc. | In Three Volumes. | London : | Sampson Low, Marston, Searle & Rivington, | Crown Buildings, 188, Fleet Street, | 1881. | [*All rights reserved.*] Post 8vo. Vol. I., pp. 312; Vol. II., pp. 275; Vol. III., pp. 269.

Harper's Magazine, European Edition, vols. 1, 2, and 3, Dec. 1880 to Dec. 1881, A LAODICEAN, by THOS. HARDY. 13 Illustrations by George du Maurier.

The original MS. was destroyed.

TWO ON A TOWER. | A ROMANCE. | By | THOMAS HARDY, | Author of 'Far from the Madding Crowd,' | 'The Trumpet-Major,' etc. | In Three Volumes. | London: | Sampson Low, Marston, Searle & Rivington, | Crown Buildings, 188, Fleet Street. | 1882. | [*All rights reserved.*] Post 8vo. Vol. I., pp. 246; Vol. II., pp. 240; Vol. III., pp. 223.

Atlantic Monthly (Boston, U.S.A.), vols. xlix. and l., Jan. to Dec. 1882, serial issue of TWO ON A TOWER, by THOMAS HARDY.

Longman's Magazine, vol. ii., July 1883, THE DORSETSHIRE LABOURER (article), by THOMAS HARDY, pp. 252-269.

THE | MAYOR OF CASTERBRIDGE: | THE LIFE AND DEATH OF A | MAN OF CHARACTER. | By | THOMAS HARDY, | Author of | 'Far from the Madding Crowd,' 'A Pair of Blue Eyes,' etc. | In Two Volumes. | London: | Smith, Elder & Co., 15 Waterloo Place. | 1886. | [*All rights reserved.*] Post 8vo. Vol. I., pp. 313; Vol. II., pp. 312.

The Graphic, Jan. 2 to May 15, 1886, THE MAYOR OF CASTERBRIDGE, by THOMAS HARDY. With 20 Illustrations by Robert Barnes.

The original MS. is in the Dorset County Museum, Dorchester.

The Athenæum, Oct. 16, 1886, Article (obituary) on THE REV. WILLIAM BARNES.

(*Reprinted in this volume by permission.*)

THE WOODLANDERS | By | Thomas Hardy | In Three Volumes | London | Macmillan and Co. | and New York | 1887 | *The Right of Translation and Reproduction is Reserved.* Post 8vo. Vol. I., pp. 302; Vol. II., pp. 328; Vol. III., pp. 316.

Macmillan's Magazine, vols. liv. and lv., May 1886 to April 1887, The Woodlanders, by Thomas Hardy.

WESSEX TALES | Strange, Lively, and Commonplace | By | Thomas Hardy, | Author of ' The Woodlanders,' etc. | In Two Volumes | London | Macmillan and Co. | and New York | 1888 | *All rights reserved* | Globe 8vo. Vol. I., pp. 247; Vol. II., pp. 212.

Contents of Vol. I.

The Three Strangers. [*March* 1883.]
The Withered Arm. [*January* 1888.]
Fellow Townsmen. [*April* 1880.]

Contents of Vol. II.

Interlopers at the Knap. [*May* 1884.]
The Distracted Preacher. [*April* 1879.]

The original MS. of *The Three Strangers* belongs to Mr. Sydney Cockerell.

The Forum (New York), March 1888, vol. v., Article, The Profitable Reading of Fiction, by Thos. Hardy, pp. 57-70.

(Not reprinted.)

New Review, Jan. 1890, vol. ii., Article, Candour in English Fiction. I. By Walter Besant. II. By E. Lynn Linton. III. By Thomas Hardy, pp. 15-21.

(Not reprinted in England.)

THREE NOTABLE STORIES | Love and Peril | To Be, or Not to Be | The Melancholy Hussar | Respectively by | The Marquis of Lorne, K.T. | Mrs. Alexander | Thomas Hardy | London | Spencer Blackett | 35, St. Bride Street, Ludgate Circus, E.C. | 1890 | [*All rights reserved*] Crown 8vo, pp. 211. [The Melancholy Hussar, by Thomas Hardy, pp. 151-211.]

A GROUP OF | NOBLE DAMES | By | Thomas Hardy | That is to say | The First Countess of Wessex | Barbara of the House of Grebe | The Marchioness of Stonehenge | Lady Mottisfont, The Lady Icenway | Squire Petrick's Lady | Anna, Lady Baxby | The Lady Penelope | The Duchess of Hamptonshire | and | The Honourable Laura |

> '. . . Store of Ladies, whose bright eyes
> Rain influence.'
>
> *L'Allegro.* |

Publishers' Device | (*and on back of title*) James R. Osgood, | McIlvaine & Co., | 45 | Albemarle Street, | London. | 1891. Post 8vo, pp. vi+271.

A large portion of the original MS. is in the Library of Congress, Washington, U.S.A., and Mr. Edmund Gosse possesses 'Wessex Folk,' the first rough draft of some of the tales afterwards called *A Group of Noble Dames*.

New Review, April 1891, The Science of Fiction, pp. 304-319. I. By Paul Bourget, pp. 304-309. II. By Walter Besant, pp. 305-315. III. By Thomas Hardy, pp. 315-319.

(*Not reprinted in England.*)

U

TESS | OF THE D'URBERVILLES | A Pure Woman | FAITHFULLY PRESENTED BY | Thomas Hardy | In Three Volumes |.

> '. . . Poor wounded name ! My bosom as a bed
> Shall lodge thee.'
> W. Shakspeare.

Publishers' Device | *All Rights* | *Reserved.* | (*and on back of title-page*) James R. Osgood, | McIlvaine and Co., | 45 | Albemarle Street | London, | 1891. Post 8vo. Vol. I., pp. viii+264; Vol. II., pp. viii+278 ; Vol. III., pp. vi+277.

In this form the book ran through four editions.

The Graphic, July 4 to Dec. 26, 1891, Tess of the D'Urbervilles, by Thomas Hardy. With 25 Illustrations by Professor Hubert Herkomer, R.A., and his pupils, Messrs. Wehrschmidt, Johnson, and Sydall.

The original MS. is in the British Museum.

Pall Mall Gazette, August 31, 1892, Article, Why I don't Write Plays. The first contribution is by Thomas Hardy.

(*Not reprinted.*)

The English Illustrated Magazine, Christmas Number, 1893, Ancient Earthworks at Casterbridge, by Thomas Hardy. With 4 Illustrations from photographs by W. Pouncy, Dorchester. Pp. 281-288.

(*Not reprinted.*)

BOOK OF THE WORDS | THE THREE WAYFARERS | A Pastoral Play in One Act | By Thomas Hardy | New York | Harper & Brothers | 1893. 16mo. 32 pp.

The dramatized version of the short story *The Three Strangers*, which was produced at Terry's Theatre, London, on June 3, 1893.

STORIES | FROM | ' BLACK AND WHITE ' | By | W. E.
NORRIS. | W. CLARK RUSSELL. | THOMAS HARDY. | MRS. E.
LYNN LINTON. | JAMES PAYN. | J. M. BARRIE. | MRS.
OLIPHANT. | GRANT ALLEN. | With Twenty-seven Illustra-
tions. | London : Chapman & Hall, Ld. | 1893. Crown
8vo, pp. viii+349. *The third contribution is* To PLEASE HIS
WIFE, by THOMAS HARDY, pp. 99-145. With Portrait and
2 Illustrations, the latter by W. J. Hennessy.

LIFE'S | LITTLE IRONIES | A SET OF TALES | with |
Some Colloquial Sketches | entitled | A FEW CRUSTED
CHARACTERS | By | THOMAS HARDY | (*Publishers' device from
block*) | *All rights* | *reserved*

On Back of Title.
Osgood, | McIlvaine and Co., | 45 |
Albemarle Street | London, | 1894

Contents.

(' Life's Little Ironies.')
The Son's Veto. [*December* 1891.]
For Conscience' Sake. [*March* 1891.]
A Tragedy of Two Ambitions. [*December* 1888.]
On the Western Circuit. [*Autumn* 1891.]
To Please his Wife. [*June* 1891.]
The Melancholy Hussar of the German Legion. [*December* 1889.]
The Fiddler of the Reels. [*May* 1893.]
A Tradition of Eighteen Hundred and Four. [*Christmas* 1882.]

(' A Few Crusted Characters.') [*March* 1891.]
　　Tony Kytes, the Arch Deceiver.
　　The History of the Hardcomes.
　　The Superstitious Man's Story.
　　Andrey Satchel and the Parson and Clerk.
　　Old Andrey's Experience as a Musician.
　　Absentmindedness in a Parish Choir.

The Winters and the Palmleys.
Incident in the Life of Mr. George Crookhill.
Netty Sargent's Copyhold.
Crown 8vo, pp. vi+301.

The Pall Mall Magazine, April 1894, AN IMAGINATIVE WOMAN, by THOMAS HARDY. With Headpiece and 6 Illustrations by A. J. Goodman, pp. 951-969.

Reprinted in *Wessex Tales*, 1898 and transferred to *Life's Little Ironies* (Vol. VIII. of the Wessex Edition) in 1912.

JUDE | THE OBSCURE | By | THOMAS HARDY | With an Etching by | H. Macbeth-Raeburn | and a Map of Wessex | 'The letter killeth.' | [*Publishers' device*] | *All rights reserved* [*On verso of title-page* :] Osgood, McIlvaine & Co., | 45 | Albemarle Street | London, | 1896 | Large Crown 8vo, pp. viii+520. Vol. VIII. of 'Thomas Hardy's Works: The Wessex Novels.'

Harper's Monthly Magazine (European Edition) vols. xxix., xxx., December 1894 to November 1895, JUDE THE OBSCURE under the title of HEARTS INSURGENT, by THOMAS HARDY. The first instalment was entitled THE SIMPLETONS. 12 Illustrations by W. Hatherell.

The original MS. is in the Fitzwilliam Museum, Cambridge.

IN SCARLET AND GREY | STORIES OF SOLDIERS AND OTHERS by | FLORENCE HENNIKER | and | THE SPECTRE OF THE REAL by | THOMAS HARDY and FLORENCE HENNIKER | London : John Lane, Vigo St. | Boston : Roberts Bros., 1896. [*The title-page printed within a design by Patten Wilson*] Vol. xxvi. of the ' Keynote Series,' pp. viii+208. [THE SPECTRE OF THE REAL, pp. 164-208.]

To-day, edited by Jerome K. Jerome, vol. ii., March 1894, THE
SPECTRE OF THE REAL, by THOMAS HARDY and FLORENCE
HENNIKER.

THE WELL-BELOVED | A SKETCH | OF A TEMPERAMENT |
By | THOMAS HARDY | With an Etching by | H. Macbeth-
Raeburn | and a Map of Wessex | ' One shape of many
names.' | P. B. SHELLEY | [*Publishers' device*] | *All rights
reserved.* [*On verso of title-page* :] Osgood, McIlvaine & Co.,
| 45 | Albemarle Street | London. | 1897 | Large Crown
8vo, pp. xii+340. Vol. XVII. of ' Thomas Hardy's Works :
The Wessex Novels.'

The Illustrated London News, October 1 to December 17, 1892.
THE PURSUIT OF THE WELL-BELOVED, by THOMAS HARDY.
Headpiece and 24 Illustrations by Walter Paget, and a full-
page portrait of the author.

WESSEX POEMS | AND OTHER VERSES | By | THOMAS
HARDY | With Thirty Illustrations | by the Author |
[*Publishers' device*] | London and New York | Harper &
Brothers | 45 Albemarle Street, W. | MDCCCXCVIII | [*On
verso of title-page*.] Copyright 1898 by Harper & Brothers |
All rights reserved. Large Crown 8vo, pp. xii+228.

The original MS. is in the Birmingham Art Gallery.

Contents.

PREFACE.	T. H. *September* 1898.	
THE TEMPORARY THE ALL.		
AMABEL.	1865.	
HAP.	1866.	
' IN VISION I ROAMED.'		
To ——.	1866.	

At a Bridal.
 To ——.   1866.

Postponement.   1866.

A Confession to a Friend in Trouble.   1866.

Neutral Tones.   1867.

She.
 At his funeral.   187–.

Her Initials.   1869.

Her Dilemma.
 (In —— Church.)   1866.

Revulsion.   1866.

She, to Him, I.   1866.
  ,,   ,, II.   1866.
  ,,   ,, III.   1866.
  ,,   ,, IV.   1866.

Ditty.
 (E. L. G.)   1870.

The Sergeant's Song.
 (1803.)   1878.
      Published in ' The Trumpet-Major,' 1880.

Valenciennes.
 (1793.)
 By Corp'l Tullidge : *see ' The Trumpet-Major.'*
 In memory of S. C. (Pensioner). Died 184–.
          1878-1897.

San Sebastian.
 (*August* 1813.)
 With thoughts of Sergeant M—— (Pensioner), who died
 185–.

The Stranger's Song.
 (*As sung by Mr. Charles Charrington in the play of ' The
 Three Wayfarers.'*)
      Printed in ' The Three Strangers,' 1883.

The Burghers.
 (17—.)

Leipzig.
 (1813.)
 Scene.—*The master-tradesmen's parlour at the Old Ship
 Inn, Casterbridge. Evening.*

THE PEASANT'S CONFESSION.
' Si le maréchal Grouchy avait été rejoint par l'officier que
Napoléon lui avait expédié la veille à dix heures du soir,
toute question eût disparu. Mais cet officier n'était point
parvenu à sa destination, ainsi que le maréchal n'a cessé
de l'affirmer toute sa vie, et il faut l'en croire, car autrement
il n'aurait eu aucune raison pour hésiter. Cet officier
avait-il été pris ? avait-il passé à l'ennemi ? C'est ce qu'on
a toujours ignoré.'—THIERS : *Histoire de l'Empire.*
"Waterloo."

THE ALARM.
(1803.)
See ' The Trumpet-Major.'
In memory of one of the Writer's Family who was a
Volunteer during the War with Napoleon.

HER DEATH AND AFTER.

THE DANCE AT THE PHOENIX.

THE CASTERBRIDGE CAPTAINS.
(Khyber Pass, 1842.)
A tradition of J. B. L——, T. G. B——, and J. L——.

A SIGN-SEEKER.

MY CICELY.
(17—.)

HER IMMORTALITY.

THE IVY-WIFE.

A MEETING WITH DESPAIR.

UNKNOWING.

FRIENDS BEYOND.

TO OUTER NATURE.

THOUGHTS OF PH—A.
At news of her death.   *March* 1890.
[Title changed to ' *Phena.*']

MIDDLE-AGE ENTHUSIASMS.
To M. H.

IN A WOOD.
See 'THE WOODLANDERS.'   1887 : 1896.

TO A LADY.
(Offended by a book of the writer's.)

To an Orphan Child.
  A Whimsey.
    [Title changed to : ' *To a Motherless Child.*']
Nature's Questioning.
The Impercipient.
  (At a cathedral service.)
At an Inn.
The Slow Nature.
  (An incident of Froom valley.   1894.
In a Eweleaze near Weatherbury.   1890.

Additions—
The Fire at Tranter Sweatley's.
  [Title changed to ' *The Bride-Night Fire.*']   *Written* 1866 ;
                                    printed 1875.
Heiress and Architect.
  For A. W. B.   1867.
The Two Men.   1866.
Lines.
  *Spoken by Miss Ada Rehan at the Lyceum Theatre, July 23,
  1890, at a performance on behalf of Lady Jeune's Holiday
  Fund for City Children.*
' I look into my Glass.'

POEMS OF THE PAST | AND THE PRESENT | By |
Thomas Hardy | *Publishers' device.* [*On the reverse of the
title-page* :] London and New York | Harper & Brothers
| 45 Albemarle Street, W. | MDCCCCII | *All rights reserved.*
Large Crown 8vo, pp. xii+264.

The original MS. of *Poems of the Past and the Present* is in the
Bodleian Library, Oxford.

Contents.

Preface.   T. H.   *August* 1901.
V. R. 1819-1901.
  A Reverie.   *Sunday night, 27th January* 1901.

WAR POEMS.

EMBARCATION.
　　(*Southampton Docks : October* 1899.)
DEPARTURE.
　　(*Southampton Docks : October* 1899.)
THE COLONEL'S SOLILOQUY.
　　(*Southampton Docks : October* 1899.)
THE GOING OF THE BATTERY.
　　Wives' Lament.
　　　(*November* 2, 1899.)
AT THE WAR OFFICE, LONDON.
　　(*Affixing the Lists of Killed and Wounded* : *December*
　　1899.)
A CHRISTMAS GHOST STORY.　　　　　*Christmas Eve*, 1899.
THE DEAD DRUMMER.
　　[Title changed to ' *Drummer Hodge.*']
A WIFE IN LONDON.
　　(*December* 1899.)
　　　I. The Tragedy.
　　　II. The Irony.
THE SOULS OF THE SLAIN.　　　　　*December* 1899.
　　　　　Note.—The ' Race ' is the turbulent sea-area off the
　　　　　Bill of Portland, where contrary tides meet.
SONG OF THE SOLDIERS' WIVES.
　　[Title changed to ' *Song of the Soldiers' Wives and Sweet-
　　hearts.*']
THE SICK GOD.
　　[Title changed to ' *The Sick Battle God.*']

POEMS OF PILGRIMAGE.

GENOA AND THE MEDITERRANEAN.
　　(*March* 1887.)
SHELLEY'S SKYLARK.
　　(*The neighbourhood of Leghorn : March* 1887.)
IN THE OLD THEATRE, FIESOLE.
　　(*April* 1887.)
ROME : ON THE PALATINE.
　　(*April* 1887.)

ROME.
  Building a New Street in the Ancient Quarter.
    (*April* 1887.)
ROME.
  The Vatican—Sala delle Muse.
    (1887.)
ROME.
  At the Pyramid of Cestius near the Graves of Shelley and
    Keats.
    (1887.)
LAUSANNE.
  In Gibbon's old Garden : 11-12 P.M.
    (*June* 27, 1897.)
    (*The 110th anniversary of the completion of the ' Decline and
    Fall,' at the same hour and place.*)
ZERMATT.
  To the Matterhorn.
    (*June—July* 1897.)
THE BRIDGE OF LODI.
    (*Spring* 1887.)
ON AN INVITATION TO THE UNITED STATES.

MISCELLANEOUS POEMS—
  THE MOTHER MOURNS.
  ' I SAID TO LOVE.'
  A COMMONPLACE DAY.
  AT A LUNAR ECLIPSE.
  THE LACKING SENSE.
    SCENE.—*A sad-coloured landscape, Wadden Vale.*
  TO LIFE.
  DOOM AND SHE.
  THE PROBLEM.
  THE SUBALTERNS.
  THE SLEEP-WORKER.
  THE BULLFINCHES.
  GOD-FORGOTTEN.
  THE BEDRIDDEN PEASANT.
    To an unknowing god.

By the Earth's Corpse.

Mute Opinion.

To an Unborn Pauper Child.

To Flowers from Italy in Winter.

On a Fine Morning.   *February* 1899.

To Lizbie Browne.

Song of Hope.

The Well-Beloved.

Her Reproach.   *Westbourne Park Villas*, 1867.

The Inconsistent.

A Broken Appointment.

' Between us now.'

' How great my Grief.'
    (*Triolets.*)

' I need not go.'

The Coquette, and after.
    (*Triolet.*)

A Spot.

Long plighted.

The Widow.
    [Title changed to, ' *The Widow Betrothed.*']

At a Hasty Wedding.
    (*Triolet.*)

The Dream-Follower.

His Immortality.   *February* 1899.

The To-be-Forgotten.

Wives in the Sere.

The Superseded.

An August Midnight.   *Max Gate*, 1899.

The Caged Thrush freed and Home again.
    (*Villanelle.*)

Birds at Winter Nightfall.
    (*Triolet.*)   *Max Gate.*

The Puzzled Game-Birds.
    (*Triolet.*)
       [Title changed to, ' *The Battue.*']

WINTER IN DURNOVER FIELD.

SCENE.—*A wide stretch of fallow ground recently sown with wheat, and frozen to iron hardness. Three large birds walking about thereon, and wistfully eyeing the surface. Wind keen from north-east : sky a dull grey.*
(*Triolet.*)

THE LAST CHRYSANTHEMUM.

THE DARKLING THRUSH.   *December* 1900.

THE COMET AT YALBURY OR YELL'HAM.

MAD JUDY.

A WASTED ILLNESS.

A MAN.
(In memory of H. of M.)

THE DAME OF ATHELHALL.

THE SEASONS OF HER YEAR.

THE MILKMAID.

THE LEVELLED CHURCHYARD.   1882.

THE RUINED MAID.   *Westbourne Park Villas*, 1866.

THE RESPECTABLE BURGHER.
On ' The Higher Criticism.'

ARCHITECTURAL MASKS.

THE TENANT-FOR-LIFE.

THE KING'S EXPERIMENT.

THE TREE.
An Old Man's Story.

HER LATE HUSBAND.
(*King's Hintock*, 182–.)

THE SELF-UNSEEING.

DE PROFUNDIS.
[Title changed to ' *In Tenebris.*']
I
' Percussus sum sicut foenum, et aruit cor meum.'—*Ps.* ci.
II
' Considerabam ad dexteram, et videbam ; et non erat qui cognosceret me. . . . Non est qui requirat animam meam.'—*Ps.* cxli.   1895-96.
III
' Heu mihi, quia incolatus meus prolongatus est ! Habitavi

cum habitantibus Cedar ; multum incola fuit anima mea.'
—*Ps.* cxix. 1896.

THE CHURCH-BUILDER.

THE LOST PYX.

> A Mediaeval Legend.
>> On a lonely table-land above the Vale of Blackmore, between High-Stoy and Bubb-Down hills, and commanding in clear weather views that extend from the English to the Bristol Channel, stands a pillar, apparently mediaeval, called Cross-and-Hand or Christ-in-Hand. Among other stories of its origin a local tradition preserves the one here given.

TESS'S LAMENT.

THE SUPPLANTER.

> A Tale.

IMITATIONS, ETC.

> SAPPHIC FRAGMENT.
>> ' Thou shalt be—Nothing.'—OMAR KHAYYÁM.
>> ' Tombless, with no remembrance.'—W. SHAKESPEARE.

> CATULLUS : XXXI.
>> (After passing Sirmione, *April* 1887.)

> AFTER SCHILLER.

> SONG FROM HEINE.

> FROM VICTOR HUGO.

> CARDINAL BEMBO'S EPITAPH ON RAPHAEL.

RETROSPECT.

> ' I HAVE LIVED WITH SHADES.' *February* 2, 1899.

> MEMORY AND I.

> ΆΓΝΩΣΤΩι ΘΕΩι.

>> NOTE.—The contents of this volume are now included in the *Wessex Poems* volume.

THE DYNASTS | A Drama | of the Napoleonic Wars, | In Three Parts, | Nineteen | Acts, & One Hundred and | Thirty Scenes | By | THOMAS HARDY | Part First. [*Part Second*] [*Part Third.*] | ' And I heard sounds of insult,

shame, and wrong, | And trumpets blown for wars.' |
London | Macmillan & Co., Limited | New York: The
Macmillan Company | 1903 *1906 1908*. | *All rights re-
served.* Crown 8vo. Vol. I., pp. xxiv+228+viii. Vol. II.,
pp. xvi+304. Vol. III., pp. xvi+356.

The original MS. is in the British Museum.

NOTE.—Part I. was originally published at the end of 1903, but
only a few copies were distributed bearing that date. In January 1904
the same volume was published with a new title-page dated 1904,
but without any other changes.

SELECT POEMS OF | WILLIAM BARNES | Chosen and
Edited | With a Preface and Glossarial Notes | By | THOMAS
HARDY | London | Henry Frowde | 1908 | Fcap. 8vo, xvi+
196 pp., Portrait frontispiece. A volume of the *Oxford
Library of Prose and Poetry* series.

TIME'S | LAUGHINGSTOCKS | AND OTHER VERSES |
By | THOMAS HARDY | Macmillan and Co., Limited | St.
Martin's Street, London | 1909. | Crown 8vo, pp. x+212.

Contents.

PREFACE.   T. H. *September* 1909.

TIME'S LAUGHINGSTOCKS.

THE REVISITATION.

A TRAMPWOMAN'S TRAGEDY.

    (182–.)

        Notes.—' Windwhistle ' (Stanza iv.). The highness
and dryness of Windwhistle Inn was impressed upon
the writer two or three years ago, when, after
climbing on a hot afternoon to the beautiful spot
near which it stands and entering the inn for tea,
he was informed by the landlady that none could
be had, unless he would fetch water from a valley
half a mile off, the house containing not a drop,

owing to its situation. However, a tantalising row of full barrels behind her back testified to a wetness of a certain sort, which was not at that time desired.

' Marshal's Elm ' (Stanza vi.) so picturesquely situated, is no longer an inn, though the house, or part of it, still remains. It used to exhibit a fine old swinging sign.

' Blue Jimmy ' (Stanza x.) was a notorious horse-stealer of Wessex in those days, who appropriated more than a hundred horses before he was caught. He was hanged at the now demolished Ivel-chester or Ilchester jail above mentioned—that building formerly of so many sinister associations in the minds of the local peasantry, and the continual haunt of fever, which at last led to its condemnation. Its site is now an innocent-looking green meadow.

April 1902.

THE TWO ROSALINDS.

A SUNDAY MORNING TRAGEDY.
    (*Circa* 186–.)   *January* 1904.

THE HOUSE OF HOSPITALITIES.

BEREFT.   1901.

JOHN AND JANE.

THE CURATE'S KINDNESS.
    A Workhouse Irony.

THE FLIRT'S TRAGEDY.
    (17—.)

THE REJECTED MEMBER'S WIFE.   *January* 1906.

THE FARM-WOMAN'S WINTER.

AUTUMN IN THE PARK.   1901.
    [Title changed to ' *Autumn in King's Hintock Park.*']

SHUT OUT THAT MOON.   1904.

REMINISCENCES OF A DANCING MAN.

THE DEAD MAN WALKING.

LOVE LYRICS.
  1967.   16 *W. P. Villas*, 1867.
  HER DEFINITION.   *W. P. V.*, *Summer*, 1866.

THE DIVISION.

ON THE DEPARTURE PLATFORM.

IN A CATHEDRAL CITY.   *Salisbury.*

' I SAY I 'LL SEEK HER.'

HER FATHER.   *Weymouth.*

AT WAKING.   *Weymouth,* 1869.

FOUR FOOTPRINTS.

IN THE CRYPTED WAY.
> [Title changed to ' *In the Vaulted Way.*']

THE PHANTOM.

THE END OF THE EPISODE.

THE SIGH.

' IN THE NIGHT SHE CAME.'

THE CONFORMERS.

THE DAWN AFTER THE DANCE.   *Weymouth,* 1869.

THE SUN ON THE LETTER.

THE NIGHT OF THE DANCE.

MISCONCEPTION.

THE VOICE OF THE THORN.

FROM HER IN THE COUNTRY.   16 *W. P. V.,* 1866.

HER CONFESSION.   *W. P. V.,* 1865-67.

TO AN IMPERSONATOR OF ROSALIND.   *21st April* 1867.
                                  8 *Adelphi Terrace.*

TO AN ACTRESS.   1867.

THE MINUTE BEFORE MEETING.   1871.

HE ABJURES LOVE.   1883.

A SET OF COUNTRY SONGS.

LET ME ENJOY.
> (Minor Key.)

AT CASTERBRIDGE FAIR.
> I. The Ballad-Singer.
> II. Former Beauties.
> III. After the Club-Dance.
> IV. The Market-Girl.
> V. The Inquiry.
> VI. A Wife Waits.

Note.—' The Bow ' (line 3). The old name for the curved corner by the cross-streets in the middle of Casterbridge. It is not now so inscribed, and the spot has to be designated by a circumlocution, to the inconvenience of market-men in their appointments.

VII. After the Fair. 1902.

Note.—' The Chimes ' (line 6) will be listened for in vain here at midnight now, having been abolished some years ago.

THE DARK-EYED GENTLEMAN.

Note.—' Leazings ' (line 1). Bundle of gleaned corn.

TO CARRY CLAVEL.

THE ORPHANED OLD MAID.

THE SPRING CALL.

JULIE-JANE.

NOTE.—It is, or was, a common custom in Wessex, and probably other country places, to prepare the mourning beside the death-bed, the dying person sometimes assisting, who also selects his or her bearers on such occasions.

' Coats ' (line 7). Old name for petticoats.

NEWS FOR HER MOTHER.

THE FIDDLER.

THE HUSBAND'S VIEW.

ROSE-ANN.

THE HOME COMING. *December* 1901.

PIECES OCCASIONAL AND VARIOUS—

A CHURCH ROMANCE.

(*Circa* 1835.)

THE RASH BRIDE.

An Experience of the Mellstock Quire.

THE DEAD QUIRE. 1897.

THE CHRISTENING. 1904.

A DREAM QUESTION.

' It shall be dark unto you, that ye shall not divine.'—*Micah* iii. 6.

BY THE BARROWS.

A WIFE AND ANOTHER.

THE ROMAN ROAD.

THE VAMPIRINE FAIR.

THE REMINDER.

THE RAMBLER.

NIGHT IN THE OLD HOME.

AFTER THE LAST BREATH.   1904.

IN CHILDBED.

THE PINE PLANTERS.
    (Marty South's Reverie.)

THE DEAR.   1901.

ONE WE KNEW.
    (M. H. 1772-1857.)   *May* 20, 1902.

SHE HEARS THE STORM.

A WET NIGHT.

BEFORE LIFE AND AFTER.

NEW YEAR'S EVE.   1906.

HIS EDUCATION.
    [Title changed to ' *God's Education.*']

TO SINCERITY.   *February* 1899.

PANTHERA.
    (For other forms of this legend—first met with in the
    second century—see Origen contra Celsum ; the Talmud ;
    Sepher Toldoth Jeschu ; quoted fragments of lost Apocry-
    phal writings ; Strauss ; Haeckel; etc.)

THE UNBORN.

THE MAN HE KILLED.   1902.

GEOGRAPHICAL KNOWLEDGE.
    (A memory of Christiana C——.)

ONE RALPH BLOSSOM SOLILOQUIZES.
    (' It being deposed that vij women who were mayds before
    he knew them have been brought upon the towne [rates ?]
    by the fornicacions of one Ralph Blossom, Mr. Maior
    inquired why he should not contribute xiv pence weekly
    toward their mayntenance.   But it being shewn that the
    sayd R. B. was dying of a purple feaver, no order was
    made.'—*Budmouth Borough Minutes* : 16——.)

THE NOBLE LADY'S TALE.
   (*Circa* 1790.)
UNREALIZED.
WAGTAIL AND BABY.
ABERDEEN.
   (*April* 1905.)
      ' And wisdom and knowledge shall be the stability of
      thy times.'—*Isaiah* xxxiii. 6.
G. M.
      1828-1909.   *May* 1909.
      [Title changed to ' *George Meredith* 1828-1909.']
YELL'HAM-WOOD'S STORY.   1902.
A YOUNG MAN'S EPIGRAM ON EXISTENCE.
                                    16 *W. P. V.*, 1866.

THE CONVERGENCE OF THE TWAIN By THOMAS
HARDY. Macmillan & Co., Limited, St. Martin's Street,
London, 1912. Small 8vo. 10 copies.

This poem was written for the Dramatic and Operatic Matinée
   in aid of the Titanic Disaster Fund, at the Royal Opera,
   Covent Garden, on May 14, 1912, and reprinted with
   additions in the *Fortnightly* for the following June.

A CHANGED MAN | The Waiting Supper | and Other Tales
| concluding with | The Romantic Adventures | of a Milk-
maid | By | THOMAS HARDY | Macmillan and Co., Limited |
St. Martin's Street, London | 1913. Crown 8vo, pp. viii+
416. Frontispiece and a double-page map of Wessex.
Vol. XVIII. of ' The Wessex Novels.'

Contents.

A Changed Man. [1900.]
The Waiting Supper. [*Autumn* 1887.]
Alicia's Diary. [1887.]
The Grave by the Handpost. [*Christmas* 1897.]
Enter a Dragoon. [*December* 1899.]
A Tryst at an Ancient Earthwork. [*March* 1885.]

What the Shepherd saw.   [*Christmas* 1881.]
A Committee-Man of ' The Terror.'   [1895.]
Master John Horseleigh, Knight.   [*Spring* 1893.]
The Duke's Reappearance.   [1896.]
A Mere Interlude.   [*October* 1885.]
The Romantic Adventures of a Milkmaid.   [*Midsummer* 1883.]

The original MS. of *The Duke's Reappearance*, dated 1896, is in
the possession of Mr. Edward Clodd.

AN APPRECIATION OF ANATOLE FRANCE.

Mr. Hardy, who was unable to be present at the banquet in
honour of M. Anatole France, held at the Savoy on December
10, 1913, sent the following message which was read by the
Chairman, Lord Redesdale, and appeared the next day in
many of the newspapers :—

‘ I particularly regret that, though one of the Committee, I am
unable to be present to meet M. Anatole France at the reception on
Wednesday.   In these days when the literature of narrative and
verse seems to be losing its qualities as an art, and to be assuming a
structureless, conglomerate character, it is a privilege that we should
have come into our midst a writer who is faithful to the principles
that make for permanence, who never forgets the value of organic
form and symmetry, the force of reserve, and the emphasis of under-
statement, even in his lighter works.'

The MS. was given by Mr. Lane to M. Anatole France as a
souvenir.

SATIRES | OF CIRCUMSTANCE | LYRICS AND REV-
ERIES | With Miscellaneous Pieces | By | THOMAS HARDY
Macmillan and Co., Limited | St. Martin's Street, Londo
| 1914. | Crown 8vo, pp. x+232.

Contents.

LYRICS AND REVERIES—
  IN FRONT OF THE LANDSCAPE.
  CHANNEL FIRING.   *April* 1914.

THE CONVERGENCE OF THE TWAIN.
  (*Lines on the loss of the 'Titanic.'*)
THE GHOST OF THE PAST.
AFTER THE VISIT.
  (*To F. E. D.*)
TO MEET, OR OTHERWISE.
THE DIFFERENCE.
THE SUN ON THE BOOKCASE.
  (*Student's Love-song.*)
'WHEN I SET OUT FOR LYONNESSE.'
A THUNDERSTORM IN TOWN.
  (*A Reminiscence.*)
THE TORN LETTER.
BEYOND THE LAST LAMP.
  (*Near Tooting Common.*)
THE FACE AT THE CASEMENT.
LOST LOVE.
'MY SPIRIT WILL NOT HAUNT THE MOUND.'
WESSEX HEIGHTS.
  (1896.)
IN DEATH DIVIDED.
THE PLACE ON THE MAP.
WHERE THE PICNIC WAS.
THE SCHRECKHORN.
  (*With thoughts of Leslie Stephen.*)
    (June 1897.)
A SINGER ASLEEP.   *Bonchurch*, 1910.
  (*Algernon Charles Swinburne*, 1837-1909.)
A PLAINT TO MAN.   1909-10.
GOD'S FUNERAL.   1908-10.
SPECTRES THAT GRIEVE.
'AH, ARE YOU DIGGING ON MY GRAVE?'

SATIRES OF CIRCUMSTANCE—
    In fifteen glimpses.
  I. AT TEA.
  II. IN CHURCH.

III. By her Aunt's Grave.
IV. In the Room of the Bride-elect.
V. At a Watering-place.
VI. In the Cemetery.
VII. Outside the Window.
VIII. In the Study.
IX. At the Altar-Rail.
X. In the Nuptial Chamber.
XI. In the Restaurant.
XII. At the Draper's.
XIII. On the Death-bed.
XIV. Over the Coffin.
XV. In the Moonlight.

Lyrics and Reveries—*continued*--
Self-Unconscious.
The Discovery.
Tolerance.
Before and after Summer.
At Day-close in November.
The Year's awakening.   *February* 1910.
Under the Waterfall.
The Spell of the Rose.
St. Launce's Revisited.

Poems of 1912-13—
    Veteris vestigia flammae.
The Going.   *December* 1912.
Your last Drive.   *December* 1912.
The Walk.
Rain on a Grave.   *January* 31, 1913.
' I found her out there.'
Without Ceremony.
Lament.
The Haunter.
The Voice.   *December* 1912.

HIS VISITOR.	1913.
A CIRCULAR.	
A DREAM OR NO.	*February* 1913.
AFTER A JOURNEY.	*Pentargan Bay.*
A DEATH-DAY RECALLED.	
BEENY CLIFF.	
March 1870—*March* 1913.	
AT CASTLE BOTEREL.	*March* 1913.
PLACES.	*Plymouth, March* 1913.
THE PHANTOM HORSEWOMAN.	

MISCELLANEOUS PIECES—

THE WISTFUL LADY.	
THE WOMAN IN THE RYE.	
THE CHEVAL-GLASS.	
THE RE-ENACTMENT.	
HER SECRET.	
' SHE CHARGED ME.'	
THE NEWCOMER'S WIFE.	
A CONVERSATION AT DAWN.	1910.
A KING'S SOLILOQUY.	*May* 1910.
On the night of his funeral.	
THE CORONATION.	1911.
AQUAE SULIS.	*Bath.*
SEVENTY-FOUR AND TWENTY.	
THE ELOPEMENT.	
' I ROSE UP AS MY CUSTOM IS.'	
A WEEK.	
HAD YOU WEPT.	
BEREFT, SHE THINKS SHE DREAMS.	
IN THE BRITISH MUSEUM.	
IN THE SERVANTS' QUARTERS.	
THE OBLITERATE TOMB.	
' REGRET NOT ME.'	
THE RECALCITRANTS.	
STARLINGS ON THE ROOF.	

THE MOON LOOKS IN.

THE SWEET HUSSY.

THE TELEGRAM.

THE MOTH-SIGNAL.
   (*On Egdon Heath*.)

SEEN BY THE WAITS.

THE TWO SOLDIERS.

THE DEATH OF REGRET.

IN THE DAYS OF CRINOLINE.

THE ROMAN GRAVEMOUNDS.   *November* 1910.

THE WORKBOX.

THE SACRILEGE.
   A Ballad-Tragedy.
      (*Circa* 182–.)

THE ABBEY MASON.
   (*Inventor of the ' Perpendicular ' Style of Gothic Architecture.*)

THE JUBILEE OF A MAGAZINE.
   (*To the Editor*.)

THE SATIN SHOES.

EXEUNT OMNES.   *June* 2, 1913.

A POET.   *July* 1914.

POSTSCRIPT—

' MEN WHO MARCH AWAY.' *
      (Song of the Soldiers.)   *September* 5, 1914.
         * This poem is included in the Mellstock Edition of
         Moments of Vision.

The original draft of ' God's Funeral ' is in the possession of
Mr. Edmund Gosse, to whom it was inscribed.   Begun in
1908 and finished in 1910.   Mr. Gosse also possesses two or
three of Mr. Hardy's other lyrics in their original form.

THE | OXEN. | By THOMAS HARDY. | Published in *The Times*,
24th December, 1915. | Reprinted at Hove, 28th December,
1915.   Demy 8vo, pp. 4.

This poem and *Song of the Soldiers* (September 16, 1914) were privately printed in a series of booklets issued solely to give away to soldiers on active service abroad.

MOMENTS OF VISION | and | Miscellaneous Verses | by | Thomas Hardy | Macmillan and Co., Limited | St. Martin's Street, London | 1917. Crown 8vo, pp. xii+256+4.

Contents.

Moments of Vision.

The Voice of Things.

'Why be at Pains ?'
  (*Wooer's song.*)

'We sat at the Window.'
  (*Bournemouth*, 1875.)

Afternoon Service at Mellstock.
  (*Circa* 1850.)

At the Wicket-gate.

In a Museum.   *Exeter.*

Apostrophe to an old Psalm Tune.
          Sunday, August 13, 1916.

At the Word 'Farewell.'

The Day of First Sight.
  [Title changed to '*First Sight of Her and After.*']

The Rival.

Heredity.

'You were the sort that men forget.'

She, I, and They.   1916.

Near Lanivet, 1872.

Joys of Memory.

To the Moon.

Copying Architecture in an Old Minster.
  (*Wimborne.*)

To Shakespeare.
  After three hundred years.   1916.

Quid Hic Agis ?   *The Spectator :* 1916.

On a Midsummer Eve.

Timing Her.
    (Written to an old folk-tune.)

Before Knowledge.

The Blinded Bird.

' The Wind blew Words.'

The Faded Face.

The Riddle.

The Duel.

At Mayfair Lodgings.

To my Father's Violin.   1916.

The Statue of Liberty.

The Background and the Figure.
    (*Lover's Ditty.*)

The Change.   *Jan.—Feb.* 1913.

Sitting on the Bridge.
    (*Echo of an old song.*)   *Grey's Bridge.*

The Young Churchwarden.

' I travel as a Phantom now.'   1915.

Lines.
    To a movement in Mozart's E-flat symphony.
                      Begun November 1898.

' In the Seventies.'
    ' Qui deridetur ab amico suo sicut ego.'—*Job.*

The Pedigree.   1916.

His Heart.
    A Woman's Dream.

Where they lived.

The Occultation.

Life Laughs Onward.

The Peace-Offering.

' Something Tapped.'   *August* 1913.

The Wound.

A Merrymaking in Question.

' I said and sang Her Excellence.'
    (*Fickle Lover's Song.*)   *By Rushy-Pond.*

A JANUARY NIGHT.
   (1879.)
A KISS.
THE ANNOUNCEMENT.
THE OXEN.
THE TRESSES.
THE PHOTOGRAPH.
ON A HEATH.
AN ANNIVERSARY.   *Kingston-Maurward Eweleaze.*
' BY THE RUNIC STONE.'
THE PINK FROCK.
TRANSFORMATIONS.
IN HER PRECINCTS.   *Kingston-Maurward Park.*
THE LAST SIGNAL.
   (*October* 11, 1886.)
      A memory of William Barnes.
                  Winterborne-Came Path.
THE HOUSE OF SILENCE.
GREAT THINGS.
THE CHIMES.
THE FIGURE IN THE SCENE.   *From an old note.*
' WHY DID I SKETCH.'   *From an old note.*
CONJECTURE.
THE BLOW.
LOVE THE MONOPOLIST.
   (*Young Lover's Reverie.*)
               Begun 1871 : *finished* ——.
AT MIDDLE-FIELD GATE IN FEBRUARY.
               Bockhampton Lane.
THE YOUTH WHO CARRIED A LIGHT.   1915.
THE HEAD ABOVE THE FOG.
OVERLOOKING THE RIVER STOUR.
THE MUSICAL BOX.
ON STURMINSTER FOOT-BRIDGE.
ROYAL SPONSORS.
OLD FURNITURE.

A THOUGHT IN TWO MOODS.

THE LAST PERFORMANCE.   1912.

'YOU ON THE TOWER.'

THE INTERLOPER.

LOGS ON THE HEARTH.   *December* 1915.

THE SUNSHADE.   *Swanage Cliffs.*

THE AGEING HOUSE.

THE CAGED GOLDFINCH.

AT MADAME TUSSAUD'S IN VICTORIAN YEARS.

THE BALLET.

THE FIVE STUDENTS.

THE WIND'S PROPHECY.   *Rewritten from an old copy.*

DURING WIND AND RAIN.

HE PREFERS HER EARTHLY.

THE DOLLS.

MOLLY GONE.

A BACKWARD SPRING.   *April* 1917.

LOOKING ACROSS.   *December* 1915.

AT A SEASIDE TOWN IN 1869.
    (*Young Lover's Reverie.*)   *From an old note.*

THE GLIMPSE.

THE PEDESTRIAN.
    An incident of 1883.

'WHO'S IN THE NEXT ROOM?'

AT A COUNTRY FAIR.

THE MEMORIAL BRASS: 186–.

HER LOVE-BIRDS.

PAYING CALLS.

THE UPPER BIRCH-LEAVES.

'IT NEVER LOOKS LIKE SUMMER.'
                 Boscastle, March 8, 1913.

EVERYTHING COMES.

THE MAN WITH A PAST.

HE FEARS HIS GOOD FORTUNE.

HE WONDERS ABOUT HIMSELF.   *November* 1893.

JUBILATE.

He Revisits his First School.
' I thought, my Heart.'
Fragment.
Midnight on the Great Western.
Honeymoon-Time at an Inn.
The Robin.
' I rose and went to Rou'tor Town.'
The Nettles.
In a Waiting-Room.
The Clock-Winder.
Old Excursions. *April* 1913.
The Masked Face.
In a Whispering Gallery.
The Something that saved Him.
The Enemy's Portrait.
Imaginings.
On the Doorstep. *January* 1914.
Signs and Tokens.
Paths of Former Time. 1913.
The Clock of the Years.
   ' A spirit passed before my face ; the hair of my flesh
   stood up.' 1916.
At the Piano.
The Shadow on the Stone.
                        Begun 1913 : *finished* 1916.
In the Garden.
   (M. H.) 1915.
The Tree and the Lady.
An Upbraiding.
The Young Glass-Stainer. *November* 1893.
Looking at a Picture on an Anniversary.
                              Spring 1913.
The Choirmaster's Burial.
The Man who Forgot.
While drawing in a Churchyard.
' For life I had never cared greatly.'

Poems of War and Patriotism—
His Country.
> Written before the War.   1913.

England to Germany in 1914.   *Autumn* 1914.
On the Belgian Expatriation.   *October* 18, 1914.
An Appeal to America on behalf of the Belgian Destitute.
       December 1914.
The Pity of It.   *April* 1915.   (' *Fortnightly Review*.')
In Time of Wars and Tumults.   1915.
In Time of ' The Breaking of Nations.'   1915.
       (' *Saturday Review*.')   *Jer.* li. 20.
Cry of the Homeless.
> After the Prussian Invasion of Belgium.   *August* 1915.

Before Marching and After.
> (*In memoriam F. W. G.*)   *September* 1915.

' Often when Warring.'   1915.
Then and now.   *Written* 1915 : *published in*
       ' *The Times*,' 1917.
A Call to National Service.   *March* 1917.
The Dead and the Living One.
      1915.   (' *The Sphere*.')
A New Year's Eve in War Time.   1915—1916.
' I met a Man.'   1916.
' I looked up from my Writing.'

Finale—
The Coming of the End.
Afterwards.

JUDE THE OBSCURE | A Letter and a Foreword | Lakewood, Ohio | Printed for Private Circulation by Paul Semperley | 1917. Crown 8vo, pp. 24.

The basis of the pamphlet consists of a letter addressed by Thomas Hardy to Miss Jeannette Gilder on March 12, 1917, declining to permit himself to be interviewed on the subject of his novel *Jude the Obscure*. The recipient of the letter,

who had reviewed *Jude* in an aggressive manner, replied as
follows :—' Dear Mr. Hardy, I knew you were a great man,
but I did not appreciate your goodness until I received your
letter this morning.'

' Virtus post funera vivit.' | WESSEX WORTHIES | (Dorset) |
With some account of others connected with the history |
of the County, and numerous Portraits and Illustrations. |
By | J. J. FOSTER, F.S.A. | *Author of* [here follows a list of six
works] | With an introductory note by | THOMAS HARDY,
O.M. | [design] | London : | Dickensons : 37, Bedford
Street, W.C. | 1920. Quarto, xx+168 pp. 31 plates.

The 'Introductory Note' by Thomas Hardy is on p. ix and
ends with a facsimile of his signature.

LATE LYRICS | AND EARLIER | WITH MANY OTHER
VERSES | By | THOMAS HARDY | Macmillan and Co., Limited
| St. Martin's Street, London | 1922. Crown 8vo, pp. xxiv
+288.

Contents.

APOLOGY.	T. H. *February* 1922.
WEATHERS.	
THE MAID OF KEINTON MANDEVILLE.	
(A tribute to Sir H. Bishop.)	1915 or 1916.
SUMMER SCHEMES.	
EPEISODIA.	
FAINTHEART IN A RAILWAY TRAIN.	
AT MOONRISE AND ONWARDS.	
THE GARDEN SEAT.	
BARTHÉLÉMON AT VAUXHALL.	

> François Hippolite Barthélémon, first-fiddler at Vauxhall
> Gardens, composed what was probably the most popular
> morning hymn-tune ever written. It was formerly sung,
> full-voiced, every Saturday in most churches, to Bishop
> Ken's words, but is now seldom heard.

'I SOMETIMES THINK.'
    (For F. E. H.)

JEZREEL.
    On its seizure by the English under Allenby, September
    1918.   *September 24, 1918.*

A JOG-TROT PAIR.

'THE CURTAINS NOW ARE DRAWN.'
    (Song.)   1913.

'ACCORDING TO THE MIGHTY WORKING.'   1917.

'I WAS NOT HE.'
    (Song.)

THE WEST-OF-WESSEX GIRL.
                      Begun in Plymouth, March 1913.

WELCOME HOME.

GOING AND STAYING.

READ BY MOONLIGHT.

AT A HOUSE IN HAMPSTEAD.
    Sometime the dwelling of John Keats.   *July* 1920.

A WOMAN'S FANCY.

HER SONG.

A WET AUGUST.   1920.

THE DISSEMBLERS.

TO A LADY PLAYING AND SINGING IN THE MORNING.

'A MAN WAS DRAWING NEAR TO ME.'

THE STRANGE HOUSE.
    (*Max Gate*, A.D. 2000.)

'AS 'TWERE TO-NIGHT.'
    (Song.)

THE CONTRETEMPS.   *Weymouth.*

A GENTLEMAN'S EPITAPH ON HIMSELF AND A LADY, WHO
    WERE BURIED TOGETHER.

THE OLD GOWN.
    (Song.)

A NIGHT IN NOVEMBER.   (?) 1913.

A DUETTIST TO HER PIANOFORTE.
    Song of Silence.
        (E. L. H.—H. C. H.)

' WHERE THREE ROADS JOINED.'

' AND THERE WAS A GREAT CALM.'
    (On the signing of the Armistice, *November* 11, 1918.)

HAUNTING FINGERS.
    A Phantasy in a Museum of Musical Instruments.

THE WOMAN I MET.   *London*, 1918.

' IF IT 'S EVER SPRING AGAIN.'
    (Song.)

THE TWO HOUSES.

ON STINSFORD HILL AT MIDNIGHT.

THE FALLOW DEER AT THE LONELY HOUSE.

THE SELF SAME SONG.

THE WANDERER.

A WIFE COMES BACK.

A YOUNG MAN'S EXHORTATION.
                       Westbourne Park Villas, 1867.

AT LULWORTH COVE A CENTURY BACK.   *September* 1920.
            Note.—In September 1820 Keats, on his way to
            Rome, landed one day on the Dorset coast, and
            composed the sonnet, ' Bright star ! would I were
            steadfast as thou art.' The spot of his landing is
            judged to have been Lulworth Cove.

A BYGONE OCCASION.
    (Song.)

TWO SERENADES.
    I. *On Christmas Eve.*
    II. *A year later.*   *From an old copy.*

THE WEDDING MORNING.

END OF THE YEAR 1912.

THE CHIMES PLAY ' LIFE 'S A BUMPER ! '   1913.

' I WORKED NO WILE TO MEET YOU.'
    (Song.)

AT THE RAILWAY STATION, UPWAY.

SIDE BY SIDE.

DREAM OF THE CITY SHOPWOMAN.
                       Westbourne Park Villas, 1866.

A MAIDEN'S PLEDGE.
    (Song.)

THE CHILD AND THE SAGE.   *December* 21, 1908.
MISMET.
AN AUTUMN RAIN-SCENE.   *October* 1904.
MEDITATIONS ON A HOLIDAY.
    (A new theme to an old folk-jingle.)   *May* 1921.
AN EXPERIENCE.
THE BEAUTY.
        Note.—' The Regent Street beauty, Miss Verrey,
        the Swiss confectioner's daughter, whose personal
        attractions have been so mischievously exaggerated,
        died of fever on Monday evening, brought on by
        the annoyance she had been for some time subject
        to.'—London paper, *October* 1828.
THE COLLECTOR CLEANS HIS PICTURE.
    Fili hominis, ecce ego tollo a te desiderabile oculorum
    tuorum in plaga.—*Ezech.* xxiv. 16.
THE WOOD FIRE.
    (A Fragment.)
SAYING GOOD-BYE.
    (Song.)
ON THE TUNE CALLED THE OLD-HUNDRED-AND-FOURTH.
THE OPPORTUNITY.
    (For H. P.)
EVELYN G. OF CHRISTMINSTER.
THE RIFT.
    (Song : *Minor Mode.*)
VOICES FROM THINGS GROWING IN A CHURCHYARD.
        It was said her real name was Eve Trevillian or
        Trevelyan ; and that she was the handsome mother
        of two or three illegitimate children, *circa* 1784-95.
ON THE WAY.
' SHE DID NOT TURN.'
GROWTH IN MAY.   *Near Chard.*
THE CHILDREN AND SIR NAMELESS.
AT THE ROYAL ACADEMY.
HER TEMPLE.
A TWO-YEARS' IDYLL.

BY HENSTRIDGE CROSS AT THE YEAR'S END.
> (From this centuries'-old cross-road the highway leads east to London, north to Bristol and Bath, west to Exeter and the Land's End, and south to the Channel coast.)
>> *During the War.*

PENANCE.
'I LOOK IN HER FACE.'
> (Song : *Minor*.)

AFTER THE WAR.
'IF YOU HAD KNOWN.'   1920.

THE CHAPEL-ORGANIST.
> (A.D. 185–.)

FETCHING HER.
'COULD I BUT WILL.'
> (Song : *Verses 1, 3, key major ; verse 2, key minor*.)

SHE REVISITS ALONE THE CHURCH OF HER MARRIAGE.

AT THE ENTERING OF THE NEW YEAR.
> I. (Old Style).
> II. (New Style).   *December 31. During the War.*

THEY WOULD NOT COME.

AFTER A ROMANTIC DAY.

THE TWO WIVES.
> (Smoker's Club-story.)

'I KNEW A LADY.'
> (Club Song.)

A HOUSE WITH A HISTORY.

A PROCESSION OF DEAD DAYS.

HE FOLLOWS HIMSELF.

THE SINGING WOMAN.

WITHOUT, NOT WITHIN HER.

'O I WON'T LEAD A HOMELY LIFE.'
> (*To an old air*.)

IN THE SMALL HOURS.

THE LITTLE OLD TABLE.

VAGG HOLLOW.
> Vagg Hollow is a marshy spot on the old Roman road near Ilchester where 'things' are seen. Merchandise was

formerly fetched inland from the canal-boats at Load-Bridge by waggons this way.

THE DREAM IS—WHICH ?   *March* 1913.

THE COUNTRY WEDDING.
  (A fiddler's story.)

FIRST OR LAST.
  (Song.)

LONELY DAYS.   *Versified from a Diary.*

' WHAT DID IT MEAN ? '

AT THE DINNER-TABLE.

THE MARBLE TABLET.   *St. Juliot : September* 8, 1916.

THE MASTER AND THE LEAVES.   1917.

LAST WORDS TO A DUMB FRIEND.   *October* 2, 1904.

A DRIZZLING EASTER MORNING.

ON ONE WHO LIVED AND DIED WHERE HE WAS BORN.

THE SECOND NIGHT.
  (Ballad.)

SHE WHO SAW NOT.

THE OLD WORKMAN.

THE SAILOR'S MOTHER.   *From ' To Please His Wife.'*

OUTSIDE THE CASEMENT.
  (A Reminiscence of the War.)

THE PASSER-BY.
  (L. H. recalls her romance.)

' I WAS THE MIDMOST.'

A SOUND IN THE NIGHT.
  (Woodsford Castle : 17—.)

ON A DISCOVERED CURL OF HAIR.   *February* 1913.

AN OLD LIKENESS.
  (Recalling R. T.)

HER APOTHEOSIS.
  ' Secretum meum mihi.'
    (Faded Woman's Song.)

' SACRED TO THE MEMORY.'
  (Mary H.)

TO A WELL-NAMED DWELLING.

THE WHIPPER-IN.

A MILITARY APPOINTMENT.
    (Scherzando.)
THE MILESTONE BY THE RABBIT-BURROW.
    (On Yell'ham Hill.)
THE LAMENT ON THE LOOKING-GLASS.
CROSS-CURRENTS.
THE OLD NEIGHBOUR AND THE NEW.
THE CHOSEN.
    'Ατινά ἐστιν ἀλληγορούμενα.'
THE INSCRIPTION.
    (A Tale.)   *October* 30, 1907.
THE MARBLE-STREETED TOWN.   *Plymouth* (1914 ?).
A WOMAN DRIVING.
A WOMAN'S TRUST.
BEST TIMES.   *Rewritten from an old draft.*
A CASUAL ACQUAINTANCE.
INTRA SEPULCHRUM.
THE WHITEWASHED WALL.
JUST THE SAME.
THE LAST TIME.
THE SEVEN TIMES.
THE SUN'S LAST LOOK ON THE COUNTRY GIRL.
    (M. H.)   *December* 1915.
IN A LONDON FLAT.
DRAWING DETAILS IN AN OLD CHURCH.
RAKE-HELL MUSES.   189–.
THE COLOUR.
    (*The following lines are partly made up, partly remembered from a Wessex folk-rhyme.*)
MURMURS IN THE GLOOM.
    (Nocturne.)   *September* 22, 1899.
EPITAPH.
AN ANCIENT TO ANCIENTS.
AFTER READING PSALMS XXXIX., XL., ETC.   187–.
SURVIEW.
    ' Cogitavi vias meas.'

The original MSS. of ' At a House in Hampstead ' and ' And There was a Great Calm ' are in the possession of Thomas Wise, Esq.

I CAN REMEMBER | ROBERT LOUIS STEVENSON | Edited by | ROSALINE MASSON | W. & R. Chambers, Limited | Edinburgh : 339 High Street | London : 38 Soho Square, W. 1 | 1922.
Pp. 214, 215, 216, by Thomas Hardy, O.M.

The London Mercury, February 1923, p. 344, ON THE PORTRAIT OF A WOMAN ABOUT TO BE HANGED (Poem) by THOMAS HARDY, dated 6th January 1923.

LIST OF BOOKLETS privately printed for CLEMENT SHORTER, Esq., by Messrs. EYRE AND SPOTTISWOODE. First Editions.

SONG | OF THE | SOLDIERS | By | THOMAS HARDY.

(The title-page printed within a one-line border). Fcap. 4to, pp. 8. 12 copies, September 12, 1914.

The Times, September 9, 1914, *Song of the Soldiers* by THOMAS HARDY.

Reprinted in *Satires of Circumstance* as a Postscript.

LETTERS | ON | THE WAR | By | THOMAS HARDY.

(The title-page printed within a one-line border). Fcap. 4to, pp. 8. 12 copies, November 9, 1914.

The first of these letters appeared in *The Times* and certain other newspapers, October 7, 1914, the other in the *Manchester Guardian*, October 12, 1914.

THE | DYNASTS | By | THOMAS HARDY | The Prologue and Epilogue.

(The title-page printed within a one-line border). Fcap. 4to, pp. 8. 12 copies. December 1, 1914.

An abridged version of *The Dynasts* was produced by Granville Barker on November 25, 1914. The *Prologue* was included in the programme of the play, but the *Epilogue* had not then appeared elsewhere.

IN TIME OF | ' THE BREAKING | OF NATIONS ' | By | Thomas Hardy.

(The title-page printed within a one-line border).   Fcap. 4to, pp. 4.   25 copies.   February 1, 1915.

BEFORE | MARCHING | AND AFTER | By | Thomas Hardy.

(The title-page printed within a one-line border).   Fcap. 4to, pp. 7.   25 copies.   November 1915.

DOMICILIUM | By | Thomas Hardy.

(The title-page printed within a one-line border).   Fcap. 4to, pp. 7.   25 copies.   April 5, 1916.

Domicilium is the earliest extant poem written by Thomas Hardy.   It was composed between 1857 and 1860 and had never before been printed.

A DULL DAY IN LONDON | By | Dora Sigerson Shorter. | A Prefatory Note | By | Thomas Hardy.

Crown 4to, pp. 2.   12 copies.   1920.

LIST OF BOOKLETS privately printed for Mrs. HARDY at THE CHISWICK PRESS. First Editions.

TO SHAKESPEARE AFTER | THREE HUNDRED YEARS | By THOMAS HARDY.

(The title-page printed within a one-line border). Fcap. 4to, pp. 6. 50 copies. 1916.

The original MS. is in the possession of Thomas Wise, Esq.

ENGLAND TO GERMANY. | THE PITY OF IT. I MET A | MAN. A NEW YEAR'S EVE | IN WAR TIME. | By THOMAS HARDY.

(The title-page as above). Fcap. 4to, pp. 8. 25 copies. February 1917.

A CALL TO NATIONAL SERVICE | AN APPEAL TO AMERICA | CRY OF THE HOMELESS | By THOMAS HARDY.

(The title-page as above). Fcap. 4to, pp. 6. 25 copies. May 1917.

THE FIDDLER'S STORY | A JINGLE ON THE TIMES | By THOMAS HARDY.

(The title-page as above). Fcap. 4to, pp. 8. 25 copies. October 1917.

'WHEN I WEEKLY KNEW' | By THOMAS HARDY.
(The title-page as above).   Demy 8vo, pp. 5.   25 copies.   1916.

JEZREEL | THE MASTER AND THE LEAVES | By
  THOMAS HARDY.

(The title-page as above).   Fcap. 4to, pp. 6.   25 copies.
  September 1919.

'AND THERE WAS A GREAT CALM' | 11 NOVEMBER
  1918 | By THOMAS HARDY.

(The title-page as above).   Fcap. 4to, pp. 5.   25 copies.
  December 1920.

The original MS. is in the possession of Thomas Wise, Esq.

HAUNTING FINGERS | VOICES FROM THINGS
  GROWING | TWO PHANTASIES | By | THOMAS HARDY.

(The title-page as above).   Fcap. 4to. pp. 9.   25 copies.
February 1922.

WILLIAM BARNES

A BIOGRAPHICAL NOTE

By THOMAS HARDY

THE REV. WILLIAM BARNES, B.D.

By THOMAS HARDY

(Reprinted by permission, from *The Athenæum*
of October 16, 1886.)

UNTIL within the last year or two there were few figures more familiar to the eye in the county town of Dorset on a market day than an aged clergyman, quaintly attired in caped cloak, knee-breeches, and buckled shoes, with a leather satchel slung over his shoulders, and a stout staff in his hand. He seemed usually to prefer the middle of the street to the pavement, and to be thinking of matters which had nothing to do with the scene before him. He plodded along with a broad, firm tread, notwithstanding the slight stoop occasioned by his years. Every Saturday morning he might have been seen thus trudging up the narrow South Street, his shoes coated with mud or dust according to the state of the roads between his rural home and Dorchester, and a little grey dog at his heels, till he reached the four cross-ways in the centre of the town. Halting here, opposite the public clock, he would pull his old-fashioned watch from its deep fob, and set it with great precision to London time. This, the invariable first act of his market visit, having been completed to his satisfaction, he turned round and methodically proceeded about his other business.

This venerable and well-characterized man was William Barnes, the Dorsetshire poet and philologer, by whose death last week at the ripe age of eighty-six the world has lost not only a lyric writer of a high order of genius, but probably the most interesting link between present and past forms of rural life that England possessed. The date of his birth at the very beginning of the century is less explanatory of his almost unique position in this respect than the remoteness, even from contemporary provincial civilization, of the pastoral recesses in which his earlier years were passed—places with whose now obsolete customs and beliefs his mind was naturally imbued. To give one instance of the former tardiness of events in that part of the country : it was a day almost within his remembrance when, amidst the great excitement and applause of the natives, who swept the street with brooms in honour of its arrival, a stage-coach made its first entry into Sturminster Newton, the little market town nearest to the hamlet of Bagbere, the home of his parents. And there used to come to a little bridge, close to his father's door, till quite recently, a conjurer or ' white wizard,' who cured afflicted persons by means of the toad-bag—a small piece of linen having a limb from a living toad sewn up inside, to be worn round the sufferer's neck and next his skin, the twitching movements of which limb gave, so it was said, ' a turn ' to the blood of the wearer, and effected a radical change in his constitution.

Born so long ago as February 22nd, 1800 (1801 has been given, but I believe incorrectly), amid such surroundings, a thorough son of the soil, and endowed with great retentiveness and powers of observation, it is no wonder that Barnes became a complete repertory of forgotten manners, words, and sentiments, a store which he afterwards turned to such good use in his writings on ancient British and Anglo-Saxon speech, customs, and folklore ; above all, in the systematic study of his native dialect, as a result of which he has shown the world that far from being, as popularly supposed, a corruption of correct English, it is a distinct branch of Teutonic speech, regular in declension and conjugation, and richer in many classes of words than any other tongue known to him. As an instance of the latter he used to mention the pronouns with particular pride, there being no fewer than four demonstratives to set against the current English two. He would also instance any natural object, such as a tree, and show that there were double as many names for its different parts in the Dorset dialect as those available in the standard tongue.

It was a proud day for young William Barnes when, some time in the year 1814 or 1815, a local solicitor, the late Mr. Dashwood, entered the village school and inquired if there was a boy clever enough with his pen to come and copy deeds in his office in a clerkly hand. The only lad who at all approximated to such a high description was Barnes, and the scene of testing him with the long quill pen and paper, and his selection by the lawyer, must have been one to which Mulready alone could have done justice. The youth thus found himself at a solicitor's desk, and, what was more, in a position to help himself in some degree to the grammars and glossaries his soul desired, and by whose diligent perusal at odd hours through many laborious years he became familiar with an astonishing number of languages and dialects. A more notable instance of self-help has seldom been recorded, considering the date in the century, the young man's circumstances, and the remote place of his residence, for it appears that he still lived on at the hamlet, walking to and from the town—or rather townlet—every day. In later years academic scholars were sometimes found to remark upon the unsystematic character of his linguistic attainments, but it cannot be gainsaid that he was almost always ready with definite and often exclusive information on whatever slightly known form of human speech might occur to the mind of his questioner, from Persian to Welsh, from the contemporary vernaculars of India to the tongues of the ancient British tribes. Over and above these subjects, his mind was occupied after his removal to Dorchester, to judge from his letters to old local newspapers, with investigations of Roman remains, theories on the origin of Stonehenge, and kindred archæological matters ; while among his other hobbies about this time was engraving on wood and on silver, crests and initials upon old pieces of plate in the neighbourhood still remaining to testify to his skill in the art.

Though Barnes's first practical step in life had brought him to the office of a solicitor, his instincts were towards tuition ; and when, some years later, he had become well settled in the county town he opened a school. As schoolmaster he was fairly successful from the first, and as time went by and he obtained, as a ten years' man, his university degree and took orders, the school grew highly popular. It was during this period—from early in the forties onwards—that he wrote at intervals the first, second, and third series of those sweet rustic poems by which his name will be best remembered.

He used to tell an amusing story of his experience on relinquishing the school at Dorchester to retire to the country rectory of Winterbourne Came, in which he has ended his days. About the very week of his translation, so to call it, the name of one of his pupils appeared in *The Times* and other papers at the head of the Indian examination list, a wide proportion of marks separating it from the name following. The novelty of these lists lent a keen interest to them in those days, and the next morning Mr. Barnes was deluged with letters from all parts of the country, requesting him at almost any price to take innumerable sons, and produce upon them the same successful effect. ' I told them it took two to do it,' he would say, adding, ' Thus a popularity which I had never known during the working years of my life came at almost the first moment when it was no longer of use to me.'

To many readers of these pages the charming idyls

z

known as Barnes's ' Poems in the Dorset Dialect ' are too familiar to need description or eulogy. Though locally distinguished on the title-page by the name of the county at large, the chief scenes of their inspiration lie more precisely in the limited district to the north and north-west of Dorsetshire, that is to say in the secluded Vale of Blackmore, whose margin formed the horizon of his boyhood, and was, as he himself sings in one of the poems, the end of the world to him then. This fertile and sheltered tract of country, where the fields are never brown and the springs never dry, is bounded on the south by the bold chalk ridge that embraces the prominences of Hambledon Hill, Bulbarrow, Nettlecombe Tout, Dogbury, and High-Stoy. The prospect northwards from each of these heights is one which rivals, and in many points surpasses, those much admired views of Surrey and Buckinghamshire from Richmond Hill and the terrace at Windsor Castle, while the portion of the landscape immediately beneath the spectator is the abiding-place of the people whose daily doings, sayings, and emotions have been crystallized in the poet's verse. Occasionally, it is true, we find among the men and women presented in Mr. Barnes's volumes some who are housed in hamlets lying nominally beyond the Vale, but to my mind these characters are in a great measure Blackmore people away from home, bearing with them still the well-marked traits which distinguish the Vale population from that of the neighbouring uplands. The same may be said of his backgrounds and scenery. Moreover, when, moved by the pervading instinct of the nineteenth century, he gives us whole poems of still life, unaffected and realistic as a Dutch picture, the slow green river Stour of the same valley, with its deep pools, whence the trout leaps to the may-fly undisturbed by anglers, is found to be the stream dearest to his memory and the inspirer of some of his happiest effusions.

Unlike Burns, Béranger, and other poets of the people, Mr. Barnes never assumed the high conventional style; and he entirely leaves alone ambition, pride, despair, defiance, and other of the grander passions which move mankind great and small. His rustics are, as a rule, happy people, and very seldom feel the sting of the rest of modern mankind—the disproportion between the desire for serenity and the power of obtaining it. One naturally thinks of Crabbe in this connexion; but though they touch at points, Crabbe goes much further than Barnes in questioning the justice of circumstance. Their pathos, after all, is the attribute upon which the poems must depend for their endurance; and the incidents which embody it are those of everyday cottage life, tinged throughout with that ' light that never was,' which the emotional art of the lyrist can project upon the commonest things. It is impossible to prophesy, but surely much English literature will be forgotten when ' Woak Hill ' is still read for its intense pathos, ' Blackmore Maidens ' for its blitheness, and ' In the Spring ' for its Arcadian ecstasy.

Notwithstanding the wide appreciation of his verse both here and in America, so largely local were the

poet's interests that it may be questioned if the enthusiasm which accompanied his own readings of his
works in the town-halls of the shire was not more
grateful to him than the admiration of a public he had
never seen. The effect, indeed, of his recitations upon
an audience well acquainted with the *nuances* of the
dialect—impossible to impart to outsiders by any kind
of translation—can hardly be imagined by readers of
his lines acquainted only with English in its customary
form. The poet's own mild smile at the boisterous
merriment provoked by his droll delivery of such pieces
as ' The Shy Man,' ' A Bit o' Sly Coorten,' and ' Dick
and I,' returns upon the memory as one of the most
characteristic aspects of a man who was nothing if not
genial ; albeit that, while the tyranny of his audience
demanded these broadly humourous productions, his
own preferences were for the finer and more pathetic
poems, such as ' Wife a-lost,' ' Woak Hill,' and ' Jaäy
a-past.'

To those who knew Mr. Barnes in his prime, it may
have been a matter for conjecture why a man of his
energies should not at some point or other of his career
have branched off from the quiet byways of his early
manhood into the turmoils of the outer world, particularly as his tastes at that time were somewhat general,
and the direction of his labours was dictated in the
main by his opportunities. The explanation seems
to be that the poetic side of his nature, though not
always dominant, was but faintly ruled by the practical
at any time, that his place-attachment was strong
almost to a fault, and that his cosmopolitan interests,

though lively, were always subordinate to those local hobbies and solicitudes whence came alike his special powers and his limitations.

Few young people who have seen him only in latter years, since the pallor and stoop of old age overcame him, can realize the robust, upright form of his middle life, the ruddy cheek, and the bright quick eye. The last, indeed, dimmed but slightly, and even on his death-bed his zest for the subject of speech-form was strong as ever.   In one of his latest conversations he became quite indignant at the word ' bicycle.' ' Why didn't they call it " wheel-saddle " ? ' he exclaimed.

Though not averse to social intercourse, his friendships extended over but a small area of society.   But those who, like the present writer, knew him well and long, entertained for him a warm affection ; while casual visitors from afar were speedily won to kindly regard by the simplicity of his character, his forbearance, and the charming spurts of youthful ardour which would burst out as rays even in his latest hours.

Mr. HARDY'S MSS.

Mr. Lane will be very glad to hear from any other owners of Mr. Hardy's MSS., either stories or poems, with a view to adding the information to any later editions of this book.

Date Due